Classical Black Nationalism

Classical Black Nationalism

■ ■ ■

From the American Revolution to Marcus Garvey

Edited by

Wilson Jeremiah Moses

New York University Press / New York and London

The following letters are used with the permission of the Board
of Trustees of the New Bedford Free Public Library:
Paul Cuffe to Peter Williams, August 30, 1816
Paul Cuffe to James Forten, January 8, 1817
James Forten to Paul Cuffe, January 25, 1817

New York University Press
New York and London

© 1996 by New York University

Library of Congress Cataloging-in-Publication Data
Classical Black nationalism : from the American Revolution to Marcus
Garvey / edited by Wilson Jeremiah Moses.
p.   cm.
Includes bibliographical references and index.
ISBN 0-8147-5524-0 (cloth : alk. paper). — ISBN 0-8147-5533-X
(pbk. : alk. paper)
1. Afro-Americans—History—Sources.   2. Black nationalism—United
States—History—Sources.   3. Pan-Africanism—History—Sources.
I. Moses, Wilson Jeremiah, 1942–
E148.6.C62   1996
973'.0496073—dc20   95-44335
                              CIP

New York University Press books are printed on acid-free paper, and
their binding materials are chosen for strength and durability.

Manufactured in the United States of America

10 9 8 7 6 5 4 3 2 1

For my students

Contents

Three   *Black Nationalist Revival, 1895–1925*

Acknowledgments

Since this volume is intended not as a scholarly edition but as a teaching text, I have dedicated it to my students who, over the past quarter century, have taught me how to teach this material. While aimed at the mid-career college undergraduate, the volume should also be useful to graduate students, whose prior work in African American history has focused on the heroic and necessary struggles of the civil rights movement to the neglect of the equally important self-help tradition. Much of this material will be interesting and familiar to high school students who have been exposed to black nationalist values in their homes, churches, and other social institutions, although it may appear esoteric to persons whose understanding of African American sentiments and traditions derives from standard classroom treatments or from commercialized popular culture. Traditional black nationalist and Pan-Africanist feeling is very much alive in America, as symbolized by the many red, black, and green banners of the Garvey movement displayed during the Million Man March on Washington of October 16, 1995. It may, therefore, be assumed that the documents reprinted in this volume will interest persons entirely outside academic environments. The introduction, head notes, index, and short bibliography should be useful to persons embarking on a scholarly study of the origins of black nationalism, Afrocentrism, and Pan-Africanism.

Some of the ideas contained in the introduction to this work represent a rethinking of my book *The Golden Age of Black Nationalism, 1850–1925,* published by Archon books in 1978 and reprinted by Oxford University Press in 1988. I wrote a short article on black nationalism for the sixth edition of *The Negro Almanac: A Reference Work on the African American* (Detroit: Gale Research, 1994), which the editors granted me permission to rework for use in this project, although, as it turns out, my introduction to the present volume is five times the length of that essay and does not recycle its contents.

Since the early stages of this project, I have piled up debts with such old and new friends as Gary Gallagher, Robert A. Hill, Lloyd Monroe, Carl Senna, William Van Deburg, and Vernon Williams. I am deeply thankful to Timothy Bartlett, who acquired the manuscript for the New York University Press. I also express my thanks to Despina Papazoglou Gimbel and her staff, whose diligence and professionalism helped me to discipline my prose, clarify my ideas, and fortify my documentation. Any stylistic idiosyncracies that persist are due to my own stubbornness and have survived despite editorial warnings. In this, as in all my past work, I have been helped immeasurably by my wife, Maureen Joan Moses, who subjected the page proofs to several close readings and assumed primary responsibility for the index.

Introduction

"Black nationalism," "Afrocentrism," and "Pan-Africanism" are terms widely in use on college campuses today, but few students realize that these concepts had their origins in documents dating as far back as the American Revolutionary period. The purpose of this volume is to offer an introduction to these documents, and to chart the origins of these concepts. Classical black nationalism is defined here as an ideology whose goal was the creation of an autonomous black nation-state, with definite geographical boundaries—usually in Africa. Classical black nationalism originated in the 1700s, reached its first peak in the 1850s, underwent a decline toward the end of the Civil War, and peaked again in the 1920s, as a result of the Garvey movement.

Although few living black Americans are classical black nationalists, in the sense that they intend to pack up and migrate to a new homeland, most black Americans have at some time or another felt a quickening of the pulse when black nationalist notions are discussed. Whether leftist or conservative, most African Americans have experienced feelings of sympathy for such ideas as "self-help" and "self-determination" for black communities. Persons as different as Justice Clarence Thomas and the Reverend Jesse Jackson have declared support for the sentiments of black nationalism as expressed by Malcolm X, Elijah Muhammad, or Marcus Garvey. The recent resurgence of interest in Malcolm X demonstrates the affinity of many black Americans to a tradition of black separatism. In American cities everywhere, African Americans display the red, black, and green colors of the Garvey movement. African American bookstores in black communities do a thriving business in the writings of Elijah Muhammad and are well stocked with Afrocentric, black nationalist, and Pan-Africanist literature. The symbols of black nationalism and African American cultural separatism do not seem to be disappearing from the contemporary American scene.

My purpose in compiling this collection has been to provide college students and professors with a basic set of texts for courses in African American history. The documents, many of which are reprinted in full, trace the historical roots of the popular black nationalism that attracts so many African Americans today. The following paragraphs will provide a few definitions and outline the history of the ideas that are treated in the documents.

Definition of the Concept

Classical black nationalism, which reached its fullest expression in the years from 1850 to 1925, may be defined as the effort of African Americans to create a sovereign nation-state and formulate an ideological basis for a concept of a national culture.[1] Classical black nationalism's goal of establishing a national homeland in Africa or elsewhere signified something more than a dissatisfaction with conditions in the United States. It indicated a desire for independence and a determination to demonstrate the ability of black people to establish a republican form of government. Some historians have defined black nationalism broadly enough to include the kindred ideology of Pan-Africanism, a movement to develop sentiments of unity among peoples of African descent throughout the world and advance the supposedly similar interests of these diverse peoples, regardless of where they may live.[2] Properly speaking, such a definition of black nationalism is too broad to be meaningful. The essential feature of classical black nationalism is its goal of creating a black nation-state or empire with absolute control over a specific geographical territory, and sufficient economic and military power to defend it.

The major proponents of classical black nationalism in the nineteenth century invariably believed that the hand of God directed their movement. Their religious beliefs led to a black nationalist conception of history in which Divine Providence would guide the national destiny to an early fulfillment, once the work was taken up. With God at the center of their ideological conceptions of black history, it was not surprising that they had utopian visions of the society they hoped to establish. Classical black nationalism may seem mystical by the standards of modern secular society, but to its adherents it provided a means of preserving shreds of dignity and self-respect in the face of the almost universal military, technological, and economic domination by whites over blacks. With its religious optimism, black nationalism met the need for psychological resistance to the slavery, colonialism, and racism imposed by Europeans and white Americans.

In addition to their religious historicism, nineteenth-century black nationalists frequently demonstrated an interest in developing a distinctive tradition in art, architecture, music, and letters. Such concerns are usually grouped under the rubric of "cultural nationalism," but classical black nationalists did not employ the term "cultural nationalism," which was not coined until the twentieth century. Ironically, the cultural ideals of nineteenth-century black nationalists usually resembled those of upper-class Europeans and white Americans, rather than those of the native African or African American masses. Classical black nationalists were quick to claim an ancestral connection with Egypt and Ethiopia, but showed little enthusiasm for the cultural expressions of sub-Saharan Africa. They certainly were not inclined to sentimentalize the manners and morals of the enslaved masses in the Southern United States. Black cultural nationalism of the classical period must, therefore, be carefully distinguished from that of the late twentieth century. The nationalism of Alexander Crummell and Marcus Garvey was situated in a "high culture" aesthetic, which admired symbols of imperial power, military might, and aristocratic refinement. Post-Garveyite nationalism, reflecting the influences of twentieth-century anthropology, has tended to idealize African village life, sentimentalize the rural South, and romanticize the urban ghetto.

To define black nationalism we must first define its two component terms, "black" and "nation." What most African Americans seem to imply by "black" is a special status, owned by any person who is recognized or identified as having ancestral origins among the black peoples of sub-Saharan Africa, or any person possessing a set of physical traits that would seem to identify him or her with black African ancestry. Among African Americans this category is often extended to include individuals who, despite their lack of those physical traits associated with black Africa, can nonetheless claim some "Negro" ancestry, and who claim some connection with the political interests of African Americans or other black peoples.

A nation may be defined as any group of people who view themselves as bound together by ties of kinship, history, and heritage, and who believe themselves to be distinct and separate from other groups by virtue of common beliefs, behaviors, and ways of thinking.[3] The members of a national group tend to think of themselves as sharing a distinguishing and unifying history and destiny that separate them from other peoples. This tendency to separatism is usually reinforced by outsiders whose behavior toward that national group reinforces its self-perception as a separate entity. A nation comes into existence when such a group seeks to perpetuate its separation from outsiders and attempts to exercise self-determination. A nation thus seeks to establish or maintain possession of a self-governing, independent, sovereign state. To this end, the national group usually attempts to acquire or defend, by force of arms, some clearly defined geographical unit, usually some territory with which the group has a historical and/or sentimental affinity. Nationalism views the nation-state as the natural unit around which the life of a society ought to be organized.

In ordinary conversation, the terms "nation" and "state" are frequently used interchangeably, although in precise speech, "nation" and "state" do not always mean the same thing. We frequently use the word "nation" to designate any sovereign territorial entity, but the term subtly cloaks a more sinister meaning. The concept of nationalism is accompanied by a belief in consanguinity, a commitment to the conservation of racial or genetic purity, a myth of commonality and purity of "blood." The nation is seen as an organic segment of humanity, and like the family, "an organism or ordinance of God," whose members own a common ancestry and ties of ethnic kinship.[4] In this view, national purity must be preserved by means of an ethos of endogamy. Marital and other sexual pairings should be restricted to members of the national group. If for some reason a member of a given nation forms a sexual union outside the national group, the outsider must be acceptable to the national group and suitable for assimilation into it. The children of such unions are expected to manifest a loyalty to the nation, even more obsessive than that practiced by children of endogamous unions.

Black nationalism, as manifested in the nineteenth-century United States, was a racial nationalism, premised on the assumption that membership in a race could function as the basis of a national identity. This idea, although not peculiar to American black nationalists, was a spurious one. Most nineteenth-century nationalists—Japanese, Italians, and Germans, for example—based their ideologies not on race but on economic exigencies, military ambitions, geographical circumstances, and commonalities of language. In each of these instances nationalist rhetoric often revealed conflicts among peoples of the same race. The contempt of Japanese nationalists for Koreans is legendary, although European anthropologists have lumped together both peoples in a category called "the Asian race." Italian nationalists resented Austrian imperialists, although both groups were racially white. Throughout the nineteenth century, the Germans and the French squabbled over national boundaries. Each of these nationalisms represented concerns with preserving the distinctive identities that separated each nationality from other nationalities of the same race. American black nationalists stubbornly ignored the possibility of legitimate competing national interests arising within the black race. They perceived, correctly enough, that all African peoples were oppressed by whites, but rashly assumed that this common experience of oppression could be the basis of a pan-racial national consciousness.

History of the Movement

The ideology of black nationalism has gone through several phases of rise and decline: from its "protonationalistic" phase in the late 1700s to its hiatus in the 1830s, from its flourishing in the 1850s to its eclipse in the 1870s, from its apex in the Garvey movement to its comparatively feeble recrudescence in the 1960s.[5] Classical black nationalism in the nineteenth- and early-twentieth-century United States developed at a time when there were no African nation-states. American black nationalists defined their national goals as racial goals, because race had such primary importance in the American environment. Even today, many African Americans, when asked to specify their nationality, will respond with the simple assertion that they are "African" or "black." But Africa is a continent, not a nationality, and there is no such thing as a black passport. Therefore, black nationalists have sometimes proposed (as did Marcus Garvey) to fuse the entire continent of Africa into a superstate, in which all black persons might claim citizenship.

Classical black nationalism in the United States, defined as the ideology that argued for the self-determination of African Americans within the framework of an independent nation-state, came into existence at the end of the eighteenth century. It is therefore one of the earliest expressions of nationalism; while it originated in unison with the American and French Revolutions, it was not an imitation of North American or European nationalism. Black nationalism was an expression of the impulse toward self-determination among Africans transplanted to the New World by the slave trade. This protonationalistic drive toward self-determination in the Americas is readily identifiable in the creation of the Brazilian republic of Palmares in the 1600s.[6] It can also be seen among the enslaved Africans who managed to gain their freedom by taking refuge in "Maroon societies," isolated strongholds of resistance in wilderness areas, most notably in Jamaica and Suriname.[7] Maroon communities are known to have existed in North America, and references are frequently made to instances in Florida where African fugitives linked their destinies to those of the Seminoles.[8]

It would be incorrect to attribute full-blown nationalistic motives to most North American slave uprisings. Slave revolts were frequently no more than opportunistic expressions of resentment, revealing an alienation from existing sociopolitical structures, but not necessarily indicating concrete plans for an alternative social order.[9] On the other hand, as several historians have shown, the existence of slave revolts and conspiracies provides ample evidence of a discontent among the African population that was often linked to a desire for self-determination. The fact that white communities were constantly reporting and reacting to rumors of revolt and conspiracy, sometimes attributing them to international intrigues and "papist plots," provides evidence that the African slave population was viewed by contemporaries as potentially insurrectionary.[10]

A dearth of contemporary written records makes it impossible to determine precisely when African Americans began to develop a nationalistic ideology, although evidence of such thinking predates the American Declaration of Independence. In 1773 a group of four Boston slaves expressed a desire to return to Africa and petitioned the legislature for the right to set aside one day a week during which they could earn money toward the purchase of their freedom. The petition reveals its authors' racial cosmopolitanism, as they made reference to the condition of Africans in Latin America and appealed to the belief of Anglo-American colonists that Anglo-Americans were culturally superior to their Hispanic counterparts. "Even the Spaniards," who did not possess the same "sublime ideas of freedom that English men have," allowed their enslaved Africans "to work for themselves, to enable them to earn money to purchase the residue of their time." Although the rhetoric of this document is not that of full-blown nationalism, it is clearly the language of self-determination.

We are willing to submit to such regulations and laws, as may be made relative to us, until we leave the province, which we determine to do, as soon as we can, from our joynt labours, procure money to transport ourselves to some part of the Coast of Africa, where we propose a settlement. We are very desirous that you should have instructions relative to us, from your town, therefore we pray you to communicate this letter to them, and ask this favor for us.[11]

These sentiments were protonationalistic, as opposed to truly nationalistic. The petitioners did not articulate any sense of national destiny or any intention of creating a nation-state with a distinctive national culture. African American thinking moved in that direction around the time of the American Revolution, as the black population was caught up in the ideology and rhetoric of national independence. While in some African Americans the Revolution instilled hopes of eventually gaining American citizenship rights, in others it inflamed a desire for self-determination. Some African Americans understood their interests to lie on the side of the Revolution, and therefore fought alongside the white colonials for American independence. On the other hand, there were African American "loyalists," who sided with the British Empire. During and immediately following the Revolution, many of those Africans who had remained loyal to the Crown were evacuated with the British. Some of the evacuees were resettled in Nova Scotia; others were carried back to England. In 1787 the British transported a group of British residents, known as the "black poor," to Sierra Leone, West Africa. A segment of the Nova Scotian community was "repatriated" in Sierra Leone along with the black poor. In 1800 the British also settled a group of Jamaican Maroons in Sierra Leone, which eventually became a dropping-off place for "recaptives"—Africans recaptured by the British fleet after 1811, when the British became actively engaged in suppressing the West African slave trade.[12]

In the years following the American Revolution some "Free Africans," as they called themselves, began to express a desire to return to the land of their fathers. Speaking for a group of seventy-three "African blacks," Prince Hall, leader of the African Lodge in Boston, led a delegation to petition the General Court of Massachusetts in 1787 with a plan for resettlement in Africa, due to the "disagreeable and disadvantageous circumstances" that attended them in the United States.

This and other considerations which we need not here particularly mention induce us to return to Africa, our native country, which warm climate is more natural and agreeable to us; and for which the God of nature has formed us; and where we shall live among our equals and be more comfortable and happy, than we can be in our present situation; and at the same time, may have a prospect of usefulness to our brethren there.[13]

The delegation expressed goals that seemed to be truly nationalistic. They spoke of their desire to "form themselves into a civil society, united by a political constitution," and also expressed their commitment to set up a Christian church under the headship of "blacks ordained as their pastors or Bishops." The plan would be for the purpose of both Christianizing and "civilizing" the indigenous peoples, setting up missionary schools, and establishing domestic and international commerce. The concerns of the Prince Hall delegation thus demonstrated not only a desire to escape from American oppression, but also a commitment to what might be called Pan-Africanism. Their goals were Pan-African in the sense that they linked the concerns of African Americans to the advancement of African peoples on the African continent. American black nationalism has usually been associated with such a desire to elevate the status of Africa and its indigenous peoples.

Prince Hall and other black leaders at the end of the eighteenth century found considerable inspiration in the Haitian revolt (1790–1804). In a *Charge Delivered to the African Lodge on June 24th, 1797 at Metonomy [Now West Cambridge] Mass.*, Hall wrote as follows:

My brethren let us not be cast down under these and many other abuses we at present are laboring under,—for the darkest hour is just before the break of day. My brethren, let us remember what a dark day it was with our African brethren, six years ago, in the French West Indies. Nothing but the snap of the whip was heard, from morning to evening. Hanging, breaking on the wheel, burning, and all manner of tortures, were inflicted on those unhappy people. But, blessed be God, the scene is changed. They now confess that God hath no respect of persons, and therefore, receive them as their friends and treat them as brothers. Thus doth Ethiopia stretch forth her hand from slavery, to freedom and equality.

Prince Hall's address preceded the truly nationalistic phase of the Haitian struggle, and was thus intended to celebrate a triumph of abolitionism rather than an achievement of nationalistic goals in that country. As the nineteenth century progressed, however, references to Haiti became frequent in the rhetoric of black nationalism and Pan-Africanism. The leader of the revolt in its nationalist phase, Toussaint L'Ouverture, became a central figure in the black nationalist pantheon of heroes.[14]

Documents illustrating the ideology of black nationalism began to appear during the late eighteenth century. The historian Elie Kedourie has argued that nationalism is a European idea in its origins, and that the American and French Revolutions gave birth to conceptions of the nation-state that came to dominate political thought not only in the North Atlantic but also among African and Asian peoples.[15] Other historians, notably W. E. B. Du Bois and Eugene Genovese, have argued that the slave revolt and seizure of the state in Haiti was both a cause and an effect of rising conceptions of nationalism and manifest destiny in France and the United States.[16]

Be that as it may, the Haitian revolt was certainly an inspiration to black nationalism among both the slaves and the "Free Africans" in North America's black population. The historian Imanuel Geiss has referred to documents that appeared around this time as representing "proto–Pan-Africanism," and pays particular attention to a work produced in 1787 by Gustavus Vassa, an African living in England:

Population, the bowels and surface of Africa, abound in valuable and useful returns; the hidden treasures of centuries will be brought to light and into circulation. Industry, enterprise, and mining will have their full scope proportionally as they civilize. In a word, it lays open an endless field of commerce to the British manufacturers and merchant adventurer. The manufacturing interest and the general interest are synonymous. The abolition of slavery would be in reality an universal good.[17]

Vassa was not a nationalist, but he believed that the African condition could be improved by the repatriation of Afro-Europeans to Africa. Eventually he came to abandon that plan, but he remained committed to the destruction of African slavery through the agencies of Christianity, commerce, and civilization.[18]

The case of Vassa illustrates that black nationalism, from its earliest origins, has been closely associated with the doctrine of Pan-Africanism, the idea that Africans everywhere should work together for their mutual benefit and for the uplift of the mother continent. The ideology of African emigrationism, as expressed by American black nationalists, has seldom attempted to justify itself purely in terms of African American interests. Black nationalist emigrants to Africa have recognized that their moral position would be ill-served if they were to adopt the ruthless expansionist principles of a settler-state. Thus, American black nationalists have never *openly* advocated the displacement or oppression of indigenous African populations. At least in their speeches and writings they have always made the claim of a commitment to the universal improvement of the African condition.

On the American side of the Atlantic, Thomas Jefferson's *Notes on the State of Virginia* (an excerpt of which is reprinted in this volume) presented a version of the repatriationism that had originated in England. Like the English repatriationists, Jefferson claimed to be motivated primarily by altruism. He favored emancipation on moral grounds, but argued that one of the most important obstacles to emancipation was the problem of what to do with the freed persons of African descent. He held it self-evident that it would be impossible to incorporate African Americans into the national fabric, because of their history as a nation in bondage, but more importantly because of their racial distinctiveness.

Deep rooted prejudices entertained by the whites; ten thousand recollections, by the blacks, of the injuries they have sustained; new provocations; the real distinctions which nature has made; and many other circumstances, will divide us into parties, and produce convulsions which will probably never end but in the extermination of the one or the other race.—To these objections, which are political, may be added others, which are physical and moral.

One should neither deny nor overstate the philanthropic aspect of Jefferson's ideas, which were linked to a proposal for the complete, if gradual, abolition of slavery. Nonetheless, his plan, whether discussed in terms of benevolence or racism, was undeniably a proposal by an outsider, and rooted in an extreme color prejudice. Black nationalism must amount to more than a simple accommodation to white separatism, and thus black Americans whose thinking was consistent with Jefferson's often justified their position in terms of idealistic and sentimental goals. Early black colonization schemes were frequently cloaked in the rhetoric of self-sacrifice and missionary altruism, promising the "redemption of Africa" from industrial backwardness and "heathenism."

But nationalism must have a practical side, and must in some way be linked to enlightened self-interest. It must, in other words, have an economic element, and this ingredient was supplied by two African American capitalists. Captain Paul Cuffe, a shipowner, and James Forten, a sail manufacturer, were among the earliest advocates of a back-to-Africa movement, inspired by that healthy bourgeois commercialism that seems to accompany all successful nationalisms. Their economic nationalism was nonetheless steeped in a religious impulse, and they hoped to develop Christianity along with commerce and civilization in Africa, while at the same time providing a homeland for African Americans. Like the New England merchants and Virginia planters who founded the United States, they were driven as much by economic desire as by political idealism. As entrepreneurs in the maritime industries, Forten and Cuffe had much to gain by supporting a back-to-Africa movement. They looked toward the development of a Pan-African commercial system. Paul Cuffe was, in fact, more interested in the development of a trading empire than he was in becoming an African pioneer.[19]

In 1815 Cuffe managed to resettle thirty-eight emigrants in Sierra Leone, which, with its Pan-African population of "repatriates" from England, Jamaica, North America, and other regions of Africa, was a logical focus for Cuffe's enterprise. Cuffe had high hopes that "the people of color might establish a mercantile line of business from the United States to Africa." In a letter of 1817 (reprinted in this volume), he wrote to his friend James Forten, describing the overtures of Robert Finley, a white "gentleman in the city of Washington announcing to me the concern that rests at the seat of government for the welfare of the people of color. They mention to me whether I will join them in going to England and Africa to seek a place where the people of color might be colonized."

At first Cuffe gained some sympathy from African Americans, including Forten and possibly Richard Allen, the leader of the African Methodist Episcopal Church in Philadelphia.[20] By 1817, the year of Cuffe's death, however, hostility to all forms of African emigration was mounting among the black population of the United States. This rising hostility to the movement was due to the activities of Henry Clay, Andrew Jackson, and other white American slaveholders, who met in the nation's capital in 1817 to found the American Society for Colonizing the Free People of Color in the United States, usually called the American Colonization Society or simply the ACS. To be sure, some white American colonizationists were philanthropists like Robert Finley, who endorsed a Jeffersonian brand of antislavery and believed that African colonization would be a means of encouraging slaveholders to free their slaves. Soon, however, colonization became the project of anti-abolitionists, and the ACS expressly denied any sympathy for abolition. According to its constitution, the ACS would exist solely for the purpose of deporting the "free people of color," and as it became clear that the society was to be under the control of proslavery forces, African Americans became increasingly hostile to it.

In a letter to Cuffe on January 25, 1817 (reprinted here), Forten described the mounting pressure against the African movement, and it was not long before African Americans who supported the American Colonization Society or who migrated under its auspices became the objects of extreme vituperation. Even Forten was profoundly influenced by the rise of emotional opposition to the resettlement movement, and within a few months of Richard Allen's Philadelphia meeting, he had completely shifted his position. Forten eventually became a prominent anticolonizationist, giving financial as well as moral support to the white abolitionist William Lloyd Garrison, and he is believed to have influenced Garrison's conversion to adamant anticolonization.[21]

By the 1830s the majority of black leaders were staunch opponents of colonization, but an important exception was Rev. Peter Williams Jr. of St. Philip's Episcopal Church in New York. Williams eulogized Paul Cuffe and defended the decision of "any man of color, [who] after carefully considering the subject has thought it best to emigrate to Africa." Williams remained friendly to John Russwurm, one of the founders of *Freedom's Journal,* even when Russwurm decided to migrate to Liberia and was burned in effigy by anticolonizationists. Williams had been openly critical of the ACS in 1830, but under pressure from his bishop, who endorsed colonization, he resigned from the New York Antislavery Society in 1834 because of its vociferous hostility to the ACS.[22]

Opposition to emigration and colonization sometimes coexisted with expressions of an intense racial messianism. David Walker's *Appeal in Four Articles* (excerpts of which are reprinted here) is a case in point. It made use of a "chosen people" rhetoric, comparing blacks to the biblical Hebrews, and whites to their Egyptian oppressors, but it bespoke no desire to abandon the American Egypt in pursuit of an African Zion. The document condemned racial separatism as unchristian, and contained many bitter references to

Jefferson's assertion in *Notes on the State of Virginia* that emancipation could never be effected unless accompanied by deportation, "beyond the reach of mixture." The document contained a seething digression against American laws banning intermarriage.

Addressed to "the colored citizens of the world," Walker's *Appeal* presupposed that black people everywhere were morally bound to revolt against their common heritage of oppression. It is thus unquestionably an example of militant Pan-Africanism, but its ties to black nationalism are problematic. The historian Sterling Stuckey has viewed Walker's *Appeal* as "the most all-embracing black nationalist formulation to appear in America during the nineteenth century," but Walker was ambivalent with respect to separatism. Although he viewed African Americans as a "nation in bondage," he did not advocate a separate national destiny. Furthermore, while Walker was filled with revolutionary anger, and assured the slaves that God would be on their side if they rose up and destroyed their oppressors, his ultimate objective was the social, political, and cultural assimilation of black Americans into American society. Walker's *Appeal* concluded with the hope that black and white Americans would ultimately become a "united and happy people," an admirable goal, but not compatible with classical black nationalism, which always aimed at the creation of a separate nation-state.[23]

As observed previously, Walker's *Appeal* began with the assumption that African Americans are a distinct people, with a special God-given historical identity resembling that of the Israelites in Egypt. Walker's analogy between the condition of African Americans and that of the biblical Hebrews was incomplete, however, for his interpretation of deliverance referred only to release from the condition of slavery, not to any desire to depart the "house of bondage." His hostility to "the Colonization Plan" was rooted in an aversion for Africa, as well as the American Colonization Society, an institution that Walker had once viewed as benevolent. In this respect Walker's *Appeal* must be contrasted to an article he published two years earlier in *Freedom's Journal* (December 19,

1828), where he offered the highest praise for the colonization agent Jehudi Ashmun's efforts in the establishment of Liberia, and heralded the day when "the children of Africa will take their stand among the nations of the earth." For unknown reasons Walker had ceased to praise colonizationists by the time he published the first edition of his *Appeal* in 1829. Walker asserted that if African Americans felt they must emigrate, they should not attempt to set up a republic in Africa, but should "go to those who have been for many years, and are now our greatest earthly friends and benefactors—the English," or, as a second choice, resettle in Haiti.

Walker's warning to white America was in the tradition of the "jeremiad," so named for the prophet Jeremiah, who preached the coming judgment of God on the unrighteous. His *Appeal* is also an illustration of what has been called "Ethiopianism," a tradition based on the cryptic prophecy of Psalms 68:31, "Princes shall come out of Egypt, Ethiopia shall soon stretch out her hands unto God." Civilizations in the past had risen and fallen according to their adherence to the laws of God and nature. Americans, if they obeyed the divine commandment and abolished slavery, could escape the cycles of decline and fall. In this context, Walker pointed to the example of Catholic Spain. He accepted, or at least made rhetorical use of, the Anglo-Christian tradition in which Spanish Catholics, more than English Protestants, bore the great responsibility for the origins of the slave trade, and English Protestants were viewed as comparatively less culpable. Walker internalized the biases that predominated in American society, and viewed Catholics and Iberians as culturally decadent and morally inferior to Northern European Protestants. By accepting this convention, known as the "black legend," Walker revealed his own unconscious acceptance of Anglo-Protestant racism. He provided an interesting twist to the legend, however, attributing the warfare and revolution experienced by Spain and her colonies during the 1820s to slavery. Similar disorders would befall North Americans if they continued their persecution of the African peoples, who, by the fact of their oppression, claimed the special protection of a just God.[24]

Walker's *Appeal* did not anticipate the cultural black nationalism of the twentieth century. Aside from his willingness to claim an identity with ancient Egypt and Ethiopia, Walker's attitude toward Africa was negative. He was, furthermore, historically removed from that modern brand of multiculturalism that romanticizes peasant and proletarian folkways. His contempt for the "vernacular" culture of the black masses was revealed in his chapter on "Our Wretchedness in Consequence of Ignorance," where he dismissed the distinctive features of black speech simply as manifestations of "ignorance," and implied that they should be eradicated. He demonstrated, as Sterling Stuckey has observed in *The Ideological Origins of Black Nationalism,* a "tendency to exaggerate the degree of acquiescence to oppression by the masses of black people." On the other hand, Walker's rhetoric had a convincingly nationalistic ring when he predicted, with obvious relish, the collapse of America under the weight of its sins. "Our sufferings will come to an *end,* in spite of all the Americans this side of *eternity.* Then we will want all the learning and talents among ourselves, and perhaps more, to govern ourselves.——'Every dog must have its day,' the American's is coming to an end."

The Ethiopian prophecy, interpreted by Walker as a prediction of the African's rise, accompanied by America's fall, was also an inspiration to Robert Alexander Young's *Ethiopian Manifesto,* which is reprinted here. The prophetic Young hailed the coming of a black messiah: "As came John the Baptist, of old, to spread abroad the forthcoming of his master, so alike are intended these our words, to denote to the black African or Ethiopian people, that God has prepared for them a leader, who awaits but for his season to proclaim to them his birthright." Like Walker, Young wrote in a messianic tradition, filled with Old Testament rhetoric, and viewed African Americans as living among the ungodly. It is impossible to determine, however, based on a reading of Young, whether God intended that his chosen people should "come out from among them."

Maria Stewart wrote in the same messianic tradition as Robert

Alexander Young and David Walker, and embodied the same contradictions. She denounced the United States with strident jeremiadic rhetoric, while never abandoning a desire to become part of American society. She viewed black Americans as a captive nation with a distinct national destiny, but never took the step of advocating a separate nation-state. She referred to herself as an African, as did most of her contemporaries in the 1830s, but was hostile to the colonization movement. While ambivalent with respect to black separatism, she engaged in a rhetoric that was infused with racial messianism and biblical images of chosen peoplehood. In an 1833 speech, which is reproduced in this volume, Stewart declared,

America has become like the great city of Babylon. . . . She is indeed a seller of slaves and the souls of men; she has made the Africans drunk with the wine of her fornication; she has put them completely beneath her feet, and she means to keep them there; her right hand supports the reins of government, and her left hand the wheel of power, and she is determined not to let go her grasp.

"America has risen to her meridian," she said in the introduction to her literary *Productions,* published in 1835. "When you begin to thrive, she will begin to fall." Stewart thus represented a bitter prophetic tradition in African American thought. Her unrequited longing for citizenship rights was transformed into hostility toward the United States, and although she opposed emigration, she felt that African Americans had a separate and distinct national destiny apart from that of other Americans.[25]

Walker's *Appeal,* with its kindred sentiments of messianic—but stateless—nationalism, appeared shortly before Nat Turner's slave revolt of 1831, which had an identifiable messianic current, although no causal connections have ever been demonstrated. Messianic nationalism of the variety represented in Stewart, Walker, and Young has sometimes been identified with the slave conspiracies of Gabriel Prosser (1800) and Denmark Vesey (1820). Messianic or not, Prosser had political aspirations beyond the simple taking of revenge; according to trial testimony, he planned a seizure of the state of Virginia. Vesey was aware of the Haitian revolt and is reputed to have sought the establishment of a black empire in the Caribbean. Most of the evidence of black nationalism in the United States is found among the free black population of the North, however. People like David Walker and Maria Stewart found their audiences in the so-called Free African Societies, which for obvious reasons could not flourish in the deep South. Although such communities did not harbor much enthusiastic support for colonization, they did nurture a sense of history and national destiny among African Americans. During the 1830s and 1840s, messianic rhetoric was consistently associated with religious leadership, such as that provided by Richard Allen, who sustained a belief in a special God-given mission for black Americans as a people, despite his steadfast opposition to the American Colonization Society.[26]

Black nationalism received little support from the majority of black leaders in the twenty years from 1830 to 1850. African colonization was so firmly associated in their minds with the nefarious scheme of the American Colonization Society that emigrationists were constantly on the defensive. The rise of militant abolitionism provided forceful black leaders with ample opportunities to denounce slavery, and encouraged their hopes that the United States might yet evolve into a truly egalitarian democracy. Then came the federal Fugitive Slave Act of 1850, which ruled, in effect, that every black person in the United States was a slave unless he or she could prove otherwise. The law increased the power of alleged owners to sue for the return of their escaped "property." It had a chilling effect on the hopes of Free Africans, many of whom began at this point to consider migration to Canada or South America, although hostility to the American Colonization Society still prevailed.

The first phase of classical black nationalism in the United States dates from the Fugitive Slave Act of 1850 to the Emancipation Proclamation of 1862, and is dominated by a renewed interest in emigration. The antebellum generation of black nationalists did not deem it important to define an African or a mass-folk-cultural basis for their movement. They were not interested in the celebration of slave folkways, and they seldom showed much appreciation for indigenous African manners and customs. Their goals were political, military, and economic, as they sought to create a black republic in which they would be able to maintain their cherished values of bourgeois "respectability." They ultimately came to believe that the abolition of slavery depended on the elevation of the Free Africans, and that they could best work for abolition by bringing a powerful black nation into existence.

In its strictest form, classical black nationalism must be defined as the effort by African Americans to create a modern nation-state with distinct geographical boundaries. In a broader sense, it may indicate a spirit of Pan-African unity and an emotional sense of solidarity with the political and economic struggles of African peoples throughout the world. In a very loose sense, it may refer simply to any feelings of pride in a distinct ethnic heritage. However, this last variety of black nationalism, sometimes called "cultural black nationalism," did not manifest itself strongly in the classical period. Antebellum black nationalists showed little inclination to celebrate a mass culture that was associated with slavery. Slavery was a clear and ever present horror, and classical black nationalists, unlike their twentieth-century successors, had no inclination to pen learned treatises on the beauties of slave culture that might be misused as justifications for slavery, with its heritage of illiteracy and superstition.

Black nationalism during the classical period was invariably obsessed with uplifting and "civilizing" the race. Black nationalists defined their mission as a movement for "African civilization." In the nineteenth century, they referred to their civilizing mission as the African movement. Later they employed such terms as "Pan-Negroism," "Pan-Africanism," and, in Marcus Garvey's case, "universal Negro improvement." Certain of these terms revealed the goal of cultural uplift for all African peoples, including those who were dispersed by the slave trade into Europe or the Americas, as well as those who had never left Africa. Pan-Africanism always revealed a concern for the universal cultural improvement of all African peoples, and the desire to bring modern economic, industrial, and military development to the African continent.[27]

Classical black nationalism had its most influential defender in Edward Wilmot Blyden (1832–1912). A native of the Danish West Indies, Blyden arrived in the United States in 1850, hoping to enroll in Rutgers Theological College. He left within months, having been denied admission to Rutgers and two other institutions, and migrated to Liberia under the auspices of the American Colonization Society. Blyden was a staunch defender of Liberia, and his writings amounted to a systematic theoretical justification for African nationalism. Blyden's Christian nationalistic theories were intertwined with the Ethiopianism of Psalms 68:31, already discussed in connection with David Walker and Maria Stewart. In 1856 Blyden published *A Voice from Bleeding Africa,* in which he expressed what scholars have called the "redemptionist" approach to black nationalism. The national mission of Liberia was "the redemption of Africa, and the disenthralment and elevation of the African race." He believed, as did many Liberians, that the emergence of a powerful African civilization would contribute to the overthrow of the slave power. Thus, Blyden denied the old canard that black nationalists had turned their backs on their brothers and sisters who remained in slavery, and insisted that the people of Liberia were committed to the destruction of "the nefarious system." Blyden later published *The Call of Providence to the Descendants of Africa in America* (reprinted here), where he further developed his redemptionism, arguing that God had allowed the enslavement and subjugation of the African American people so that they might be converted to Christianity. Divine Providence was known to bring forth good out of evil. It was now the manifest destiny of the African American people to return to their ancestral homeland, bringing the benefits of Christianity and civilization.[28]

Alexander Crummell (1819–1898) emigrated to Liberia in 1853 because of a desire to bring up his children "under black men's institutions." Like Blyden, he wrote in the Ethiopian redemptionist tradition and spoke of the duties of African Americans to their ancestral continent. Contemporary readers are frequently put off by elements in Crummell's writing that they perceive as elitist. Sterling Stuckey in *Slave Culture* and Anthony Appiah in *My Father's House* have accused him of too readily accepting the cultural values of the Victorian bourgeoisie. The observation is not without merit, but one must remember that Crummell did not have the blessing of being introduced to twentieth-century anthropology, with its doctrines of multiculturalism and cultural relativism. He could not appreciate such quaint West African customs as clitorectomy or trial by ordeal, so thoroughly was he immersed in European cultural modes. He hoped to promote a political economy similar to that of England or the United States, but this, he believed, must be preceded by the transfer of modern technology to Africa, and this must in turn be preceded by the transfer of European culture. For this reason he favored Christianity and the English language as means of advancing the "civilization" of West Africa. In this respect Crummell did not differ from Blyden or other nationalists, and it is important to understand that none of the nineteenth-century nationalists would have understood the criticism that they were "Eurocentric." Despite their now outmoded attitudes toward African culture, however, they were unequivocally committed to the development of Africa as an economic, industrial, and military power controlled by Africans.

Martin R. Delany (1812–1885) was another figure whose nationalist position solidified in the 1850s. Delany, a physician, became an active emigrationist after being dismissed from Harvard Medical School on purely racial grounds.[29] In 1852 he published *The Condition, Elevation, Emigration, and Destiny of the Colored People of the United States,* excerpts of which are reprinted here. In August 1854 he called a National Emigration Convention in Cleveland, Ohio, seemingly interested in migration to some portion of North or South America, but secret sessions of the convention apparently focused on Africa. Appended to the published convention proceedings was a lengthy paper written by Delany, "The Political Destiny of the Colored Race." [30]

In *The Condition, Elevation, Emigration, and Destiny of the Colored People,* Delany described colored people as powerless, although he recognized the accomplishments of several African Americans in the realm of business. For the most part, however, Delany asserted, African Americans were objects of pity; he saw the rest of the world "looking upon us, with feelings of commisseration, sorrow, and contempt."

Delany admonished black Americans to observe how white folk have raised "massive buildings," launched swift vessels "with their white sheets spread to the winds of heaven," built railroads "flying with the velocity of the swallow." Such monuments of white enterprise stood "rebuking us with scorn." African Americans had been described by Frederick Douglass as "the sick man of America" and by Alexander Crummell as "the withered arm of humanity." [31] Delany, with cruel bluntness, observed that throughout the world, "the white race predominates over the colored; or in other words, wherever there is one white person, that one rules and governs two colored persons. This is a living undeniable truth, to which we call the especial attention of the colored reader in particular."

As a remedy for this condition, Delany proposed a vigorous program of self-help. Inheriting the hostility of the older generation toward the American Colonization Society, Delany saw no hope for Liberia as the center of national enterprise. "*Its geographical position* [was] objectionable," he argued, "being located in the *sixth degree* of latitude North of the equator, in a district signally unhealthy." Furthermore, it owed its existence to a scheme got up by slaveholders "to *exterminate* the free colored of the American continent." Finally, Liberia was "not an Independent Republic . . . but a poor *miserable mockery*—a *burlesque* on a government—a pitiful dependency on the American Colonizationists" (emphasis in original). He was willing to consider the prospects for emigration to Canada as a temporary measure, but the finger of God seemed to be pointing in the direction of Mexico, South America, or the West Indies. As an afterthought, he appended the suggestion that African Americans also be willing to consider a settlement in East Africa.

Delany was not the only colorizationist who attempted to maintain a commitment to emigration while rejecting the aims of the American Colonization Society. Mary Ann Shadd Cary favored removal to Canada, where she lived and edited the *Provincial Freeman*. Samuel Ringgold Ward resettled in Jamaica, and James T. Holly, whose work is excerpted in this volume, argued the case for Haiti, where he eventually resettled. Most black nationalists preferred to draw a distinction between themselves and those African Americans who migrated under the auspices of the hated American Colonization Society. This may be attributed partially to their suspicion of the society's motives, but it was due also to their fear that Africa was not conducive to progress. Frederick Douglass toyed with the prospect of migration to Haiti, but was convinced that the environment of equatorial Africa produced racial degeneracy.[32] Delany uncritically accepted the hysterical claims of William Nesbit, who had migrated in 1853 and claimed that the streets of Liberia were "so grown up with bramble bushes [that] elephants might hide in perfect safety," and that the country was "one magnificent swamp. . . . A great deal of the disease of the country is produced by the effluvia arising from these swamps." Nesbit also asserted that "elephants, leopards and tiger cats [were] numerous, often coming into the settlements." In short, the revival of black nationalism in the wake of the Fugitive Slave Act was seldom accompanied by any good feelings toward the American Colonization Society, or what were interpreted as its pro-slavery aims.[33]

Although the Fugitive Slave Act stimulated much talk of emigration, even the most fervent nationalists insisted that they were entitled to the rights of American citizenship. In 1857 the Dred Scott decision shook convictions on that score, and provided an additional painful stimulus to black nationalism and emigrationism. Dred Scott, a slave in Missouri, had resided with his legal owner for a time on free soil, where Congress had prohibited slavery with the Missouri Compromise of 1820. On returning to Missouri, Scott sued for his freedom on the grounds that his residence on free soil had made him a free man. Scott won his suit in the lower court, but lost in the Missouri Supreme Court. The case was then tried in Federal District Court and appealed to the United States Supreme Court, which ruled in *Dred Scott v. Sanford* that Congress had no right to prohibit slavery in the territories.

In his *obiter dictum* on the case (excerpts of which are reprinted in this volume), Chief Justice Roger B. Taney ironically presented an argument for black nationalism—not that he cared. Nor was this a statement from which the nationalists could take much comfort. Taney maintained that the Constitution did not recognize African Americans as citizens, or even as individuals, but as a class of persons "whose ancestors were Negroes of the African race. . . . [and] were not intended to be included, under the word 'citizens' in the Constitution." He defined African Americans as a people both "subordinate and inferior." Taney proclaimed, in effect, that in the eyes of the founding fathers, a free black individual had been an anomaly. The framers of the Constitution, he argued, had considered Africans a subject people, a nation in bondage, a class eternally separate from the American people, and in a state of subordination to them. Some scholars have noted the inconsistency of the evidence regarding the intentions of the founding fathers on the citizenship status of African Americans. On the one hand, scholars have observed that the federal statute of 1790 limiting naturalization to "free white persons" indicated a belief in the inferiority and subordinate status of the African population. On the other hand, state laws often accorded Free Africans the same citizenship privileges as whites. The pattern of federal government action was likewise inconsistent. In 1834 Robert Purvis and his wife, Harriet, wealthy Philadelphia mulattoes, were issued passports stating that they were citizens of the United States. In general, however, American law dealt with African Americans as a "subordinate and inferior class," rather than as equal individual citizens. The Dred Scott decision convinced many African Americans that the black nationalist position made sense.[34]

Willing to consider emigration, but leery of the American Colonization Society, a number of black nationalists established an organization called the African Civilization Society, with Henry Highland Garnet as president. According to its founders, this latter society was founded to promote "the civilization and Christianization of Africa and of the descendants of African ancestors in any portion of the earth." It was Pan-Africanistic in that it did not confine its emigrationism to the African prospect, but also encouraged migration to the Caribbean. Garnet's boyhood acquaintance Samuel Ringgold Ward had migrated to Jamaica in 1855, and Garnet had lived as a missionary in Jamaica from 1852 to 1856. The African Civilization Society supported Caribbean emigration, and frequently discussed plans for a black empire that would encompass all the islands, and perhaps even some portions of the Southern United States. The Caribbean interest is best illustrated by James Theodore Holly, who had participated in Delany's emigration convention and in 1857 published his pamphlet on Haiti, *A Vindication of the Capacity of the Negro Race for Self-Government and Civilized Progress,* sections of which are reprinted here.[35]

The African Civilization Society was not only Pan-Africanistic, but nationalistic, as it was committed by its constitution to "the principle of an African Nationality, the African race being the ruling element of the nation, controlling and directing their own affairs." The society's constitution declared its dedication to undermining the African slave trade, and it contained an article specifying that no one sent to Africa under the society's auspices could uphold doctrines justifying slavery. This was rather mild language, however, in comparison to the radical abolitionism of the day. The society aroused suspicions among militant abolitionists by its declaration that it would "act in harmony with all other societies, whose objects were similar to those of this Association." The only similar societies at the time were the various state colonization societies and the disreputable American Colonization Society itself, whose initials were also ACS. Frederick Douglass was thoroughly suspicious of the African Civilization Society, and in an editorial reprinted in the present volume, he expressed his conviction that the organization was no more than a front for the other ACS.[36]

Indeed, by the late 1850s, black nationalists were becoming less squeamish about cooperating with the American Colonization Society, or at least with those of its members who favored abolition. When Martin R. Delany sailed for West Africa in 1859, on an "expedition of exploration," he left on a ship bearing the Liberian flag, and headed, astonishingly, for Liberia, with Henry Highland Garnet's best wishes, if not his open endorsement. Confusion persists as to the relationship between Garnet and Delany at this point in their careers. The African Civilization Society apparently supported a rival West African expedition headed by Robert Campbell, who set off earlier, but arrived in Liberia later. In Liberia, Delany was toasted and feted by Blyden and Crummell, and he denied that he had ever said anything negative about the republic. Eventually Delany and Campbell teamed up in the region of West Africa that is now Nigeria. Campbell arrived there first, Delany having been delayed by a bout with "the fever." In Lagos they signed a treaty with King Docemo, who seemed receptive to the idea of an African American settlement within his territories. However, when American abolitionists charged that the Kingdom of Lagos condoned slavery, Garnet stated publicly that neither Campbell nor Delany were commissioners of the African Civilization Society, "and probably never will be." Nonetheless, Campbell always claimed that he represented Garnet's organization, and Delany pretended that he and Campbell had cooperated all along.[37]

By the early 1860s, black nationalists were expressing their ideas openly through the medium of the *Weekly Anglo-African,* a weekly newspaper published by the black emigrationist Robert Hamilton and featuring Garnet among its contributing editors. The period also witnessed the growth of a cooperative spirit between Delany's "African movement" and Garnet's African Civilization Society. Whatever his earlier position, Garnet endorsed the "African movement" in his speech at Cooper's Institute, New York City, 1860, which is included in the present collection. By November 1861, Delany was playing a prominent role in the African Civilization Society, and his name appeared in a list of the ACS board of vice presidents, which also included the names of some prominent white supporters of colonization. Delany and Garnet no longer found it necessary to deny one another, once they had both owned up to the informal, but very real, connections of their respective enterprises to the American Colonization Society.[38]

Colonization received a rather ethereal endorsement in 1862 when Abraham Lincoln met with a delegation of African Americans to discuss a proposal for emigration to Latin America or the Caribbean. The occasion was remarkable because neither Delany nor Garnet was part of the delegation (the transcript of the meeting is reprinted in this collection). Also conspicuously absent were Blyden and Crummell, who happened to be in the United States at the time, and Joseph Jenkins Roberts, former president of Liberia, who had met with Lincoln shortly before. The relatively obscure figures who made up the African American delegation, after listening to Lincoln's proposal, replied that "they would hold a consultation and in a short time give an answer." The president responded, "Take your full time—no hurry at all." Some African Americans took his proposal seriously. In 1862 Daniel A. Payne, in "An Open Letter to the Colored People" (reprinted here), advised African Americans to give it careful consideration. There is reason to believe, however, that Lincoln had secretly abandoned any serious consideration of African deportation by 1862, although he disingenuously continued public discussion of colonization, in order to disarm potential critics of his Emancipation Proclamation, which had already been drafted.[39]

African Americans did not immediately abandon all interest in emigration when the Emancipation Proclamation was announced in September 1862, but when the proclamation took effect, on January 1, 1863, attitudes shifted. By then the war, which had begun with the aim of keeping the slave states within the Union, was being transformed into a war for the abolition of slavery. As black troops were mustered into the army, Martin Delany was awarded a commission at the rank of major, and after the war he went into South Carolina politics, taking advantage of the opportunities offered by the ascendancy of the Republican Party. With the failure of Reconstruction, Delany changed course again, to support a back-to-Africa movement in 1878. Generally speaking, however, classical black nationalism commanded few followers in the late nineteenth century, and there was not much interest in emigration from the end of the Civil War to World War I.

Some scholars have detected a nationalistic impulse in the migration of blacks who left the South in the "Kansas Exodus" of the 1870s and those who founded all-black settlements in Oklahoma during the migration of the 1890s. Certainly there were separatist, messianic elements in both movements, but if nationalism is defined as the impulse to create a sovereign nation-state, then these migrations do not meet the definition. A truer manifestation of nationalism arose in the 1890s, in a movement headed by Henry McNeal Turner, a strong-minded and assertive bishop of the African Methodist Episcopal Church. Turner maintained that he had been a consistent supporter of colonization, after being converted by an address of Alexander Crummell in 1862. He maintained ties with Edward Wilmot Blyden, who still occasionally visited the United States during the nineties. Known for his doctrine that "God is a Negro," Turner attempted to resuscitate the religiously based black nationalism of the antebellum period. His program, which called for a mass migration to Africa, may be contrasted with the black nationalism of the mid-nineteenth century, however, in that it failed to make much headway among bourgeois intellectuals. As a Pan-Africanist, Turner is remembered for his missionary expeditions to South Africa, where his efforts on behalf of African Methodism encouraged an independent church movement with an enduring strain of Christian black nationalism. While talk of emigration had little currency with black leadership during the late nineteenth century, Pan-Africanism, as represented by Turner's South African activities, remained strong.[40]

Alexander Crummell made his final departure from the Republic of Liberia in 1872, having come to believe that African problems must be solved by "indigenous" Africans themselves. In 1882 he preached his famous "Eulogium on the life of Henry Highland Garnet," who had gone to Liberia as United States Minister Resident in that year, but died almost immediately, presumably of tropical disease. Crummell still believed in a universal uplift movement for the elevation of the entire African race and did not abandon his commitment to "African civilization." He continued to advocate separate black institutions for racial uplift, and to that end he founded the American Negro Academy in 1897. Edward Wilmot Blyden and James T. Holly were elected to the academy as "foreigners of distinction." The academy's original members included John E. Bruce and William H. Ferris, who were to become important figures in Marcus Garvey's Universal Negro Improvement Association. Another of the academy's original members was a young college professor, W. E. B. Du Bois.

William Edward Burghardt Du Bois (1869–1963) was not a classical black nationalist. He never advocated a mass migration of African Americans to Africa, nor did he favor the creation of a separate, geographically based nation-state for the African American population. He was a founder of the NAACP and editor of its official publication, the *Crisis*. Although he crusaded for integration, he nonetheless kept up a lifelong commitment to ideological Pan-Africanism, and organized or contributed to six Pan-African conferences from 1919 to 1945. As is well known, he migrated to Ghana shortly before his death, to become a staunch supporter of the Pan-Africanist policies of the country's president, Kwame Nkrumah. In his 1897 address before the first meeting of the American Negro Academy, reprinted in this volume, Du Bois called for "the rearing of a race ideal in America and Africa, to the glory of God and the uplifting of the Negro people," and asserted that African Americans must "maintain their race identity," and made clear his belief in independent African American cultural and social institutions.[41]

The member of the American Negro Academy most closely associated with classical black nationalism was Orishatukeh Faduma, whose career seemed to epitomize Pan-Africanism. He was born in the Bahamas to parents of Yoruba ancestry, but grew up in Sierra Leone after his parents migrated there. Known originally as S. J. Davies, he studied at London University and at Yale. Faduma lived at different times in Sierra Leone, Gambia, the Gold Coast, and the American midwest. In 1913 he was a missionary in Boley, Oklahoma, and around that time, became involved with Chief Alfred C. Sam, a chief of the Apasu region in the Gold Coast of West Africa, now Ghana. Sam founded the Akim Trading Company and purchased the steamship *Curityba*, which he renamed the *S.S. Liberia*. In 1914 Faduma accompanied a number of African Americans, many of them from Oklahoma, aboard the *S.S. Liberia* to the Gold Coast, where they were cordially received, but met with little success as colonists. Stranded without food and stricken with malaria, the majority of the emigrants became disillusioned and returned to the United States.[42]

With Blyden's death in 1912, Bishop Turner's death in 1915, and Chief Sam's tragic failure that same year, the African movement appeared to be moribund, but Marcus Garvey arrived in the United States the following spring. Marcus Moziah Garvey (1887–1940), the last and most significant of the classical black nationalists, was born at Saint Ann's Bay, Jamaica. His father, Marcus Garvey Sr., was a skilled bricklayer and a bibliophile; his mother came from a family of small farmers. In his early teens, Garvey was apprenticed to his godfather, Alfred Ernest Burrowes, a man of wide reading and broad interests, who operated a printery at Saint Ann's Bay. Garvey eventually took over the management of Burrowes's branch office in Port Maria, then worked as a compositor in Kingstown. As a young man he traveled to Costa Rica and Panama, where he established small newspapers. Garvey's experiences as a journalist and printer later served him well in the United States, where he became a successful newspaperman and demonstrated true genius as a publicist. From 1912 to 1914 he lived in London, where he matriculated informally at Birkbeck College, an institution for working people that was later recognized as a school of the University of London. During the London years he published an article with Duse Mohamed Ali, an Egyptian-born Pan-Africanist, publisher of the *African Times and Orient Review*, and corresponding member of the American Negro Academy.[43]

Garvey haunted the libraries and bookstores, reading voraciously. He studied the works of Edward Wilmot Blyden. At some point he read Booker T. Washington's autobiography *Up from Slavery*, which told the story of the founding of Tuskegee Institute, an agricultural and mechanical college in Alabama. Washington was neither a militant nor a nationalist, but Garvey was much impressed by Washington's devotion to practical education, economic self-sufficiency, and material self-help. He may have been aware of Washington's International Conference on the Negro, held at Tuskegee in 1912. Perhaps he was aware that Duse Mohamed had corresponded with Washington. Or he may even have been aware of Washington's angry 1896 condemnation of the British imperialists who had mown down Africans with Maxim guns "simply because they tried to defend their homes, their wives and their children."[44] Garvey asked himself,

"Where is the black man's government?" "Where is his King and his kingdom?" "Where is his President, his country, and his ambassador, his army, his navy, his men of big affairs?" I could not find them, and then I declared, I will help to make them.[45]

He returned to Jamaica in 1914, founded the Universal Negro Improvement Association (UNIA), and in 1916, began to travel and organize in the United States.

Garvey soon discovered that black nationalist and emigrationist movements were traditional among black Americans. With remarkable brilliance, he began to tap the reservoirs of Pan-African consciousness that he discovered among stable working people, aspiring entrepreneurs, religious leaders, and educated "race men," many of them a generation older than himself. The United States had not yet entered World War I, but the effects of the "Great War" were already being felt by black Americans by the time of his arrival. Large numbers were streaming into Northern cities as the result of severe hardship in the South and the diminished supply of immigrant labor due to the disruption of Europe. Garvey discovered a diverse population of black Americans, including West Indian immigrants, transplanted peasants from the South, a small class of skilled workers, petty capitalists, and a clergy with political ambitions. The Harlem community had already demonstrated that it could maintain a press, a labor movement, a network of women's clubs, and a variety of fraternal institutions. Furthermore, there was a tradition of messianic black nationalism, extant since the late eighteenth century. Garvey's ability to make his personality felt in each of these areas gave him enduring popularity and lasting influence.

In the pages of his weekly newspaper, *Negro World,* Garvey claimed the mission of leading all progressive and upstanding Negroes back to Africa. His elaborate plan for African commerce and transatlantic shipping, the Black Star Line, followed in the tradition of Paul Cuffe and the nineteenth-century African civilization movement. African American "repatriation" was to be a means of implanting Christianity, commerce, and civilization in "the land of our fathers." But Garvey ran afoul of the civil rights establishment, much as had his predecessors Russwurm and Garnet in earlier generations. Integrationist leaders launched a "Garvey must go" campaign. The loftily independent W. E. B. Du Bois launched his own campaign against Garvey in the *Crisis*. Although Garvey was unsuccessful as a repatriationist, he enjoyed tremendous success as a journalist and ideologue of Pan-Africanism. There was also a strong religious component to Garveyism; he echoed the assertion of Henry McNeal Turner that God is black.[46]

With its emphasis on ancient African history, particularly the civilization of Egypt, *Negro World* followed in the tradition of *Freedom's Journal*. This "Afrocentric tradition," as we call it today, had been maintained by Edward Wilmot Blyden, who stressed the ties of ancient Egypt to the rest of Africa in his voluminous writings, and made a pilgrimage to the Great Pyramid. Frederick Douglass also visited the Great Pyramid, and claimed the Egyptians as long lost relatives with a "strong affinity and a direct relationship" to the rest of the African race. In his view, members of the African race were "but one people." William Wells Brown was not a classical black nationalist, and he never visited Egypt, but he spoke nonetheless of "the image of the Negro . . . engraved upon the monuments of Egypt, not as a bondman, but as the master of art." In a similar vein Marcus Garvey's *Philosophy and Opinions* proclaimed, "When the great white race of today had no civilization of its own, when white men lived in caves and were counted as savages, this race of ours boasted of a wonderful civilization on the Banks of the Nile. . . . Ancient Egypt gave the world Civilization . . . Greece and Rome have robbed Egypt of her arts and letters, and taken all the credit to themselves." Garvey noted, with acerbic irony, that "whenever a black man accomplishes anything of importance he is no longer a Negro." Who or what was a Negro? The European definition was obvious: a Negro was "a person of dark complexion or race, who has not accomplished anything and to whom others are not obligated for any useful service."[47]

The Afrocentricity and Pan-Africanism of Marcus Garvey became sources of inspiration to many African nationalists. His name came to be widely recognized among masses of simple people in Africa and the Americas. In the United States, however, he incurred the wrath of the powerful. With his exuberant black nationalism, he made many enemies outside the black community and aroused the hostility of the police, the FBI, and the attorney general of the state of New York. In 1925 he was convicted of using the mails to defraud, and after spending two years in the federal prison in Atlanta, he was deported in 1927. Garvey made attempts to revitalize his movement in Jamaica, and in 1935 he moved his base to London, but he was never able to regain the power that he had known in the Harlem of the twenties, and he died in London in 1940, a frustrated and bitter man.

Black nationalism, Pan-Africanism, and Afrocentrism have persisted in the United States due partially to the persistence of those conditions that originally gave rise to them—the segregation and subordination of the African American population. While many contemporary Americans sincerely express the hope that a color-blind society will someday evolve in the United States, there is little evidence that such a society will soon come into existence. African Americans are frequently counseled to give up attitudes of racial separatism, especially in its more militant forms, but those who offer this advice give only lukewarm support (if any) to aggressive equal opportunity programs designed to speed the entry of African Americans into the mainstream. It thus seems likely that racial separatism in various forms, particularly marital and religious separatism, will continue to divide the African American people from other Americans, and that feelings of African American racial separateness will frequently find expression in black nationalism.

Notes

1. A brilliant historical definition of black nationalism is to be found in E. U. Essien-Udom, *Black Nationalism: A Search for an Identity in America* (Chicago: University of Chicago Press, 1962). Another general definition that places Pan-Africanism under the rubric of black nationalism is included in the introduction to John H. Bracey Jr., August Meier, and Elliott M. Rudwick, eds., *Black Nationalism in America* (Indianapolis: Bobbs-Merrill, 1970). Alphonso Pinkney accepts this broad definition in *Red Black and Green: Black Nationalism in the United States* (New York: Cambridge University Press, 1976). Also see Sterling Stuckey, ed., *The Ideological Origins of Black Nationalism* (Boston: Beacon Press, 1972). Some standard works on nationalism include Hans Kohn, *The Idea of Nationalism: A Study in Its Origins and Backgrounds* (New York: Macmillan, 1944); Louis Snyder, *The Dynamics of Nationalism* (New York: Van Nostrand, 1964); K. R. Minogue, *Nationalism* (Baltimore: Penguin, 1970).

2. "Pan-African" actually has more than one meaning. George Padmore used it in the sense of a movement to unite the continent under a United States of

Africa. See George Padmore, *Pan-Africanism or Communism? The Coming Struggle for Africa* (London: Dennis Dobson, 1956). It may also refer simply to cultural and intellectual movements or to a general sense of sympathy and mutual support-iveness among Africans and peoples of African descent. The numerous definitions and a thorough historical study are offered by Imanuel Geiss in *The Pan-African Movement* (New York: Holmes and Meier, 1974).

3. *Webster's Ninth New Collegiate Dictionary* (New York: Merriam Webster, 1990) defines a nation as "a community of people composed of one or more nationalities and possessing more or less defined territory and government." Some may find this definition puzzling, in that it allows one nation to be composed of more than one nationality. Frederick Douglass described the United States as a "nation . . . made up of a variety of nations," but he later contradicted this idea, saying that "a nation within a nation is an anomaly." See his address delivered in Albany, N.Y., in 1870, in *The Frederick Douglass Papers,* ed. John W. Blassingame and John R. McKivigan (New Haven: Yale University Press, 1992), 4:272. Also see Frederick Douglass, "The Nation's Problem" (1889), in *The Frederick Douglass Papers,* ed. Blassingame and McKivigan, 5:415. Alexander Crummell observed that, like it or not, "we are a nation set apart in this country." Alexander Crum-mell, "The Social Principle among a People" (sermon delivered in Washington, D.C., 1875), in *The Greatness of Christ and Other Sermons* (New York: Thomas Whittaker, 1882), 296, 297–98. W. E. B. Du Bois in the same vein spoke of "A Negro Nation within the Nation," *Current History,* June 1935.

4. "Races are the organism and ordinance of God," wrote Alexander Crum-mell in "The Race Problem in America" (1888), in *Africa and America* (Spring-field: Willey, 1891), 46. Compare to Edward Wilmot Blyden's equation of nation and race in "The African Problem and the Method of Its Solution," *African Repository,* July 1890, 65–79.

5. Imanuel Geiss uses the term "proto–Pan-Africanism" in *The Pan-African Movement,* 30–40.

6. Standard treatments of Palmares include Irene Diggs, "Zumbi and the Republic of Os Palmares," *Phylon* 14, no. 1 (1953): 69; R. K. Kent, "Palmares: An African State in Brazil," *Journal of African History* 6, no. 2 (1965); Charles E. Chapman, "Palmares, The Negro Numantia," *Journal of Negro History* 3 (January 1918): 29–32.

7. Richard Price, ed., *Maroon Societies: Rebel Slave Communities in the Americas* (Baltimore: Johns Hopkins University Press, 1979) is a good place to begin the study of Maroons. For a recent summary, see Vincent Bakpetu Thompson, *The Making of the African Diaspora in the Americas, 1441–1900* (London: Longman, 1987), 278–92.

8. Herbert Aptheker, "Maroons within the Present Limits of the United States," *Journal of Negro History* 24 (1939): 167–84. For more extended chapters on Seminole resistance, see Mary Francis Berry, *Black Resistance/White Law: A History of Constitutional Racism in America* (New York: Appleton Century Crofts, 1971), 35–68.

9. Marion D. de B. Kilson, "Towards Freedom: An Analysis of Slave Revolts in the United States," *Phylon* 25 (2d quarter 1964): 175–87.

10. Herbert Aptheker, *American Negro Slave Revolts* (New York: Columbia University Press, 1943). For other paranoid reactions and rumors of a papist plot, see Thomas J. Davis, *A Rumor of Revolt: The "Great Negro Plot" of Colonial New York* (New York: Free Press, 1985).

11. Herbert Aptheker, ed., *Documentary History of the Negro People in the United States* (New York: Citadel, 1971), 1:7–8. The original of this document is a printed leaflet, preserved in the New York Historical Society.

12. Ellen Gibson Wilson, *The Loyal Blacks* (New York: G. P. Putnam's Sons, 1976); Richard West, *Back to Africa: A History of Sierra Leone and Liberia* (New York: Holt, Rinehart and Winston, 1970); Mavis C. Campbell, *Back to Africa: George Ross and the Maroons: From Nova Scotia to Sierra Leone* (Trenton, N.J.: Africa World Press, 1993); W. E. F. Ward, *The Royal Navy and the Slavers* (New York: Schocken, 1970), 229.

13. Sidney Kaplan and Emma Nogrady Kaplan, *The Black Presence in the Era of the American Revolution* (Amherst: University of Massachusetts Press, 1989), 206–8.

14. For examples of nineteenth-century views of Toussaint, see William Wells Brown, *The Black Man, His Antecedents, His Genius, and His Achievements* (New York: Thomas Hamilton, 1863), 92–106; and William J. Simmons, *Men of Mark: Eminent, Progressive, and Rising* (Cleveland: Geo. M. Rewell and Co., 1887), 936–47.

15. Elie Kedourie, ed., *Nationalism in Asia and Africa* (New York: Meridian, 1970), 28–31. Cf. Elie Kedourie, *Nationalism*, 3rd ed. (Oxford: Oxford University Press, 1966), 9.

16. W. E. Burghardt Du Bois, *The Suppression of the African Slave Trade to the United States of America, 1638–1870* (1896; reprint, New York: Schocken, 1969), 70–74, 80–85, 92–94; Eugene Genovese, *From Rebellion to Revolution: Afro-American Slave Revolts in the Making of the New World* (Baton Rouge: Louisiana State University Press, 1979).

17. Gustavus Vassa, *The Interesting Narrative of the Life of Olaudah Equiano, or Gustavus Vassa, the African* (London, 1789), reprinted in *Great Slave Narratives*, comp. Arna Bontemps (Boston: Beacon, 1969), 190. Also see the new edition of Equiano's *Narrative* edited by Robert J. Allison (Boston: Bedford Books, 1995).

18. Geiss, *The Pan-African Movement*, 98 ff.

19. Lamont Thomas, *Paul Cuffe: Black Entrepreneur and Pan-Africanist* (Urbana: University of Illinois Press, 1988). Also see the excellent introduction to Sheldon Harris, ed., *Paul Cuffe: Black America and the African Return* (New York: Simon and Schuster, 1972).

20. A discussion of the possibility that Allen may have been briefly sympathetic to colonization is in the introduction by William Loren Katz to William Lloyd Garrison, *Thoughts on Colonization* (1832; reprint, New York: Arno, 1969), x.

21. For an introduction to colonization, see Philip J. Staudenraus, *The African Colonization Movement* (New York: Columbia University Press, 1961). Also essential is Floyd Miller, *The Search for a Black Nationality: Black Colonization and Emigration, 1787–1863* (Urbana: University of Illinois Press, 1975).

22. Letter of Rev. Mr. Williams to the citizens of New York, July 14, 1834, originally published in *African Repository* 10:186–88, and reprinted in *The Mind of the Negro as Reflected in Letters Written during the Crisis, 1800–1860,* ed. Carter G. Woodson (Washington, D.C.: Association for the Study of Afro-American Life and History, 1926). Williams's letter reveals his sympathies with the colonization movement.

23. See comments of Sterling Stuckey, in the fine introduction to his edition of Walker's *Appeal,* in Stuckey, *The Ideological Origins of Black Nationalism,* 9.

24. The jeremiad tradition in its connection to Walker's *Appeal* is discussed in Wilson J. Moses, *Black Messiahs and Uncle Toms* (University Park: Pennsylvania State University Press, 1982), 30–48. For a broader discussion, see David Howard-Pitney, *The Afro-American Jeremiad* (Philadelphia: Temple University Press, 1990). Charles Gibson, *The Black Legend: Anti-Spanish Attitudes in the Old World and the New* (New York: Knopf, 1971). Ethiopianism is discussed throughout St. Clair Drake, *The Redemption of Africa and Black Religion* (Chicago: Third World Press, 1970). Also see George Shepperson, "Ethiopianism and African Nationalism," *Phylon* 13, no. 1 (1st quarter 1953).

25. Maria Stewart, *Productions of Mrs. Maria W. Stewart, Presented to the First African Baptist Church and Society, of the City of Boston* (Boston: Friends of Freedom and Virtue, 1835), 20.

26. Moses, *Black Messiahs and Uncle Toms,* 36–37. John Lofton, *Denmark Vesey's Revolt: The Slave Plot that Lit a Fuse to Fort Sumter* (Kent, Ohio: Kent State University Press, 1983). Douglas R. Egerton denies the importance of religion to the Gabriel conspiracy in *Gabriel's Rebellion: The Virginia Slave Conspiracies of 1800 and 1802* (Chapel Hill: University of North Carolina Press, 1993), 179–81. For a more balanced view, see Gerald Mullin, *Flight and Rebellion: Slave Resistance in Eighteenth Century Virginia* (New York: Oxford University Press, 1972), 148–49.

27. The term "African movement" is used in *Constitution of African Civilization Society* (New Haven, 1861), reprinted in *Negro Social and Political Thought, 1850–1925,* ed. Howard Brotz (New Brunswick: Transaction Publishers, 1992). For other occurrences of the term, see William E. Bittle and Gilbert Geis, *The Longest Way Home: Chief Alfred C. Sam's Back-to-Africa Movement* (Detroit: Wayne State University Press, 1964), 83; Robert A. Hill, ed., *The Marcus Garvey and Universal Negro Improvement Association Papers* (Berkeley: University of California Press, 1983), 1:541. W. E. B. Du Bois, "Reconstruction and Africa," *Crisis,* February 1919; J. Ayodele Langley, *Pan-Africanism and Nationalism in West Africa, 1900–1945* (New York: Oxford University Press, 1973), 24, 41–58, 113, 156.

28. Edward Wilmot Blyden, *A Voice from Bleeding Africa on Behalf of Her Exiled Children* (Monrovia: G. Killian, 1856), excerpted in *Black Spokesman:*

Selected Published Writings of Edward Wilmot Blyden, ed. Hollis R. Lynch, (New York: Humanities Press, 1971). Hollis R. Lynch, *Edward Wilmot Blyden: Pan-Negro Patriot, 1832–1912* (London: Oxford University Press, 1964), 4. Also see Thomas W. Livingston, *Education and Race: A Biography of Edward Wilmot Blyden* (San Francisco: Glendessary Press, 1975).

29. Victor Ullman, *Martin R. Delany: The Beginnings of Black Nationalism* (Boston: Beacon, 1971), 38, describes Delany's travels into the American Southwest to investigate emigration possibilities.

30. See *Proceedings of the National Emigration Convention of Colored People Held at Cleveland, Ohio, on Thursday Friday and Saturday, the 24th, 25th, and 26th, of August, 1854: With a Reference Page of Contents* (Pittsburgh: A. A. Anderson, 1854).

31. Frederick Douglass said, "In the eyes of Nicholas, the Turk was the sick man of Europe—just so as the negro is now the sick man of America." "The Black Man's Future in the Southern States" (2 February 1862), in *The Frederick Douglass Papers,* ed. Blassingame, 3:503. Alexander Crummell used the "withered arm" analogy in his "Address at the Anniversary Meeting of the Massachusetts Colonization Society," in Alexander Crummell and Edward Wilmot Blyden, *Liberia, the Land of Promise* (Washington, D.C.: American Colonization Society, 1861).

32. For Douglass's thoughts on Haiti, see Waldo Martin, *The Mind of Frederick Douglass* (Chapel Hill: University of North Carolina Press, 1984), 74. For his comments on the deleterious effects of the African climate, see Frederick Douglass, "The Claims of the Negro Ethnologically Considered: An Address Delivered in Hudson, Ohio on 12 July 1854," in *The Frederick Douglass Papers,* ed. Blassingame, series 1, 2:521.

33. William Nesbit, *Four Months in Liberia: Or African Colonization Exposed* (Pittsburgh: J. T. Shryock, 1865), 13, 23. Also see Martin R. Delany's introduction to that volume, which reiterates Nesbit's points.

34. Don E. Fehrenbacher, *Slavery, Law and Politics: The Dred Scott Case in Historical Perspective* (New York: Oxford University Press, 1981), 35. On the Purvises, see Peter M. Bergman, *The Chronological History of the Negro in America* (New York: Harper and Row, 1969), 151.

35. Garnet's Jamaican sojourn is discussed in Earl Ofari, *"Let Your Motto Be Resistance": The Life and Thought of Henry Highland Garnet* (Boston: Beacon Press, 1972), 66–69. The Haitian movement is discussed in Miller, *Search for a Black Nationality,* 232–49; and Howard H. Bell, ed., *Black Separatism and the Caribbean, 1860* (Ann Arbor: University of Michigan Press, 1970), which includes the full text of Holly's *Vindication of the Capacity of the Negro Race.*

36. The complete text of the constitution of the African Civilization Society is reprinted in *Negro Social and Political Thought,* ed. Brotz, 191–96. On Douglass's reaction, see Wilson J. Moses, *The Golden Age of Black Nationalism, 1850–1925* (Hamden: Archon, 1978; reprint, New York: Oxford University Press, 1988), 38–39.

37. Delany's departure is described in Miller, *Search for a Black Nationality,* 198. For the complete texts of the Delany and Campbell expeditions, see Howard H. Bell, ed., *Search for a Place: Black Separatism and Africa* (Ann Arbor: University of Michigan Press, 1971). See Ofari, *"Let Your Motto Be Resistance"* for Garnet's financial backing of Campbell (83–84), his denial of Campbell and Delany (92), and Delany's subsequent role in the African Civilization Society (95–96). Also see Cyril W. Griffith, *The African Dream: Martin R. Delany and the Emergence of Pan-African Thought* (University Park: Pennsylvania State University Press, 1975). For a brilliant treatment of Campbell, rich in detail, see R. J. M. Blackett, *Beating against the Barriers: Biographical Essays in Nineteenth Century Afro-American History* (Baton Rouge: Louisiana State University Press, 1986), 139–84. There is also material on the African Civilization Society in David Swift, *Black Prophets of Justice: Activist Clergy before the Civil War* (Baton Rouge: Louisiana State University Press, 1989), 292–99.

38. For Delany's and Garnet's flirtations with the American Colonization Society, and their interactions with Campbell and one another, see Miller, *Search for a Black Nationality,* 170–231.

39. For further discussion of Lincoln and the Liberian delegation, see Wilson J. Moses, *Alexander Crummell: A Study of Civilization and Discontent* (New York: Oxford University Press, 1989), 143–44, 328 nn. 66–69. Lincoln's attitudes on colonization are further discussed in John Hope Franklin, *The Emancipation Proclamation* (Garden City: Doubleday, 1963), 20, 31–32, 98–99, 107–8, 131–32.

40. Henry McNeal Turner to the *Washington Post,* February 2, 1895, reprinted in *Respect Black: The Writings and Speeches of Henry McNeal Turner,* ed. Edwin S. Redkey (New Haven: Yale University Press, 1971); and Edwin S. Redkey, *Black Exodus: Black Nationalist and Back to Africa Movements, 1890–1910* (New Haven: Yale University Press, 1969), 28. Also useful is Stephen Ward Angell, *Bishop Henry McNeal Turner and African-American Religion in the South* (Knoxville: University of Tennessee Press, 1992).

41. On the nationalism of Du Bois, see Vincent Harding, "A Black Messianic Visionary," *Freedomways* 9, no. 1 (1st quarter 1969): 44–58. On Du Bois and Pan-Africanism, see Richard B. Moore, "Du Bois and Pan-Africa," *Freedomways* 5, no. 1 (winter 1965): 166–88. Also see Manning Marable, *W. E. B. Du Bois, Black Radical Democrat* (New York: Twayne, 1986), 99–120.

42. On Alfred C. Sam, see *The Marcus Garvey and Universal Negro Improvement Association Papers,* ed. Hill, 1:536–47; and Robert A. Hill, "Chief Alfred Sam and the African Movement," in *Pan-African Biography,* ed. Robert A. Hill (Los Angeles: University of California and Crossroads Press, 1987), 57–78. Author's interview with S. K. Jangaba (Jangaba Johnson), former student of Faduma, outside Monrovia, Liberia, February 1980. Also see Rina L. Okonkwo, "Orishatukeh Faduma: A Man of Two Worlds," *Journal of Negro History* 68, no. 1 (winter 1983): 24–36.

43. On Duse Mohamed Ali, see *The Marcus Garvey and Universal Negro Im-

provement Association Papers, ed. Hill, 1:519–21, which identify him as Duse Mohamed Ali, but also comment on the various forms of his name. He is identified as Mohamed Ali, Duse, in the index to Langley, *Pan-Africanism and Nationalism in West Africa, 1900–1940.* His name is given as Duse Mohamed on the facsimile title page of his partially plagiarized book, *In the Land of the Pharaohs: A Short History of Egypt* (London: Frank Cass, 1968).

44. Booker T. Washington, "Christianizing Africa," *Our Day* (December 1896): 674–75, reprinted in *The Booker T. Washington Papers,* ed. Louis Harlan (Urbana: University of Illinois Press, 1975), 4:251–52. Also see Louis Harlan, "Booker T. Washington and the Black Man's Burden," *American Historical Review* 71, no. 2 (January 1966): 441–67.

45. Marcus Garvey, *Philosophy and Opinions of Marcus Garvey,* ed. Amy Jacques Garvey (1923, 1925; reprint, New York: Atheneum, 1968), 2:126.

46. For Du Bois's attacks on Garvey, see Marable, *W. E. B. Du Bois,* 99–120. Marcus Garvey, *Philosophy and Opinions,* 1:44.

47. Edward W. Blyden, *From West Africa to Palestine* (Freetown: T. J. Sawyer, 1873), reprinted in *Black Spokesman,* ed. Lynch, 152; Douglass, "The Claims of the Negro Ethnologically Considered," 517; Brown, *The Black Man, His Antecedents, His Genius, and His Achievements,* 33; Marcus Garvey, "Who and What Is a Negro," in *Philosophy and Opinions of Marcus Garvey,* 2:18–19.

Bibliographic Note

A brief introductory essay obviously cannot serve as a complete overview of classical black nationalist movements and ideologies in the United States. Further information on classical black nationalism is available in other works by the present author, including *The Golden Age of Black Nationalism, 1850–1925* (Hamden: Archon Books, 1978; reprint, New York: Oxford University Press, 1988), which contains a basic bibliography. Also see Wilson J. Moses, *Black Messiahs and Uncle Toms: Social and Literary Interpretations of a Religious Myth,* 2d ed. (University Park: Pennsylvania State University Press, 1993). Wilson J. Moses, *Alexander Crummell: A Study of Civilization and Discontent* (New York: Oxford University Press, 1989), offers detailed information on classical black nationalism, viewed from the perspective of one of the movement's chief actors. Each of the preceding contains a bibliography. Wilson J. Moses, *The Wings of Ethiopia: Studies in African American Life and Letters* (Ames: Iowa State University Press, 1990) contains additional essays on the subject of black nationalism-classical and more recent.

Some basic works on African American intellectual history during the years covered in this volume include Howard Brotz, ed., *Negro Social and Political Thought, 1850–1920: Representative Texts* 2nd ed. (New Brunswick: Transaction Publishers, 1992); Robert C. Dick, *Black Protest: Issues and Tactics* (Westport, Conn.: Greenwood Press, 1974); August Meier, *Negro Thought in America, 1880–1915: Racial Ideologies in the Age of Booker T. Washington* (Ann Arbor: University of Michigan Press, 1963); Jane H. Pease and William H. Pease,

They Who Would Be Free: Blacks' Search for Freedom, 1830–1861 (New York: Atheneum, 1974).

General works on nationalism include K. R. Minogue, *Nationalism* (Baltimore: Penguin, 1970); Hans Kohn, "Nationalism," in *Dictionary of the History of Ideas* (New York: Scribners, 1973) contains a useful introduction to the bibliography.

The most comprehensive general introduction to the history of Pan-Africanism, Imanuel Geiss, *The Pan-African Movement* (New York: Holmes and Meier, 1974), includes an outstanding bibliography of primary sources. Also see St. Clair Drake, *The Redemption of Africa and Black Religion* (Chicago: Third World Press, 1970). For influences of American black nationalism on African nationalism, see J. Ayodele Langley, *Pan-Africanism and Nationalism in West Africa, 1900–1945* (New York: Oxford University Press, 1973); George Padmore, *Pan-Africanism or Communism? The Coming Struggle for Africa* (London: Dennis Dobson, 1956); C. L. R. James, *A History of Pan-African Revolt* (Washington, D.C.: Drum and Spear Press, 1969); Okon Edet Uya, ed., *Black Brotherhood: Afro-Americans and Africa* (Lexington, Mass.: D. C. Heath, 1971).

Studies focusing on the black nationalist tradition in the United States are Rodney Carlisle, *The Roots of Black Nationalism* (Port Washington, N.Y.: Kennikat Press, 1975); Floyd Miller, *The Search for a Black Nationality: Black Colonization and Emigration, 1787–1863* (Urbana: University of Illinois Press, 1975); Edwin S. Redkey, *Black Exodus: Black Nationalist and Back to Africa Movements, 1890–1910* (New Haven, Conn.: Yale University Press, 1969); Sterling Stuckey, ed., *The Ideological Origins of Black Nationalism* (Boston: Beacon Press, 1972). For black nationalist revival in the 1960s, see Alphonso Pinkney, *Red Black and Green: Black Nationalism in the United States* (New York: Cambridge University Press, 1976); Raymond Hall, *Black Separatism in the United States* (Hanover, N.H.: University Press of New England, 1978); and William L. Van Deberg, *New Day in Babylon: The Black Power Movement and American Culture, 1965–1975* (Chicago: University of Chicago Press, 1992).

The bibliography on Afrocentrism is rapidly growing. Among the better known works are Molefi K. Asante, *The Afrocentric Idea* (Philadelphia: Temple University Press, 1987); Martin Bernal, *Black Athena: The Afroasiatic Roots of Classical Civilization*, vol. 1, *The Fabrication of Ancient Greece*, and vol. 2, *The Archeological and Documentary Evidence* (New Brunswick: Rutgers University Press, 1987, 1991); Cheikh Anta Diop, *The African Origin of Civilization: Myth or Reality*, ed. and trans. Mercer Cook (New York: Lawrence Hill, 1974); St Clair Drake, *Black Folk Here and There: An Essay in History and Anthropology*, vols. 1 and 2 (Los Angeles: Center for Afro American Studies, UCLA, 1987, 1990); W. E. B. Du Bois, *The World and Africa* (New York: Viking Press, 1947); Drusilla Dunjee Houston, *Wonderful Ethiopians of the Cushite Empire* (Oklahoma City: Universal Publishing Co., 1926); Joel Augustus Rogers, *From "Superman" to Man* (1917; reprint, New York: Helga M. Rogers, 1957). In addition, the works of Ivan Van Sertima are of paramount importance to any study of Afrocentric ideology.

Part One

The Colonization and Emigration Controversy, Preclassical Period

1

From Notes on the State of Virginia (1781–82)

Thomas Jefferson composed Notes on the State of Virginia *toward the end of the Revolutionary War in 1781–82, in response to queries he received from the Marquis de Barbé-Marbois on conditions in Virginia and plans for future development. In the following passages, he refers to laws that have been proposed for the governance of Virginia on the conclusion of the War for Independence. Despite his well-known doctrine of small government, Jefferson revealed a belief that slavery could not be abolished without the employment of remarkably complex measures. Holding it as self-evident that black and white populations could not cooperate on an equal basis to form one united and happy people, he advocated the creation of an elaborate governmental bureaucracy to carry out the work of deporting the Free African population and replacing it with European immigrants. His methods have been characterized by the historian John Chester Miller as "draconian."*

It is ironic, and offensive to many, that Jefferson imputed to black males a preference for white women, since the widespread racial admixture that occurred in colonial America was almost synonymous with the exploitation of black women by white men. Rumors were constant in his lifetime that Jefferson was the biological father of several children born to Sally Hemings, a slave of his deceased wife. The historian Fawn Brodie evaluates the available evidence in Thomas Jefferson: An Intimate History *(1974).*

Although Jefferson's inconsistencies on several subjects are well known, he consistently maintained his opinion on emancipation and deportation for over forty years. A letter to Jared Sparks (February 4, 1824) reveals the fixity of Jefferson's belief that emancipation must be accompanied by the colonization of freed African Americans "any place on the coast of Africa." Also see his letter to James Heaton (May 20, 1826).

To emancipate all slaves born after passing the act. The bill reported by the revisors does not itself contain this proposition; but

From Thomas Jefferson, *Notes on the State of Virginia, Written in the Year 1781, Somewhat Corrected and Enlarged in the Winter of 1782, for the Use of a Foreigner of Distinction, in Answer to Certain Queries Proposed by Him* (Paris, 1784–85).

an amendment containing it was prepared, to be offered to the legislature whenever the bill should be taken up, and further directing, that they should continue with their parents to a certain age, then be brought up, at the public expence to tillage, arts or sciences, according to their geniusses, till the females should be eighteen, and the males twenty-one years of age, when they should be colonized to such place as the circumstances of the time should render most proper, sending them out with arms, implements of houshold and of the handicraft arts, feeds, pairs of the useful domestic animals, &c. to declare them a free and independent people, and extend to them our alliance and protection, till they shall have acquired strength; and to send vessels at the same time to other parts of the world for an equal number of white inhabitants; to induce whom to migrate hither, proper encouragements were to be proposed. It will probably be asked, Why not retain and incorporate the blacks into the state, and thus save the expence of supplying, by importation of white settlers, the vacancies they will leave? Deep rooted prejudices entertained by the whites; ten thousand recollections, by the blacks, of the injuries they have sustained; new provocations; the real distinctions which nature has made; and many other circumstances, will divide us into parties, and produce convulsions which will probably never end but in the extermination of the one or the other race.—To these objections, which are political, may be added others, which are physical and moral. The first difference which strikes us is that of colour. Whether the black of the negro resides in the reticular membrane between the skin and scarf-skin, or in the scarf-skin itself; whether it proceeds from the colour of the blood, the colour of the bile, or from that of some other secretion, the difference is fixed in nature, and is as real as if its seat and cause were better known to us. And is this difference of no importance? Is it not the foundation of a greater or less share of beauty in the two races? Are not the fine mixtures of red and white, the expressions of every passion by greater or less suffusions of colour in the one, preferable to that eternal monotony, which reigns in the countenances, that immovable veil of black which covers all the emotions of the other race? Add to these, flowing hair, a more elegant symmetry of form, their own judgment in favour of the whites, declared by their preference of them, as uniformly as is the preference of the Oranootan for the black women over those of his own species. . . .

Among the Romans emancipation required but one effort. The slave, when made free, might mix with, without staining the blood of his master. But with us a second is necessary, unknown to history. When freed, he is to be removed beyond the reach of mixture.

Letters to Peter Williams Jr. (1816) and James Forten (1817)

Paul Cuffe's letter to the Episcopal clergyman Peter Williams Jr. illustrates that a healthy profit motive had much to do with Cuffe's involvement in the African repatriation movement. As a Massachusetts shipbuilder and sea merchant, Cuffe was positioned to reap economic benefits from a program of resettlement overseas. The same can be said of James Forten, the Philadelphia sail manufacturer, to whom Cuffe's second letter is addressed. Forten, like Cuffe, was well situated to profit from the economic nationalism that Cuffe envisioned.

Whether these two early African American capitalists can be called black nationalists is open to debate. Cuffe's wife, Alice, was an American Indian, and his mother was also Native American. He explained in a letter to the British abolitionist William Allen that he could not permanently resettle in Africa because his wife refused to go. Forten's response to Cuffe (also reproduced in this volume) indicates something more of a desire to pursue a separate destiny away from white America, but none of his writings contain any of the messianic fervor of a "chosen people" doctrine that usually accompanies nationalistic movements. There can be little doubt, however, that Forten and Cuffe represented a spirit of economic independence that is essential to nationalism. Their enterprising spirit was a product of the environment, ideological and material, that generated the nationalism of white Yankee businessmen. It is essential to the success of nationalism that patriotic ideals go hand in hand with economic self-interest.

Westport 30 August 1816

Esteemed friend Peter Williams, Jr.—In consequence of what thee mentioned, (viz.) that we the people of color might establish a mercantile line of business from the United States to Africa, etc., should this still be your mind and you propose to carry it into effect this fall, we have no time to lose. After consulting thyself and friends, please to inform me your resolution. As, also the price of prime tobacco, soap, candles, as also what size

Cuffe to Peter Williams Jr., August 30, 1816, and Cuffe to James Forten, January 8, 1817, Free Public Library, New Bedford, Mass.

vessel would be most advantageous, and such circumstances as may occur. To the view of your mind

I rest thy assured friend (in health)

Paul Cuffe

▪ ▪ ▪

Westport 8 January 1817

Esteemed friend James Forten—I desire to be thankful for the privilege of informing thee of our being generally in health, hoping these may meet with thee & thine enjoying the same blessing, for which I desire ever to be trust thankful unto the Father of all our Mercies.

I have lately received a letter from a gentleman in the city of Washington announcing to me the concern that rests at the seat of government for the welfare of the people of color. They mention to me whether I will join them in going to England and Africa to seek a place where the people of color might be colonized. With a number of propositions & question I have answered him thereto, informing [him] at the same time of the African Institution in Philadelphia, New York, etc., in order that a correspondence might be opened with them in which they may become useful to their fellow citizens.

Give my love to the members of the African Institution and tell them I wish them a joyful New Year, hoping they have all their energies renewedly engaged to celebrate the year in behalf of the African race and to the honor and glory of God, Amen.

Paul Wainer & owners of the sloop *Resolution* have requested me to inform thee that they are bound to North Carolina and are so short of funds that it is very inconvenient for them to pay thee for their mainsail according to expectation; but were willing to allow interest, and I will pledge my word for the payment of the debt. Should the money be wanted immediately, please to inform me, and the amount shall be forwarded by thy assured friend.

Paul Cuffe

PS

Give my love to Charlotte & the children & tell them I often see them in a contemplate view. Dear James thou art often the companion of my mind. In much love I subscribe myself your affectionate and ever well-wishing friend.

Paul Cuffe

3

Letter to Paul Cuffe (1817)

In this letter, James Forten implies a commitment to Cuffe's plan for African commerce and resettlement. The sentiments seem nationalistic in that Forten assumes as a matter of course that African Americans should seek to "become a people," and that some form of physical separation from white America will be necessary if African Americans are ever to "become a people." It should be noted that Forten eventually became one of the bitterest foes of the American Colonization Society, and eventually abandoned all talk of nationalism or emigration.

Philad. January 25th 1817

Esteemed friend—Permit me to inform you that I received your friendly letter by post informing me of you and family good state of health through the blessing of Divine Providence.

In my last letter to you I mention my intention of writing you again very shortly on account of Anthony Servance's property, the sale of which I expected would have taken place in the course of a day or two. But to our utter disappointment we could not get a single bid for it. Indeed, I am very much afraid that the ground rent will eat up the whole of the property. The amount in May next will be 170 dollars. We have had but one offer for it, and that was 50 dollars clear of all encumbrances, and I believe we shall be forced to take it, which, I am very sorry, will come far short of the claim you have against him.

The African Institution met at the Rev. R. Allen's the very night your letter came to hand. I read that part to them that wished them a happy New Year, for which they desired me to return you many thanks. I must now mention to you that the whole continent seems to be agitated concerning the colonizing the people of color. You mention to me in your

Forten to Paul Cuffe, January 25, 1817, Free Public Library, New Bedford, Mass.

letter that a gentleman from Washington had written to you on the subject for your opinion. I suppose it must have been the Rev. Robert Finley from the state of New Jersey. He convened us together the other night at the Rev. A. Jones on this interesting subject. He mentioned his intention of writing you.

Indeed, the people of color here was very much frightened. At first they were afraid that all the free people would be compelled to go, particularly in the southern states. We had a large meeting of males at the Rev. R. Allen's church the other evening. Three thousand at least attended, and there was not one soul that was in favor of going to Africa. They think that the slaveholders wants to get rid of them so as to make their property more secure.

However, it appears to me that if the Father of all Mercies is in this interesting subject (for it appeared that they all think that something must and ought to be done, but do not know where nor how to begin), the way will be made straight and clear. We, however, have agreed to remain silent, as the people here, both white and color, are decided against the measure. My opinion is that they will never become a people until they come out from amongst the white people. But as the majority is decidedly against me, I am determined to remain silent, except as to my opinion which I freely give when asked.

I must now inform you of an imposter which is going the rounds of this state calling himself John Cuffe, and said he is your son. He was taken up in York County, Pennsylvania, and lodged in jail, from which he wrote John James begging him to send a description of him so that he might be liberated. I have got the letter before me. John James brought the letter to me so that I might write you. He desires to be kindly remembered with all his family to you. I was intending to have given you some extracts from the letter, but having come across a publication of him in full I will enclose it to you. The signature of the letter is John Cuffe, son of the old & esteemed Capt'n Cuffe. We know you had no son of that name.

You will please give my love to your nephews and tell them any arrangements you make will be satisfactory to me. Charlotte has been very ill with the sore throat, but thank to God she has quite recovered, but longs to see you all. thought during her indisposition could she but have seen you, it would have made her well. All the family join me in love to you all.

I remain very affectionately yours unalterably

James Forten

I shall be glad to hear from you very shortly and your opinion of the colony.

4

Mutability of Human Affairs (1827)

The theme of "mutability" in human affairs has a long history in English letters. The word implied change, but not change in the mindlessly happy sense employed by twentieth-century politicians. From the sixteenth to the eighteenth century, mutability suggested instability, incoherence, inconstancy, or decay. In the following article, the term is associated with the rise and decline of civilizations. The editors of Freedom's Journal, *from which it is taken, recognized that the turning wheel of fortune had many times in the past reduced great empires to impoverishment or even slavery. For them, mutability was associated with bittersweet reveries of a semimythical day in which Africans had exercised lordship over the lost empire of ancient Egypt.*

During a recent visit to the Egyptian Mummy, my thoughts were insensibly carried back to former times, when Egypt was in her splendor, and the only seat of chivalry, science, arts and civilization. As a descendant of Cush, I could not but mourn over her present degradation, while reflecting upon the mutability of human affairs, and upon the present condition of a people, who, for more than one thousand years, were the most civilized and enlightened.

My heart sickened as I pondered upon the picture which my imagination had drawn.—Like Marius surveying the ruins of Carthage, I wept over the fallen state of my people.—Wherefore is it, that a gloom pervades the mind, while reflecting upon the ages which have passed; and which, like the "baseless fabrick of a vision," have scarcely left a wreck behind them? But such applies not to Egypt: for her obelisks and pyramids, which attest her greatness still remain, amid the grandeur of the desert, full of magnificence and death, at once a trophy and a tomb. But her kings, to preserve whose bodies from sacrilegious hands, they were erected, where

---

"Mutability of Human Affairs," *Freedom's Journal* (New York), April 6, 1827.

are they? Have they not been torn from their "vaulted sepulchres," and exhibited to a gazing world? *Have not they too been bought and sold?* Methinks, the lesson to be derived from this, should warn other potentates, who are lavishing the hard earnings of their industrious subjects upon their costly mausoleums, of the vanity of their labours. The admirable command of our Lord to one of his disciples, who was desirous of going to bury his father, "let the dead bury their dead," should convince us that it matters little, where this corruptible body is laid, after the immortal spirit has once left it; and that nothing which we can do, can reach its ear in the dull mansions of the tomb.

In reflecting on these interesting but mournful truths; the changes which had taken place within the last fifty years, were also presented to my view. On an ideal map of the Western continent, I beheld in many parts, villages, towns and cities, arisen and arising, where thirty years ago, nought but the footsteps of the savage had ever disturbed the "deep solitude of the forest," or chased the "wild deer from his covert." In the old world, the changes which have taken place, are awfully instructive. In many parts we behold the lenient policy which swayed the government of Napoleon compelled to give place to the misrule of former days. In France, the house of Bourbon, after having been exiles for twenty years, are restored to the throne of their ancestors. But the mighty Ruler, whose word was law over the greater part of Europe; "who was gentle in the manner, but vigorous in the deed," where lies he? On the rocky shores of sea-girt St. Helena!

History informs us that Cush and Menes (the Misriam of scripture) were the sons of Ham. The former is supposed to have settled in the Arabic Nome, near the Red Sea, in Lower Egypt; whence his descendants spread over the southern regions of Asia, along the Persian Gulph, and the easterly parts of Africa, on the western borders of the Red Sea; and the latter, the Northerly parts of Africa, including Upper and Lower Egypt and Barbary.

Mankind generally allow that all nations are indebted to the Egyptians for the introduction of the arts and sciences; but they are not willing to acknowledge that the Egyptians bore any resemblance to the present race of Africans; though Herodotus, "the father of history," expressly declares that the 'Egyptians had black skins and frizzled hair.'

All we know of Ethiopia, strengthens us in the belief, that it was early inhabited by a people, whose manners and customs nearly resembled those of the Egyptians. Many of their divinities were the same: they had the same orders of priesthood and religious ceremonies: they made use of the same characters in writing: their dress was alike: and the regal sceptre in both countries was in the form of a plough. Of their philosophy little is known; their wise men, like those of the Indians, were called Gymnosophists: they discharged the sacred functions like Egyptian priests; had their distinct colleges and classes of disciples; taught their dogmas in obscure and mythological language; and were remarkable for their contempt of death. Other writers of a later date than Herodotus, have asserted that the resemblance between the two nations, as it regarded their features, was as striking, as their doctrines were similar. The celebrated Mr. Salt, in his travels in Abyssinia, discovered several monumental remains, the hieroglyphics on which bore a strong resemblance to those engraved on the sarcophagi of Egyptian mummies.

The ancient Ethiopians were considered as a blameless race, worshipping the Gods, doing no evil, exercising fortitude, and despising death: —

> "The sire of gods and all the ethereal train
> On the warm limits of the farthest main,
> Now mix with mortals, nor disdain to grace
> The feasts of Ethiopia's blameless race;
> Twelve days the powers indulge the genial rite
> Returning with the twelfth revolving light."

Believing that we have sufficiently proved to the satisfaction of every unprejudiced mind, that the Egyptians and Ethiopians were of one colour, and possessed a striking similarity of features; were equally civilized and had the same rites of religious worship, we now turn our immediate attention not only to the mutability which has attended the fortunes of their descendants, but other nations also.

If we except 130 years under the Persian yoke and 294 under the Macedonian, the kingdom of Egypt continued an independent government until the time of the second Triumvirs, when the disastrous battle of Actium, (in which Anthony lost all the laurels acquired during a whole life,) reduced it from its former splendor to a province of the Roman Empire, under Augustus. Since that period, Egypt has continually decreased in population, wealth and civilization; and had not her stately monuments stood unshaken amid the convulsions which have since rent the world; as little perhaps would have been known concerning her; as little sympathy would have been felt for her oppressed and degraded children, as for poor Ethiopia's.—For the present descendants of the ancient Egyptians are an ill-looking and slovenly people, immersed in ignorance and sloth, and presenting to the eye of the observer a very striking contrast of features from any of the specimens which have reached us of their ancestors.

But Egypt and Ethiopia are not the only kingdoms where we behold the effects of the mutability of human affairs. The extensive Empire of Macedon's proud king, has passed into other hands and even Greece, herself, bows before the proud sceptre of the Moslem.

Oh, that another Leonidas might arise in this her time of need, and drive the flag of the Crescent from the second land of freedom, arts and refinement. Awake, ye Greeks, think on the spirit of your "ancient sires;" like them, let your breasts be opposed as ramparts in defence of your country's soil; like them, die all freemen, and live not to witness the despotism of your oppressors!

Time has not spared even imperial Rome, but she and her conquests, which comprehended the greater part of the civilized world at that period have changed masters. All that remains of her and them can give but a faint idea of the one, or hardly convince us of the truth of the other. Popish writers would feign convince us that the sceptre of the Cesars had passed into their hands—that Italy, the native country of all that is stupendous, great or beautiful, either in ancient or modern times is theirs'—but O, how unlike is Rome in the nineteenth century, to the Rome of the Scipios and the Cesars! But while she remains, like her coliseum, after having passed successively into the hands of the Heruli, the Ostrogoths and the Lombards, until the final dissolution of the Western Empire, in 774, by Charlemagne; Constantinople, her sister, for whose prosperity the most christian Emperor Constantine was so solicitous, has had her share of adversity; her holy temples erected to the worship of God, have been profaned with Mahomedan rites, and the haughty Turk reigns over her provinces.—And while the ancient mistress of the world has sunk comparatively into mere insignificance, a new rival has arisen, whose name at the period to which we refer, was scarcely known; and her natives considered as a fierce and unconquerable body of barbarians. Her fleets now cover every sea, and her bold and adventurous sons every clime.

If we reflect upon the present condition of Russia, which before the time of Peter the Great was hardly considered as a civilized power; who then would have believed that in the 19th century she would have held the preponderating balance which she now does, in the politics of Europe. Spain in the loss of her South American possessions has taken a retrograde step—her cruel policy in their government—the despotism which has ruled her court, and the neglect of her own fruitful soil, have met their merited reward, and we rejoice at it.

And though our people, as a body, more particularly, have to lament the changes which have brought us into such contempt and degradation; yet we are not so selfish as to mourn at the improvement of other nations; and the great progress which man has made in the knowledge of his natural rights and privileges; with which the despotic will of the monarch has no right to interfere, and for which after having this due estimate of their importance, he has been (and we trust ever will be) willing to devote his life to maintain them untrammelled and free.

As it regards the condition of our people, how painful soever the subject may be to our feelings, we feel it our duty to touch upon it. To us the subject is ever an unpleasant one to think upon; but without feelings of animosity, desirous of doing all the possible good we can, in our day and generation, and relying firmly upon the justice of a righteous God, we believe that a fairer day is yet to dawn upon our longing eyes. When this will be we cannot tell: but we believe that a few of the disadvantages which we are now under may be avoided by a more discreet line of conduct; by practising prudence and economy in our expenditures and by showing to the world, that it is our fixed determination to put to shame the unguarded and hostile expressions of our enemies.

That as a body, we are as degraded in many parts of this happy land as we can possibly be, the casual observation of the passing traveller has often recorded. What though the proud Turk lords it over ancient Greece, and would exercise a conquerors' power over her fair sons and daughters, yet have *they been treated like our brethren?* What though Mr. E. may assert, that our brethren in the South who are still in bondage, are better provided for, and more comfortable than the peasantry in some parts of Europe, do not daily facts evidence the contrary? Do they not shew that many *good* men, through a desire to please party, assert things which their cooler judgment disapproves. Look at Russia, or Poland in their former dark state, or at the feudal times of other kingdoms; can they be compared to the *happy and enviable lot* of many of our brethren? And as human affairs are continually revolving, who will predict that the day may not come when our people shall be duly considered in the scale of nations, and respected accordingly. We are no enthusiasts, but it must certainly be considered uncommonly miraculous that mutability should attend all other nations.

We are informed that the gospel was first received in the burning sands of Africa with great eagerness. "African Christians soon formed one of the principal members of the primitive Church. During the course of the 3d century, they were animated by the zeal of Tertullian, directed by the abilities of Cyprian and Origen, and adorned by the eloquence of Lactantius. But where are their descendants to be found? Is it not time to enquire after the descendants of men who have hazarded their lives to preserve the faith of the Gospel pure and unadulterated?"

5

The Ethiopian Manifesto (1829)

The name Rednaxela (Alexander spelled backwards) is appended to The Ethiopian Manifesto, *but the document was registered under the name Robert Alexander Young by the clerk of the Southern District of New York. Almost nothing is known of the author, and only at great risk may one surmise anything about him based on this intentionally cryptic document. Young foretold the coming of a prophetic liberator of the African race, whose appearance he described in great detail. Presumably, Young wrote this description with some specific individual in mind. Note the references to the "two middle toes on each of his feet [which] were, in his conception, webbed and bearded," and "in appearance, a white man, although having been born of a black woman . . . in Grenada's Island." Historians have so far uncovered no contemporary references to anyone claiming to be a black messiah fitting this description. An interesting but unrelated coincidence is that W. D. Fard (a.k.a. W. Fard Muhammad), founder of the Nation of Islam during the 1930s, was reputed to be born of a black mother, although he was white in appearance. His messianic style of community organization was in the tradition of* The Ethiopian Manifesto, *although it bore no direct relationship to it.*

By the Omnipotent will of God, we, Rednaxela, sage, and asserter to the Ethiopian of his rights, do hereby declare, and make known, as follows:—

Ethiopians! the power of Divinity having within us, as man, implanted a sense of the due and prerogatives belonging to you, a people, of whom we were of your race, in part born, as a mirror we trust, to reflect to you from a review of ourselves, the dread condition in which you do at this day stand. We do, therefore, to the accomplishment of our purpose, issue this but a brief of our grand manifesto, herefrom requiring the attention towards us of every native, or those proceeding in descent from the Ethiopian or

Robert Alexander Young, *The Ethiopian Manifesto: Issued in Defence of the Black Man's Rights in the Scale of Universal Freedom* (New York: Robert Alexander Young, 1829).

African people; a regard to your welfare being the great and inspiring motive which leads us to this our undertaking. We do therefore strictly enjoin your attention to these the dictates from our sense of justice, held forth and produced to your notice, but with the most pure intention.

Ethiopians! open your minds to reason; let therein weigh the effects of truth, wisdom, and justice (and a regard to your individual as general good), and the spirit of these our words we know full well, cannot but produce the effect for which they are by us herefrom intended.—Know, then, in your present state or standing, in your sphere of government in any nation within which you reside, we hold and contend you enjoy but few of your rights of government within them. We here speak of the whole of the Ethiopian people, as we admit not even those in their state of native simplicity, to be in an enjoyment of their rights, as bestowed to them of the great bequest of God to man.

The impositions practised to their state, not being known to them from the heavy and darksome clouds of ignorance which so woefully obscures their reason, we do, therefore, for the recovering of them, as well as establishing to you your rights, proclaim, that duty—imperious duty, exacts the convocation of ourselves in a body politic; that we do, for the promotion and welfare of our order, establish to ourselves a people framed unto the likeness of that order, which from our mind's eye we do evidently discern governs the universal creation. Beholding but one sole power, supremacy, or head, we do of that head, but hope and look forward for succour in the accomplishment of the great design which he hath, in his wisdom, promoted us to its undertaking.

We find we possess in ourselves an understanding; of this we are taught to know the ends of right and wrong, that depression should come upon us or any of our race of the wrongs inflicted on us of men. We know in ourselves we possess a right to see ourselves justified therefrom, of the right of God; knowing, but of his power hath he decreed to man, that either in himself he stands, or by himself he falls. Fallen, sadly, sadly low indeed, hath become our race, when we behold it reduced but to an enslaved state, to raise it from its degenerate sphere, and instill into it the rights of men, are the ends intended of these our words; here we are met in ourselves, we constitute but one, aided, as we trust, by the effulgent light of wisdom to a discernment of the path which shall lead us to the collecting together of a people, rendered disobedient to the great dictates of nature, by the barbarity that hath been practised upon them from generation to generation of the will of their more cruel fellow-men. Am I, because I am a descendant of a mixed race of men, whose shade hath stamped them with the hue of black, to deem myself less eligible to the attainment of the great gift allotted of God to man, than are any other of whatsoever cast you please, deemed from being white as being more exalted than the black?

These words, which carry to the view of others the dictates of my mind. I borrow not from the sense of white men or of black: learn, my brother and fellow-Ethiopian, it is but the invigorating power of Deity instills them to my discernment. Of him do I know I derive my right; of him was I on the conception of a mother's womb created free; who then in the shape of man shall dare to rob me of my birthright as bestowed to me in my existence from God? No, I am in myself a man, and as a man will live, or as a man will die; for as I was born free of the will allotted me of the freedom of God, so do I claim and purport to establish an alike universal freedom to every son and daughter descending from the black; though however mixed in grades of colour through an intercourse of white with black; still as I am in myself, but a mixture of like, I call to witness, if the power of my mind hath not a right to claim an allegiance with all descendants of a race, for the justification of whose rights reason hath established within me the ends for their obtainment? God, an almighty, sole, and governing God, can alone direct me to the ends I have, but of his will to fulfill, be they here to the view of the universal world from him established; for as I do in myself stand upright, and claim in myself, as outwardly from myself, all my rights and prerogatives as pertaining to me in my birthright of man, so do I equally claim to the untutored black of every denomination, be he in bondage or free, an alike right; and do hereby publicly protest against the infringement of his rights, as is at this day practised by the fiendish cast of men who dare, contrary to the knowledge of justice, as hath been implanted of God in the soul of man, to hold him in bondage, adducing from his servitude a gorgeous maintenance. Accursed and damned be he in mind, soul and body, who dare after this my protest, to claim the slightest alleged right to hold a man, as regards manly visage, shape, and bearing, equal in all points, though ignorant and untaught with himself, and in intrinsic worth to the view of Deity; by far in his sacred presence, must he appear the better man, the calm submission to his fate, pointing him to the view of justice at the throne of God, as being more worthy of the rights of man, than the wretch who would claim from him his rights as a man.

I pause. Custom here points to me her accursed practises, if founded in error, as base injustice; shall they stand? nay, aught they to be allowed or sanctioned, for so to do by the cognizance of the just, the wise, the great, the good, and sound men of discretion of this world? I speak for no man, understanding but in myself my rights, that from myself shall be made known to a people, rights, which I, of the divine will of God, to them establish. Man—white man—black man—or, more properly, ye monsters incarnate, in human shape, who claim the horrid right to hold nature's untutored son, the Ethiopian, in bondage, to you I do herefrom speak. Mark me, and regard well these my words; be assured, they convey the voice of reason, dictated to you through a prophetic sense of truth. The time is at hand when many signs shall appear to you, to denote that Almighty God regards the affairs of afflicted men:— for know, the cries of bitter servitude, from those unhappy sons of men, whom ye have so long unjustly oppressed with the goading shafts of an accursed slavery, hath ascended to Deity. Your God, the great and mighty God, hath seen your degradation of your fellow brother, and mortal man; he hath long looked down with mercy on your suffering slave; his cries have called for a vindication of his rights, and know ye they have been heard of the Majesty of

Heaven, whose dignity have you not offended by deeming a mortal man, in your own likeness, as but worthy of being your slave, degraded to your brute? The voice of intuitive justice speaks aloud to you, and bids you to release your slave; otherwise stings, eternal stings, of an outraged and goading conscience will, ere long, hold all them in subjection who pay not due attention to this, its admonition. Beware! know thyselves to be but mortal men, doomed to the good or evil, as your works shall merit from you. Pride ye not yourselves in the greatness of your worldly standing, since all things are but moth when contrasted with the invisible spirit, which in yourself maintains within you your course of action. That within you will, to the presence of your God, be at all times your sole accuser. Weigh well these my words in the balance of your conscientious reason, and abide the judgment thereof to your own standing, for we tell you of a surety, the decree hath already passed the judgment seat of an undeviating God, wherein he hath said, "surely hath the cries of the black, a most persecuted people, ascended to my throne and craved my mercy; now, behold! I will stretch forth mine hand and gather them to the palm, that they become unto me a people, and I unto them their God." Hearken, therefore, oh! slaveholder, thou task inflicter against the rights of men, the day is at hand, nay the hour draweth nigh, when poverty shall appear to thee a blessing, if it but restore to thy fellow-man his rights; all worldly riches shall be known to thee then but as a curse, and in thine heart's desire to obtain contentment, when sad reverses come upon thee, then shalt thou linger for a renewal of days, that in thine end thou might not curse the spirit which called thee forth to life. Take warning, again we say, for of a surety from this, God will give you signs to know, in his decrees he regards the fallen state of the sons of men. Think not that wisdom descries not from here your vanity. We behold it, thou vain bloated upstart worldling of a slaveholder, laugh in derision of thy earthly taught and worldly sneer; but know, on thee we pronounce our judgment, and as fitting thee, point out to thy notice this our sign. Of the degraded of this earth, shall be exalted, one who shall draw from thee, as though gifted of power divine, all attachment and regard of thy slave towards thee. Death shall he prefer to a continuance of his race:—being doomed to thy vile servitude, no cohabitation shall be known between the sexes, while suffering under thy slavery; but should ungovernable passion attain over the untaught mind an ascendancy, abortion shall destroy the birth. We command it, the voice of imperative justice, though however harsh, must be obeyed. Ah! doth your expanding judgment, base slaveholder, not from here descry that the shackles which have been by you so undeservingly forged upon a wretched Ethiopian's frame, are about to be forever from him unlinked. Say ye, this can never be accomplished? If so, must indeed the power and decrees of Infinity become subservient to the will of depraved man. But learn, slaveholder, thine will rests not in thine hand: God decrees to thy slave his rights as man. This we issue forth as the spirit of the black man or Ethiopian's rights, established from the Ethiopian's Rock, the foundation of his civil and religious rights, which hereafter will be exemplified in the order of its course. Ethiopians, throughout the world in general, receive this as but a lesson presented to you from an instructive Book, in which many, many therein are contained, to the vindication of its purpose. As came John the Baptist, of old, to spread abroad the forthcoming of his master, so alike are intended these our words, to denote to the black African or Ethiopian people, that God has prepared for them a leader, who awaits but for his season to proclaim to them his birthright. How shall you know this man? By indubitable signs which cannot be controverted by the power of mortal, his marks being stamped in open visage, as equally so upon his frame, which constitutes him to have been particularly regarded in the infinite work of God to man.

Know ye, then, if a white man ever appeared on earth, bearing in himself the semblance of his former race, the man we proclaim ordained of God, to call together the black people as a nation in themselves. We say, in him will be seen, in appearance, a white man, although having been born of a black woman, his mother. The proof is strong, and in Grenada's Island, Grand Anta Estate, there, some time ago, did dwell his mother—his father then owner of the said estate. The church books of St. Georgestown, the capital of Grenada, can truly prove his birth. As another instance wherein providence decreed he should appear peculiar in his make, the two middle toes on each of his feet were, in his conception, webbed and bearded. Now, after the custom of the ancient order of men, with long and flowing hair, by like appearances may he be known; none other man, but the one bearing the alike marks, and proving his identity from the island on which he was born, can be the man of whom we speak. To him, thou poor black Ethiopian or African slave, do thou, from henceforth, place a firm reliance thereon, as trusting in him to prove thy liberator from the infernal state of bondage, under which you have been so long and so unjustly laboring. To thee he pledges himself, in life to death, not to desert thee, his trust being in the power of the Almighty, who giveth not the race to the swift nor the battle to the strong, but decrees to all men the justice he establishes. As such, we draw from him the conception of your rights, and to its obtainment we issue this to you, our first pledge of faith, binding ourselves herefrom to render to you, at all times, such services as shall tend most to your advantage in effecting a speedy deliverance from your mortal and most deadly foe, the monster of a slaveholder. We would most particularly direct you to such government of yourselves as should be responsible but to God, your maker, for the duty exacted of you to your fellow-men; but, under goading situations, where power and might is but the construction of law, it then behooves the depressed and vilely injured to bear his burthen with the firmness of his manhood:—So at this time, we particularly recommend to you, degraded sons of Africa, to submit with fortitude to your present state of suffering, relying in yourselves, from the justice of a God, that the time is at hand, when, with but the power of words and the divine will of our God, the vile shackles of slavery shall be broken asunder from you, and no man known who shall dare to own or proclaim you as his bondsman. We say it, and assert it as though by an oracle given and delivered to you from on high. God, in his holy keeping, direct thee, thou poor untaught and degraded African slave, to a full conception of these the words we have written for your express benefit. Our care and regard of you will be that of a fostering parent toward a beloved offspring. The hatred of your oppressor we fear not, nor do we his power, or any vile machinations that may be resorted to by incendiaries towards us. We hold ourself, with the aid of our God therewith, at all times ready to encounter, trusting but in God, our Creator, and not in ourselves, for a deliverance from all worldly evil.

Peace and Liberty to the Ethiopian first, as also all other grades of men, is the invocation we offer to the throne of our God.

REDNAXELA

DATED FROM THE

ETHIOPIAN'S ROCK,

IN THE

THIRTY-SEVENTH YEAR

FROM ITS

FOUNDATION,

THIS THIRTEENTH DAY OF FEBRUARY, A.D.

1829

6

From An Appeal in Four Articles (1830)

The excerpts from David Walker's Appeal in Four Articles *included in this volume were chosen to reflect the author's messianic sense of mission and his conception of African Americans as a people under the protection of a just God. Sixty years ago, the distinguished African American scholar Benjamin Brawley noted that David Walker was a man of limited education who wrote "from an overflowing heart." This was true enough, and the document has some incohesiveness, but the style and the ideas are nonetheless powerful. Some passages of the* Appeal *were so incendiary that the governors of Virginia and North Carolina wrote to Harrison Gray Otis, the mayor of Boston, demanding that it be suppressed, but Otis responded that while he did not personally approve of the pamphlet, the law could not hinder Walker in the free expression of his ideas.*

The introduction to the third edition is printed in its entirety. It contains a reference to Psalms 68:31, "Princes shall come out of Egypt, Ethiopia shall soon stretch out her hands unto God." The preamble that follows contains some of Walker's several references to the decline of civilizations brought on by the practice of slavery. He alludes to several vanished empires of the ancient world, then makes reference to the revolution in the Spanish colonies and the wars that disrupted the Iberian Peninsula during the preceding decade.

Article 1, "Our Wretchedness in Consequence of Slavery," begins with a discussion of the enslavement of the ancient Hebrews by the Egyptians. It is a response to Jefferson's assertion that American slavery is mild in comparison to other historical examples of slavery. Walker points out that the Egyptians, who were black, gave land to the children of Israel. Whether this bespeaks a desire on his part that a part of the U.S. territories should be set aside for African Americans, he does not make clear. Walker also compares Jefferson's attitude on racial mixing to that of the biblical Egyptians. The section reprinted here concludes as Walker expresses his wish to see Jefferson's charges of racial inferiority "refuted by the blacks themselves." As for white America, he predicts that God's judgment is at hand.

Article 2, "Our Wretchedness in Consequence of Ignorance," covers a number of subjects. Walker begins with references to a time when Africans stood at the peak of civilization, and argues, as do twentieth-century Afrocentrists, that all the arts and sciences of Greece and Rome derived from the civilization of the Nile. He claims the

---

From David Walker, *An Appeal in Four Articles; Together with a Preamble to the Colored Citizens of the World, but in Particular, and Very Expressly, to Those of the United States of America,* 3d ed. (Boston: David Walker, 1830).

civilization of Carthage for the black race and attributes the fall of its general Hannibal to the failure of the Carthaginians to unite behind him. Walker predicts that God will raise up a new Hannibal, who will come as a racial deliverer, and charges his readers "to lay no obstacle in his way." He describes the ignorance of African Americans, who assist slaveholders in keeping them in bondage. After a transitional passage, and some additional outrage directed at Thomas Jefferson, the article closes with some random thoughts on education, which reveal the author's belief that ignorance is intentionally encouraged among the Free Africans as well as among the slaves.

Article 3, "Our Wretchedness in Consequence of the Preachers of the Religion of Jesus Christ," contains some of Walker's most fiery rhetoric, which is self-explanatory. The title of the article is deceptive, for Walker was obviously a devout Christian who believed that God would punish the sin of slaveholding. Article 4, "Our Wretchedness in Consequence of the Colonizing Plan," reveals Walker's hostility to African colonization. It concludes with his statement of the hope that blacks and whites can live together as a "united and happy people." It is clear that Walker believed that African Americans were a national entity in the same sense that the Old Testament Hebrews had been a nation, but Walker's Appeal, despite its continuing popularity with black nationalists, cannot be said to represent classical black nationalism, because it does not call specifically for a separate nation-state.

Walker died shortly after publication of the third edition of his Appeal, and as Benjamin Brawley put it, "the belief was persistent that he met with foul play." Henry Highland Garnet, whose work is also covered in this volume, issued a reprint of Walker's Appeal in 1848, in the same volume with his own incendiary Address to the Slaves of the United States. Garnet's introduction to the 1848 edition is the source for most of what is known of the life of David Walker.

Introduction to the Third Edition

It will be recollected, that I, in the first edition of my "Appeal,"[1] promised to demonstrate in the course of which, viz. in the course of my Appeal, to the satisfaction of the most incredulous mind, that we Coloured People of these United States, are, the most wretched, degraded and abject set of beings that ever lived since the world began, down to the present day, and, that, the white Christians of America, who hold us in slavery (or, more properly speaking, pretenders to Christianity), treat us more cruel and barbarous than any Heathen nation did any people whom it had subjected, or reduced to the same condition, that the Americans (who are, notwithstanding, looking for the Millennial day) have us. All I ask is, for a candid and careful perusal of this the third and last edition of my Appeal, where the world may see that we, the Blacks or Coloured People, are treated more cruel by the white Christians of America, than devils themselves ever treated a set of men, women and children on this earth.

It is expected that all coloured men, women and children,[2] of every nation, language and tongue under heaven, will try to procure a copy of this Appeal and read it, or get some one to read it to them, for it is designed more particularly for them. Let them remember, that though our cruel oppressors and murderers, may (if possible) treat us more cruel, as Pharaoh did the children of Israel, yet the God of the Etheopians, has been pleased to hear our moans in consequence of oppression; and the day of our redemption from abject wretchedness draweth near, when we shall be enabled, in the most extended sense of the word, to stretch forth our hands to the LORD Our GOD, but there must be a willingness on our part, for GOD to do these things for us, for we may be assured that he will not take us by the hairs of our head against our will and desire, and drag us from our very, mean, low and abject condition. . . .

Preamble

. . . I will not here speak of the destructions which the Lord brought upon Egypt, in consequence of the oppression and consequent groans of the oppressed—of the hundreds and thousands of Egyptians whom God hurled into the Red Sea for afflicting his people in their land—of the Lord's suffering people in Sparta or Lacedemon, the land of the truly famous Lycurgus—nor have I time to comment upon the cause which produced the fierceness with which Sylla usurped the title, and absolutely acted as dictator of the Roman people—the conspiracy of Cataline—the conspiracy against, and murder of Caesar in the Senate house—the spirit with which Marc Antony made himself master of the commonwealth— his associating Octavius and Lipidus with himself in power—their dividing the provinces of Rome among themselves—their attack and defeat, on the plains of Phillippi, of the last defenders of their liberty (Brutus and Cassius)—the tyranny of Tiberius, and from him to the final overthrow of Constantinople by the Turkish Sultan, Mahomed II. A.D. 1453.

I say, I shall not take up time to speak of the *causes* which produced so much wretchedness and massacre among those heathen nations, for I am aware that you know too well, that God is just, as well as merciful!—I shall call your attention a few moments to that *Christian* nation, the Spaniards—while I shall leave almost unnoticed, that avaricious and cruel people, the Portuguese, among whom all true hearted Christians and lovers of Jesus Christ, must evidently see the judgments of God displayed. To show the judgments of God upon the Spaniards, I shall occupy but a little time, leaving a plenty of room for the candid and unprejudiced to reflect.

All persons who are acquainted with history, and particularly the Bible, who are not blinded by the God of this world, and are not actuated solely by avarice—who are able to lay aside prejudice long enough to view candidly and impartially, things as they were, are, and probably will be—who are willing to admit that God made man to serve Him *alone,* and that man should have no other Lord or Lords but Himself—that God Almighty is the *sole proprietor* or *master* of the WHOLE human family, and will not on any consideration admit of a colleague, being unwilling to divide his glory with another—and who can dispense with prejudice long enough to admit that we are *men,* notwithstanding our *improminent noses* and *woolly heads,* and believe that we feel for our fathers, mothers, wives and children, as well as the whites do for theirs.—I say, all who are permitted to see and believe these things, can easily recognize the judgments of God among the Spaniards. Though others may lay the cause of the fierceness with which they cut each other's throats, to some other circumstances, yet they who believe that God is a God of justice, will believe that SLAVERY *is the principal cause.*

While the Spaniards are running about upon the field of battle cutting each other's throats, has not the Lord an afflicted and suffering people in the midst of them, whose cries and groans in consequence of oppression are continually pouring into the ears of the God of justice? Would they not cease to cut each other's throats, if they could? But how can they? The very support which they draw from government to aid them in perpetrating such enormities, does it not arise in a great degree from the wretched victims of oppression among them? And yet they are calling for PEACE!—PEACE!! Will any peace be given unto them? Their destruction may indeed be procrastinated awhile, but can it continue long, while they are oppressing the Lord's people? Has He not the hearts of all men in His hand? Will he suffer one part of his creatures to go on oppressing another like brutes always, with impunity? And yet, those avaricious wretches are calling for PEACE!!!! I declare, it does appear to me, as though some nations think God is asleep, or that he made the Africans for nothing else but to dig their mines and work their farms, or they cannot believe history, sacred or profane.

I ask every man who has a heart, and is blessed with the privilege of believing—Is not God a God of justice to *all* his creatures? Do you say he is? Then if he gives peace and tranquillity to tyrants, and permits them to keep our fathers, our mothers, ourselves and our children in eternal ignorance and wretchedness, to support them and their families, would he be to us a God of *justice?* I ask, O ye *Christians!!!* who hold us and our children in the most abject ignorance and degradation, that ever a people were afflicted with since the world began—I say, if God gives you peace and tranquillity, and suffers you thus to go on afflicting us, and our children, who have never given you the least provocation—would he be to us *a God of justice?* If you will allow that we are MEN, who feel for each other, does not the blood of our fathers and of us their children, cry aloud to the Lord of Sabaoth against you, for the cruelties and murders with which you have, and do continue to afflict us. But it is time for me to close my remarks on the suburbs, just to enter more fully into the interior of this system of cruelty and oppression.

Article I. Our Wretchedness in Consequence of Slavery

MY BELOVED BRETHREN:—The Indians of North and of South America—the Greeks—the Irish, subjected under the king of Great Britain—the Jews, that ancient people of the Lord—the inhabitants of the islands of the sea—in fine, all the inhabitants of the earth (except however, the sons of Africa), are called *men,* and of course are, and ought to be free. But we (coloured people), and our children are *brutes!!* and of course are, and *ought to be* SLAVES to the American people and their children forever!! to dig their mines and work their farms; and thus go on enriching them, from one generation to another with our *blood* and our *tears!!!!*

I promised in a preceding page to demonstrate to the satisfaction of the most incredulous, that we (coloured people of these United States of America), are the *most wretched, degraded* and *abject* set of beings that *ever lived* since the world began, and that the white Americans having reduced us to the wretched state of *slavery,* treat us in that condition *more cruel* (they being an enlightened and Christian people), than any heathen nation did any people whom it had reduced to our condition. These affirmations are so well confirmed in the minds of all unprejudiced men, who have taken the trouble to read histories, that they need no elucidation from me. But to put them beyond all doubt, I refer you in the first place to the children of Jacob, or of Israel in Egypt, under Pharaoh and his people. Some of my brethren do not know who Pharaoh and the Egyptians were—I know it to be a fact, that some of them take the Egyptians to have been a gang of *devils,* not knowing any better, and that they (Egyptians) having got possession of the Lord's people, treated them *nearly* as cruel as *Christian Americans* do us, at the present day. For the information of such, I would only mention that the Egyptians, were Africans or coloured people, such as we are—some of them yellow and others dark—a mixture of Ethiopians and the natives of Egypt—about the same as you see the coloured people of the United States at the present day.—I say, I call your attention then, to the children of Jacob, while I point out particularly to you his son Joseph, among the rest, in Egypt.

"And Pharaoh, said unto Joseph, thou shalt be over my house, and according unto thy word shall all my people be ruled: only in the throne will I be greater than thou."[3]

"And Pharaoh said unto Joseph, see, I have set thee over all the land of Egypt."[4]

"And Pharaoh said unto Joseph, I am Pharaoh, and without thee shall no man lift up his hand or foot in all the land of Egypt."[5]

Now I appeal to heaven and to earth, and particularly to the American people themselves, who cease not to declare that our condition is not *hard,* and that we are comparatively satisfied to rest in wretchedness and misery, under them and their children. Not, indeed, to show me a coloured President, a Governor, a Legislator, a Senator, a Mayor, or an Attorney at the Bar.—But to show me a man of colour, who holds the low office of a Constable, or one who sits in a Juror Box, even on a case of one of his wretched brethren, throughout this great Republic!!—But let us pass Joseph the son of Israel a little farther in review, as he existed with that heathen nation.

"And Pharaoh called Joseph's name Zaphnathpaaneah; and he gave him to wife Asenath the daughter of Potipherah priest of On. And Joseph went out over all the land of Egypt."[6]

Compare the above, with the American institutions. Do they not institute laws to prohibit us from marrying among the whites? I would wish, candidly, however, before the Lord, to be understood, that I would not give a *pinch of snuff* to be married to any white person I ever saw in all the days of my life. And I do say it, that the black man, or man of colour, who will leave his own colour (provided he can get one, who is good for any thing) and marry a white woman, to be a double slave to her, just because she is *white,* ought to be treated by her as he surely will be, viz.: as a NIGER!!!! It is not, indeed, what I care about inter-marriages with the whites, which induced me to pass this subject in review; for the Lord knows, that there is a day coming when they will be glad enough to get into the company of the blacks, notwithstanding, we are, in this generation, levelled by them, almost on a level with the brute creation: and some of us they treat even worse than they do the brutes that perish. I only made this extract to show how much lower we are held, and how much more cruel we are treated by the Americans, than were the children of Jacob, by the Egyptians.—We will notice the sufferings of Israel some further, under *heathen Pharaoh,* compared with ours under the *enlightened Christians of America.*

"And Pharaoh spake unto Joseph, saying, thy father and thy brethren are come unto thee:"

"The land of Egypt is before thee: in the best of the land make thy father and brethren to dwell; in the land of Goshen let them dwell: and if thou knowest any men of activity among them, then make them rulers over my cattle."[7]

I ask those people who treat us so *well,* Oh! I ask them, where is the most barren spot of land which they have given unto us? Israel had the most fertile land in all Egypt. . . .

We, and the world wish to see the charges of Mr. Jefferson refuted by the black *themselves,* according to their chance; for we must remember that what the whites have written respecting this subject, is other men's labours, and did not emanate from the blacks. I know well, that there are some talents and learning among the coloured people of this country, which we have not a chance to develop, in consequence of oppression; but our oppression ought not to hinder us from acquiring all we can. For we will have a chance to develop them by and by. God will not suffer us, always to be oppressed. Our sufferings will come to an *end,* in spite of all the Americans this side of *eternity.* Then we will want all the learning and talents among ourselves, and perhaps more, to govern ourselves. — "Every dog must have its day," the American's is coming to an end. . . .

Article II. Our Wretchedness in Consequence of Ignorance

IGNORANCE, my brethren, is a mist, low down into the very dark and almost impenetrable abyss in which, our fathers for many centuries have been plunged. The Christians, and enlightened of Europe, and some of Asia, seeing the ignorance and consequent degradation of our fathers, instead of trying to enlighten them, by teaching them that religion and light with which God had blessed them, they have plunged them into wretchedness ten thousand times more intolerable, than if they had left them entirely to the Lord, and to add to their miseries, deep down into which they have plunged them tell them, that they are an *inferior* and *distinct race* of beings, which they will be glad enough to recall and swallow by and by. Fortune and misfortune, two inseparable companions, lay rolled up in the wheel of events, which have from the creation of the world, and will continue to take place among men until God shall dash worlds together.

When we take a retrospective view of the arts and sciences — the wise legislators — the Pyramids, and other magnificent buildings — the turning of the channel of the river Nile, by the sons of Africa or of Ham, among whom learning originated, and was carried thence into Greece, where it was improved upon and refined. Thence among the Romans, and all over the then enlightened parts of the world, and it has been enlightening the dark and benighted minds of men from then, down to this day. I say, when I view retrospectively, the renown of that once mighty people, the children of our great progenitor I am indeed cheered. Yea further, when I view that mighty son of Africa, HANNIBAL, one of the greatest generals of antiquity, who defeated and cut off so many thousands of the white Romans or murderers, and who carried his victorious arms, to the very gate of Rome, and I give it as my candid opinion, that had Carthage been well united and had given him good support, he would have carried that cruel and barbarous city by storm. But they were dis-united, as the coloured people are now, in the United States of America, the reason our natural enemies are enabled to keep their feet on our throats.

Beloved brethren—here let me tell you, and believe it, that the Lord our God, as true as he sits on his throne in heaven, and as true as our Saviour died to redeem the world, will give you a Hannibal, and when the Lord shall have raised him up, and given him to you for your possession, O my suffering brethren! remember the divisions and consequent sufferings of *Carthage* and of *Hayti*. Read the history particularly of Hayti, and see how they were butchered by the whites, and do you take warning. The person whom God shall give you, give him your support and let him go his length, and behold in him the salvation of your God. God will indeed, deliver you through him from your deplorable and wretched condition under the Christians of America. I charge you this day before my God to lay no obstacle in his way, but let him go. . . .

. . . There have been and are at this day in Boston, New-York, Philadelphia, and Baltimore, coloured men, who are in league with tyrants, and who receive a great portion of their daily bread, of the moneys which they acquire from the blood and tears of their more miserable brethren, whom they scandalously delivered into the hands of our *natural enemies!!!!!!*

To show the force of degraded ignorance and deceit among us some farther, I will give here an extract from a paragraph, which may be found in the Columbian Centinel of this city, for September 9, 1829, on the first page of which, the curious may find an article headed

Affray and Murder

Portsmouth, (Ohio) Aug. 22, 1829

A most shocking outrage was committed in Kentucky, about eight miles from this place, on 14th inst. A negro driver, by the name of Gordon, who had purchased in Maryland about sixty negroes, was taking them, assisted by an associate named Allen, and the wagoner who conveyed the baggage, to the Mississippi. The men were handcuffed and chained together, in the usual manner for driving those poor wretches, while the women and children were suffered to proceed without incumbrance. It appears that, by means of a file the negroes, unobserved, had succeeded in separating the iron which bound their hands, in such a way as to be able to throw them off at any moment. About 8 o'clock in the morning, while proceeding on the state road leading from Greenup to Vanceburg, two of them dropped their shackles and commenced a fight, when the wagoner (Petit) rushed in with his whip to compel them to desist. At this moment, every negro was found to be perfectly at liberty; and one of them seizing a club, gave Petit a violent blow on the head, and laid him dead at his feet; and Allen, who came to his assistance, met a similar fate, from the contents of a pistol fired by another of the gang. Gordon was then attacked, seized and held by one of the negroes, whilst another fired twice at him with a pistol, the ball of which each time grazed his head, but not proving effectual, he was beaten with clubs, and left for dead. They then commenced pillaging the wagon, and with an axe split open the trunk of Gordon, and rifled it of the money, about $2,400. Sixteen of the negroes then took to the woods; Gordon, in the mean time, not being materially injured, was enabled, by the assistance of one of the women, to mount his horse and flee; pursued, however, by one of the gang on another horse, with a drawn pistol; fortunately he escaped with his life barely, arriving at a plantation, as the negro came in sight; who then turned about and retreated.

The neighbourhood was immediately rallied, and a hot pursuit given—which, we understand, has resulted in the capture of the whole gang and the recovery of the greatest part of the money. Seven of the negro men and one woman, it is said were engaged in the murders, and will be brought to trial at the next court in Greenupsburg.

Here, my brethren, I want you to notice particularly in the above article, the *ignorant* and *deceitful actions* of this coloured woman. I beg you to view it candidly, as for ETERNITY!!!! Here a *notorious wretch,* with two other confederates had SIXTY of them in a gang, driving them like *brutes*—the men all in chains and hand-cuffs, and by the help of God they got their chains and hand-cuffs thrown off, and caught two of the wretches and put them to death, and beat the other until they thought he was dead, and left him for dead; however, he deceived them, and rising from the ground, this *servile woman* helped him upon his horse, and he made his escape.

Brethren, what do you think of this? Was it the natural *fine feelings* of this woman, to save such a wretch alive? I know that the blacks, take them half enlightened and ignorant, are more humane and merciful than the most enlightened and refined European that can be found in all the earth. Let no one say that I assert this because I am prejudiced on the side of my colour, and against the whites or Europeans. For what I write, I do it candidly, for my God and the good of both parties: Natural observations have taught me these things; there is a solemn awe in the hearts of the blacks, as it respects *murdering* men: [8] whereas the whites (though they are great cowards), where they have the advantage, or think that there are any prospects of getting it, they murder all before them, in order to subject men to wretchedness and degradation under them. This is the natural result of pride and avarice. But I declare, the actions of this black woman are really insupportable. For my own part, I cannot think it was any thing but servile deceit, combined with the most gross ignorance: for we must remember that *humanity, kindness* and the *fear of the Lord,* does not consist in protecting *devils.*

Here is a set of wretches, who had *SIXTY* of them in a gang, driving them around the country like *brutes,* to dig up gold and silver for them (which they will get enough of yet). Should the lives of such creatures be spared? Are God and Mammon in league? What has the Lord to do with a gang of desperate wretches, who go *sneaking about the country like robbers*—light upon his people wherever they can get a chance, binding them with chains and hand-cuffs, beat and murder them as they would *rattle-snakes?* Are they not the Lord's enemies? Ought they not to be destroyed? Any person who will save such wretches from destruction, is fighting against the Lord, and will receive his just recompense. The black men acted like *blockheads*. Why did they not make sure of the wretch? He would have made sure of them, if he could. It is just the way with black men—eight white men can frighten fifty of them; whereas, if you can only get courage into the blacks, I do declare it, that one good black man can put to death six white men; and I give it as a fact, let twelve black men get well armed for battle, and they will kill and put to flight fifty whites.—The reason is, the blacks, once you get them started, they glory in death. The whites have had us under them for more than three centuries, murdering, and treating us like brutes; and, as Mr. Jefferson wisely said, they have never *found us out*—they do not know, indeed, that there is an unconquerable disposition in the breasts of the blacks, which, when it is fully awakened and put in motion, will be subdued, only with the destruction of the animal existence. Get the blacks started, and if you do not have a gang of tigers and lions to deal with, I am a deceiver of the blacks and of the whites.

How sixty of them could let that wretch escape unkilled, I cannot conceive—they will have to suffer as much for the two whom, they secured, as if they had put one hundred to death: If you commence, make sure work—do not trifle, for they will not trifle with you—they want us for their slaves, and think nothing of murdering us in order to subject us to that wretched condition—therefore, if there is an *attempt* made by us, kill or be killed. Now, I ask you, had you not rather be killed than to be a slave to a tyrant, who takes the life of your mother, wife, and dear little children? Look upon your mother, wife and children, and answer God Almighty! and believe this, that it is no more harm for you to kill a man, who is trying to kill you, than it is for you to take a drink of water when thirsty; in fact, the man who will stand still and let another murder him, is worse than an infidel, and, if he has common sense, ought not to be pitied.

The actions of this deceitful and ignorant coloured woman, in saving the life of a desperate wretch, whose avaricious and cruel object was to drive her, and her companions in miseries, through the country like cattle, to make his fortune on their carcasses, are but too much like that of thousands of our brethren in these states: if any thing is whispered by one, which has any allusion to the melioration of their dreadful condition, they run and tell tyrants, that they may be enabled to keep them the longer in wretchedness and miseries. Oh! coloured people of these United States, I ask you, in the name of that God who made us, have we, in consequence of oppression, nearly lost the spirit of man, and, in no very trifling degree, adopted that of brutes? Do you answer, no?—I ask you, then, what set of men can you point me to, in all the world, who are so abjectly employed by their oppressors, as we are by our *natural enemies?*

How can, Oh! how can those enemies but say that we and our children are not of the HUMAN FAMILY, but were made by our Creator to be an inheritance to them and theirs for ever? How can the slave-holders but say that they can bribe the best coloured person in the country, to sell his brethren for a trifling sum of money, and take that atrocity to confirm them in their avaricious opinion, that we were made to be slaves to them and their children? How could Mr. Jefferson but say,⁹ "I advance it therefore as a suspicion only, that the blacks, whether originally a distinct race, or made distinct by time and circumstances, are *inferior* to the whites in the endowments both of body and mind?" "It," says he, "is not against experience to suppose, that different species of the same genus, or varieties of the same species, may possess different qualifications." [Here, my brethren, listen to him.] "Will not a lover of natural history, then, one who views the gradations in all the races of *animals* with the eye of philosophy, excuse an effort to keep those in the department of MAN as *distinct* as nature has formed them?"—I hope you will try to find out the meaning of this verse—its widest sense and all its bearings: whether you do or not, remember the whites do. This very verse, brethren, having emanated from Mr. Jefferson, a much greater philosopher the world never afforded, has in truth injured us more, and has been as great a barrier to our emancipation as any thing that has ever been advanced against us. I hope you will not let it pass unnoticed. He goes on further, and says: "This *unfortunate* difference of colour, and *perhaps of faculty,* is a powerful obstacle to the emancipation of these people. Many of their advocates, while they wish to vindicate the liberty of human nature, are anxious also to preserve its *dignity* and *beauty.* Some of these, embarrassed by the question, 'What further is to be done with them?' join themselves in opposition with those who are actuated by sordid avarice only."

Now I ask you candidly, my suffering brethren in time, who are candidates for the eternal worlds, how could Mr. Jefferson but have given the world these remarks respecting us, when we are so submissive to them, and so much servile deceit prevail among ourselves—when we so *meanly* submit to their murderous lashes, to which neither the Indians nor any other people under Heaven would submit? No, they would die to a man, before they would suffer such things from men who are no better than themselves, and *perhaps not so good.* Yes, how can our friends but be embarrassed, as Mr. Jefferson says, by the question, "What further is to be done with these people?" For while they are working for our emancipation, we are, by our treachery, wickedness and deceit, working against ourselves and our children—helping ours, and the enemies of God, to keep us and our dear little children in their infernal chains of slavery!!! Indeed, our friends cannot but relapse and join themselves "with those who are actuated by *sordid avarice* only!!!"

For my own part, I am glad Mr. Jefferson has advanced his positions for your sake; for you will either have to contradict or confirm him by your own actions, and not by what our friends have said or done for us; for those things are other men's labours, and do not satisfy the Americans, who are waiting for us to prove to them ourselves, that we are MEN, before they will be willing to admit the fact; for I pledge you my sacred word of honour, that Mr. Jefferson's remarks respecting us, have sunk deep into the hearts of millions of the whites, and never will be removed this side of eternity.—For how can they, when we are confirming him every day, by our *groveling submissions* and *treachery?* I aver, that when I look over these United States of America, and the world, and see the ignorant deceptions and consequent wretchedness of my brethren, I am brought ofttimes solemnly to a stand, and in the midst of my reflections I exclaim to my God, "Lord didst thou make us to be slaves to our brethren, the whites?" But when I reflect that God is just, and that millions of my wretched brethren would meet death with glory—yea, more, would plunge into the very mouths of cannons and be torn into particles as minute as the atoms which compose the elements of the earth, in preference to a mean submission to the lash of tyrants, I am with streaming eyes, compelled to shrink back into nothingness before my Maker, and exclaim again, thy will be done, O Lord God Almighty. . . .

I must close this article by relating the very heart-rending fact, that I have examined school-boys and young men of colour in different parts of the country, in the most simple parts of Murray's English Grammar, and not more than one in thirty was able to give a correct answer to my interrogations. If anyone contradicts me, let him step out of his door into the streets of Boston, New-York, Philadelphia, or Baltimore (no use to mention any other, for the Christians are too charitable further south or west!)—I say, let him who disputes me, step out of his door into the streets of either of those four cities, and promiscuously collect one hundred school-boys, or young men of colour, *who have been to school,* and who are considered by the coloured people to have received an excellent education, because, perhaps, some of them can write a good hand, but who, notwithstanding their neat writing, may be almost as ignorant, in comparison, as a horse.—And, I say it, he will hardly find (in this enlightened day, and in the midst of this *charitable* people) five in one hundred, who, are able to correct the false grammar of their language.—The cause of this almost universal ignorance among us, I appeal to our schoolmasters to declare.

Here is a fact, which I this very minute take from the mouth of a young coloured man, who has been to school in this state (Massachusetts) nearly nine years, and who knows grammar this day, *nearly* as well as he did the day he first entered the school-house, under a white master. This young man says: "My master would never allow me to study grammar." I asked him, why? "The school committee," said he "forbid the coloured children learning grammar—they would not allow any but the white children to study grammar." It is a notorious fact, that the major part of the white Americans, have, ever since we have been among them, tried to keep us ignorant, and make us believe that God made us and our children to be slaves to them and theirs. *Oh! my God, have mercy on Christian Americans!!!*

Article III. Our Wretchedness in Consequence of the Preachers of the Religion of Jesus Christ

. . . I remember a Camp Meeting in South Carolina, for which I embarked in a Steam Boat at Charleston, and having been five or six hours on the water, we at last arrived at the place of hearing, where was a very great concourse of people, who were no doubt, collected together to hear the word of God (that some had collected barely as spectators to the scene, I will not here pretend to doubt, however, that is left to themselves and their God).

Myself and boat companions, having been there a little while, we were all called up to hear; I among the rest went up and took my seat—being seated, I fixed myself in a complete position to hear the word of my Saviour and to receive such as I thought was authenticated by the Holy Scriptures; but to my no ordinary astonishment, our Reverend gentleman got up and told us (coloured people) that slaves must be obedient to their masters—must do their duty to their masters or be whipped—the whip was made for the backs of fools, &c. Here I pause for a moment, to give the world time to consider what was my surprise, to hear such preaching from a minister of my Master, whose very gospel is that of peace and not of blood and whips, as this pretended preacher tried to make us believe. What the American preachers can think of us, I aver this day before my God, I have never been able to define. They have newspapers and monthly periodicals, which they receive in continual succession, but on the pages of which, you will scarcely ever find a paragraph respecting slavery, which is ten thousand times more injurious to this country than all the other evils put together; and which will be the final overthrow of its government, unless something is very speedily done; for their cup is nearly full.—Perhaps they will laugh at or make light of this; but I tell you Americans! that unless you speedily alter your course, *you* and your *Country are gone!!!!!!* For God Almighty will tear up the very face of the earth!!!

Will not that very remarkable passage of Scripture be fulfilled on Christian Americans? Hear it Americans!! "He that is unjust, let him be unjust still:—and he which is filthy, let him be filthy still: and he that is righteous, let him be righteous still: and he that is holy, let him be holy still."[10] I hope that the Americans may hear, but I am afraid that they have done us so much injury, and are so firm in the belief that our Creator made us to be an inheritance to them for ever, that their hearts will be hardened, so that their destruction may be sure. This language, perhaps is too harsh for the American's delicate ears. But Oh Americans! Americans!! I warn you in the name of the Lord (whether you will hear, or forbear), to repent and reform, or you are ruined!!!

Do you think that our blood is hidden from the Lord, because you can hide it from the rest of the world, by sending out missionaries, and by your charitable deeds to the Greeks, Irish, &c.? Will he not publish your secret crimes on the house top? Even here in Boston, pride and prejudice have got to such a pitch, that in the very houses erected to the Lord, they have built little places for the reception of coloured people, where they must sit during meeting, or keep away from the house of God, and the preachers say nothing about it—much less go into the hedges and highways seeking the lost sheep of the house of Israel, and try to bring them in to their Lord and Master. There are not a more wretched, ignorant, miserable, and abject set of beings in all the world, than the blacks in the Southern and Western sections of this country, under tyrants and devils. The preachers of America cannot see them, but they can send out missionaries to convert the heathens, notwithstanding. Americans! unless you speedily alter your course of proceeding, if God Almighty does not stop you, I say it in his name, that you may go on and do as you please for ever, both in time and eternity—never fear any evil at all!!!!!!!!

ADDITION.—The preachers and people of the United States form societies against Free Masonry and Intemperance, and write against Sabbath breaking, Sabbath mails, Infidelity, &c. &c. But the fountain head,[11] compared with which, all those other evils are comparatively nothing, and from the bloody and murderous head of which, they receive no trifling support, is hardly noticed by Americans. This is a fair illustration of the state of society in this country—it shows what a bearing *avarice* has upon a people, when they are nearly given up by the Lord to a hard heart and a reprobate mind, in consequence of afflicting their fellow creatures. God suffers some to go on until they are ruined for ever!!!!! Will it be the case with the whites of the United States of America?—We hope not—we would not wish to see them destroyed notwithstanding, they have and do now treat us more cruel than any people have treated another, on this earth since it came from the hands of its Creator (with the exceptions of the French and the Dutch, they treat us nearly as bad as the Americans of the United States). The will of God must however, in spite of us, *be done.*

The English are the best friends the coloured people have upon earth. Though they have oppressed us a little and have colonies now in the West Indies, which oppress us *sorely.*—Yet notwithstanding they (the English) have done one hundred times more for the melioration of our condition, than all the other nations of the earth put together. The blacks cannot but respect the English as a nation, notwithstanding they have treated us a little cruel. . . .

Article IV. Our Wretchedness in Consequence of the Colonizing Plan

Extract from the Speech of Mr. John Randolph, of Roanoke. Said he: —

It had been properly observed by the Chairman, as well as by the gentleman from this District [meaning Messrs. Clay and Caldwell] that there was nothing in the proposition submitted to consideration which in the smallest degree touches another very important and delicate question, which ought to be left as much out of view as possible [Negro Slavery.] [12]

There is no fear [Mr. R. said], that this proposition would alarm the slave-holders; they had been accustomed to think seriously of the subject.—There was a popular work on agriculture, by John Taylor of Caroline, which was widely circulated, and much confided in, in Virginia. In that book, much read because coming from a practical man, this description of people [referring to us half free ones] were pointed out as a great evil. They had indeed been held up as the greater bugbear to every man who feels an inclination to emancipate his slaves, not to create in the bosom of his country so great a nuisance. If a place could be provided for their reception, and a mode of sending them hence, there were hundreds, nay thousands of citizens who would, by manumitting their slaves, relieve themselves from the cares attendant on their possession. The great slave-holder [Mr. R. said], was frequently a mere sentry at his own door—bound to stay on his plantation to see that his slaves were properly treated, &c. [Mr. R. concluded by saying] that he had thought it necessary to make these remarks being a slave-holder himself, to shew that, so far from being connected with abolition of slavery, the measure proposed would prove one of the greatest securities to enable the master to keep in possession his own property.

Here is a demonstrative proof, of a plan got up, by a gang of slave-holders to select the free people of colour from among the slaves, that our more miserable brethren may be the better secured in ignorance and wretchedness, to work their farms and dig their mines, and thus go on enriching the Christians with their blood and groans. What our brethren could have been thinking about, who have left their native land and home and gone away to Africa,

I am unable to say. This country is as much ours as it is the whites', whether they will admit it now or not, they will see and believe it by and by. They tell us about prejudices—what have we to do with it? Their prejudices will be obliged to fall like lightning to the ground, in succeeding generations; not, however, with the will and consent of all the whites, for some will be obliged to hold on to the old adage, viz.: the blacks are not men, but were made to be an inheritance to us and our children for ever!!!!!! I hope the residue of the coloured people, will stand still and see the salvation of God and the miracle which he will work for our delivery from wretchedness under the Christians!!!!!!

ADDITION.—If any of us see fit to go away, go to those who have been for many years, and are now our greatest earthly friends and benefactors—the English. If not so, go to our brethren, the Haytians, who, according to their word, are bound to protect and comfort us. . . .

I speak Americans for your good. We must and shall be free I say, in spite of you. You may do your best to keep us in wretchedness and misery, to enrich you and your children, but God will deliver us from under you. And wo, wo, will be to you if we have to obtain our freedom by fighting. Throw away your fears and prejudices then, and enlighten us and treat us like men, and we will like you more than we do now hate you, and tell us now no more about colonization, for America is as much our country, as it is yours.—

Treat us like men, and there is no danger but we will all live in peace and happiness together. For we are not like you, hard hearted, unmerciful, and unforgiving. What a happy country this will be, if the whites will listen. What nation under heaven, will be able to do any thing with us, unless God gives us up into its hand? But Americans, I declare to you, while you keep us and our children in bondage, and treat us like brutes, to make us support you and your families, we cannot be your friends. You do not look for it, do you? Treat us then like men, and we will be your friends. And there is not a doubt in my mind, but that the whole of the past will be sunk into oblivion, and we yet, under God, will become a united and happy people. The whites may say it is impossible, but remember that nothing is impossible with God.

Notes

1. See my Preamble in first edition, first page. See also 2nd edition, Article 1, page 9.

2. Who are not deceitful, abject, and servile to resist the cruelties and murders inflicted upon us by the white slave holders, our enemies by nature.

3. See Genesis, chap. xli.

4. xli. 44.

5. xli. 44.

6. xli. 45.

7. Genesis, chap. xlvii, 5, 6.

8. Which is the reason the whites take the advantage of us.

9. See his Notes on Virginia, page 213.

10. See Revelation, chap. xxii. II.

11. Slavery and oppression.

12. "Niger," is a word derived from the Latin, which was used by the old Romans, to designate inanimate beings, which were black; such as soot, pot, wood, house, &c. Also, animals which they considered inferior to the human species, as a black horse, cow, hog, bird, dog, &c. The white Americans have applied this term to Africans, by way of reproach for our colour, to aggravate and heighten our miseries, because they have their feet on our throats.

7

Address at the African Masonic Hall (1833)

Maria Stewart's address, like Walker's Appeal in Four Articles, *may be called a statement of nationalism only in the sense that it contains a biblically inspired perception of African Americans as a people with a special God-given mission and destiny. Steward employs the rhetoric of the Old Testament and the Apocalypse to portray America as a modern Babylon, and condemns the United States for inflicting sinfulness on African Americans. Nonetheless, her hostility to the idea of African emigration is unmistakable and unequivocal; she vows that "before I go, the bayonet shall pierce me through." Steward was a resident of Boston and a friend of David Walker, of whom she says, "although he sleeps, his memory lives." She paid a similar tribute in a sermon on "Religion and the Pure Principles of Morality," which she delivered in Boston on October 31, 1831: "Though Walker sleeps, yet he lives, and his name shall be had in everlasting remembrance."*

African rights and liberty is a subject that ought to fire the breast of every free man of color in these United States, and excite in his bosom a lively, deep, decided and heart-felt interest. When I cast my eyes on the long list of illustrious names that are enrolled on the bright annals of fame among the whites, I turn my eyes within, and ask my thoughts, "Where are the names of *our* illustrious ones?" It must certainly have been for the want of energy on the part of the free people of color, that they have been long willing to bear the yoke of oppression. It must have been the want of ambition and force that has given the whites occasion to say, that our natural abilities are not as good, and our capacities by nature inferior to theirs. They boldly assert, that, did we possess a natural independence of soul, and feel a love for liberty within our breasts,

Maria Stewart, Address at the African Masonic Hall, Boston, February 27, 1833, in *Productions of Mrs. Maria W. Stewart, Presented to the First African Baptist Church and Society, of the City of Boston* (Boston: Friends of Freedom and Virtue, 1835).

some one of our sable race, long before this, would have testified it, notwithstanding the disadvantages under which we labor. We have made ourselves appear altogether unqualified to speak in our own defence, and are therefore looked upon as objects of pity and commiseration. We have been imposed upon, insulted and derided on every side; and now, if we complain, it is considered as the height of impertinence. We have suffered ourselves to be considered as dastards, cowards, mean, faint-hearted wretches; and on this account, (not because of our complexion,) many despise us, and would gladly spurn us from their presence.

These things have fired my soul with a holy indignation, and compelled me thus to come forward, and endeavor to turn their attention to knowledge and improvement; for knowledge is power. I would ask, is it blindness of mind, or stupidity of soul, or the want of education, that has caused our men who are 60 or 70 years of age, never to let their voices be heard, nor their hands be raised in behalf of their color? Or has it been for the fear of offending the whites? If it has, O ye fearful ones, throw off your fearfulness, and come forth in the name of the Lord, and in the strength of the God of Justice, and make yourselves useful and active members in society; for they admire a noble and patriotic spirit in others; and should they not admire it in us? If you are men, convince them that you possess the spirit of men; and as your day, so shall your strength be. Have the sons of Africa no souls? feel they no ambitious desires? shall the chains of ignorance forever confine them? shall the insipid appellation of "clever negroes," or "good creatures," any longer content them? Where can we find among ourselves the man of science, or a philosopher, or an able statesman, or a counsellor at law? Show me our fearless and brave, our noble and gallant ones. Where are our lecturers on natural history, and our critics in useful knowledge? There may be a few such men among us, but they are rare. It is true, our fathers bled and died in the revolutionary war, and others fought bravely under the command of Jackson, in defence of liberty. But where is the man that has distinguished himself in these modern days by acting wholly in the defence of African rights and liberty? There was one, although he sleeps, his memory lives.

I am sensible that there are many highly intelligent gentlemen of color in these United States, in the force of whose arguments, doubtless, I should discover my inferiority; but if they are blest with wit and talent, friends and fortune, why have they not made themselves men of eminence, by striving to take all the reproach that is cast upon the people of color, and in endeavoring to alleviate the woes of their brethren in bondage? Talk, without effort, is nothing; you are abundantly capable, gentlemen, of making yourselves men of distinction; and this gross neglect, on your part, causes my blood to boil within me. Here is the grand cause which hinders the rise and progress of the people of color. It is their want of laudable ambition and requisite courage.

Individuals have been distinguished according to their genius and talents, ever since the first formation of man, and will continue to be while the world stands. The different grades rise to honor and respectability as their merits may deserve. History informs us that we sprung from one of the most learned nations of the whole earth; from the seat, if not the parent of science; yes, poor, despised Africa was once the resort of sages and legislators of other nations, was esteemed the school for learning, and the most illustrious men in Greece flocked thither for instruction. But it was our gross sins and abominations that provoked the Almighty to frown thus heavily upon us, and give our glory unto others. Sin and prodigality have caused the downfall of nations, kings and emperors; and were it not that God in wrath remembers mercy, we might indeed despair; but a promise is left us; "Ethiopia shall again stretch forth her hands unto God."

But it is of no use for us to boast that we sprung from this learned and enlightened nation, for this day a thick mist of moral gloom hangs over millions of our race. Our condition as a people has been low for hundreds of years, and it will continue to be so, unless, by true piety and virtue, we strive to regain that which we have lost. White Americans, by their prudence, economy and exertions, have sprung up and become one of the most flourishing nations in the world, distinguished for their knowledge of the arts and sciences, for their polite literature. While our minds are vacant, and starving for want of knowledge, theirs are filled to overflowing. Most of our color have been taught to stand in fear of the white man, from their earliest infancy, to work as soon as they could walk, and call "master," before they scarce could lisp the name of *mother*. Continual fear and laborious servitude have in some degree lessened in us that natural force and energy which belong to man; or else, in defiance of opposition, our men, before this, would have nobly and boldly contended for their rights. But give the man of color an equal opportunity with the white from the cradle to manhood, and from manhood to the grave, and you would discover the dignified statesman, the man of science, and the philosopher. But there is no such opportunity for the sons of Africa, and I fear that our powerful ones are fully determined that there never shall be. Forbid, ye Powers on high, that it should any longer be said that our men possess no force. O ye sons of Africa, when will your voices be heard in our legislative halls, in defiance of your enemies, contending for equal rights and liberty? How can you, when you reflect from what you have fallen, refrain from crying mightily unto God, to turn away from us the fierceness of his anger, and remember our transgressions against us no more forever. But a God of infinite purity will not regard the prayers of those who hold religion in one hand, and prejudice, sin and pollution in the other; he will not regard the prayers of self-righteousness and hypocrisy. Is it possible, I exclaim, that for the want of knowledge, we have labored for hundreds of years to support others, and been content to receive what they chose to give us in return? Cast your eyes about, look as far as you can see; all, all is owned by the lordly white, except here and there a lowly dwelling which the man of color, midst deprivations, fraud and opposition, has been scarce able to procure. Like king Solomon, who put neither nail nor hammer to the temple, yet received the praise; so also have the white Americans gained themselves a name, like the names of the great men that are in the earth, while in reality we have been their principal foundation and support. We have pursued the shadow, they have obtained the substance; we have performed the labor, they have received the profits; we have planted the vines, they have eaten the fruits of them.

I would implore our men, and especially our rising youth, to flee from the gambling board and the dance-hall; for we are poor, and have no money to throw away. I do not consider dancing as criminal in itself, but it is astonishing to me that our young men are so blind to their own interest and the future welfare of their children, as to spend their hard earnings for this frivolous amusement; for it has been carried on among us to such an unbecoming extent, that it has became absolutely disgusting. "Faithful are the wounds of a friend, but the kisses of an enemy are deceitful." Had those men among us, who have had an opportunity, turned their attention as assiduously to mental and moral improvement as they have to gambling and dancing, I might have remained quietly at home, and they stood contending in my place. These polite accomplishments will never enrol your names on the bright annals of fame, who admire the belle void of intellectual knowledge, or applaud the dandy that talks largely on politics, without striving to assist his fellow in the revolution, when the nerves and muscles of every other man forced him into the field of action. You have a right to rejoice, and to let your hearts cheer you in the days of your youth; yet remember that for all these things, God will bring you into judgment. Then, O ye sons of Africa, turn your mind from these perishable objects, and contend for the cause of God and the rights of man. Form yourselves into temperance societies. There are temperate men among you; then why will you any longer neglect to strive, by your example, to suppress vice in all its abhorrent forms? You have been told repeatedly of the glorious results arising from temperance, and can you bear to see the whites arising in honor and respectability, without endeavoring to grasp after that honor and respectability also?

But I forbear. Let our money, instead of being thrown away as heretofore, be appropriated for schools and seminaries of learning for our children and youth. We ought to follow the example of the whites in this respect. Nothing would raise our respectability, add to our peace and happiness, and reflect so much honor upon us, as to be ourselves the promoters of temperance, and the supporters, as far as we are able, of useful and scientific knowledge. The rays of light and knowledge have been hid from our view; we have been taught to consider ourselves as scarce superior to the brute creation; and have performed the most laborious part of American drudgery. Had we as a people received one half the early advantages the whites have received, I would defy the government of these United States to deprive us any longer of our rights.

I am informed that the agent of the Colonization Society has recently formed an association of young men, for the purpose of influencing those of us to go to Liberia who may feel disposed. The colonizationists are blind to their own interest, for should the nations of the earth make war with America, they would find their forces much weakened by our absence; or should we remain here, can our "brave soldiers," and "fellow-citizens," as they were termed in time of calamity, condescend to defend the rights of the whites, and be again deprived of their own, or sent to Liberia in return? Or, if the colonizationists are real friends to Africa, let them expend the money which they collect, in erecting a college to educate her injured sons in this land of gospel light and liberty; for it would be most thankfully received on our part, and convince us of the truth of their professions, and save time, expense and anxiety. Let them place before us noble objects, worthy of pursuit, and see if we prove ourselves to be those unambitious negroes they term us. But ah! methinks their hearts are so frozen towards us, they had rather their money should be sunk in the ocean than to administer it to our relief; and I fear, if they dared, like Pharaoh, king of Egypt, they would order every male child among us to be drowned. But the most high God is still as able to subdue the lofty pride of these white Americans, as He was the heart of that ancient rebel. They say, though we are looked upon as *things,* yet we sprang from a scientific people. Had our men the requisite force and energy, they would soon convince them by their efforts both in public and private, that they were men, or things in the shape of men. Well may the colonizationists laugh us to scorn for our negligence; well may they cry, "Shame to the sons of Africa." As the burden of the Israelites was too great for Moses to bear, so also is our burden too great for our noble advocate to bear. You must feel interested, my brethren, in what he undertakes, and hold up his hands by your good works, or in spite of himself, his soul will become discouraged, and his heart will die within him; for he has, as it were, the strong bulls of Bashan to contend with.

It is of no use for us to wait any longer for a generation of well educated men to arise. We have slumbered and slept too long already; the day is far spent; the night of death approaches; and you have sound sense and good judgment sufficient to begin with, if you feel disposed to make a right use of it. Let every man of color throughout the United States, who possesses the spirit and principles of a man, sign a petition to Congress, to abolish slavery in the District of Columbia, and grant you the rights and privileges of common free citizens; for if you had had faith as a grain of mustard seed, long before this the mountains of prejudice might have been removed. We are all sensible that the Anti-Slavery Society has taken hold of the arm of our whole population, in order to raise them out of the mire. Now all we have to do is, by a spirit of virtuous ambition to strive to raise ourselves; and I am happy to have it in my power thus publicly to say, that the colored inhabitants of this city, in some respects, are beginning to improve. Had the free people of color in these United States nobly and boldly contended for their rights, and showed a natural genius and talent, although not so brilliant as some; had they held up, encouraged and patronized each other, nothing could have hindered us from being a thriving and flourishing people. There has been a fault among us. The reason why our distinguished men have not made themselves more influential is, because they fear that the strong current of opposition through which they must pass, would cause their downfall and prove their overthrow. And what gives rise to this opposition? Envy. And what has it amounted to? Nothing. And who are the cause of it? Our whited sepulchres, who want to be great, and don't know how; who love to be called of men "Rabbi, Rabbi," who put on false sanctity, and humble themselves to their brethren, for the sake of acquiring the highest place in the synagogue, and the uppermost seats at the feast. You, dearly beloved, who are the genuine followers of our Lord Jesus Christ, the salt of the earth and the light of the world, are not so culpable. As I told you, in the very first of my writing, I tell you again, I am but as a drop in the bucket—as one particle of the small dust of the earth. God will surely raise up those among us who will plead the cause of virtue, and the pure principles of morality, more eloquently than I am able to do.

It appears to me that America has become like the great city of Babylon, for she has boasted in her heart,—"I sit a queen, and am no widow, and shall see no sorrow"? She is indeed a seller of slaves and the souls of men; she has made the Africans drunk with the wine of her fornication; she has put them completely beneath her feet, and she means to keep them there; her right hand supports the reins of government, and her left hand the wheel of power, and she is determined not to let go her grasp. But many powerful sons and daughters of Africa will shortly arise, who will put down vice and immorality among us, and declare by Him that sitteth upon the throne, that they will have their rights; and if refused, I am afraid they will spread horror and devastation around. I believe that the oppression of injured Africa has come up before the Majesty of Heaven; and when our cries shall have reached the ears of the Most High, it will be a tremendous day for the people of this land; for strong is the arm of the Lord God Almighty.

Life has almost lost its charms for me; death has lost its sting and the grave its terrors; and at times I have a strong desire to depart and dwell with Christ, which is far better. Let me entreat my white brethren to awake and save our sons from dissipation, and our daughters from ruin. Lend the hand of assistance to feeble merit, plead the cause of virtue among our sable race; so shall our curses upon you be turned into blessings; and though you should endeavor to drive us from these shores, still we will cling to you the more firmly; nor will we attempt to rise above you: we will presume to be called your equals only.

The unfriendly whites first drove the native American from his much loved home. Then they stole our fathers from their peaceful and quiet dwellings, and brought them hither, and made bond-men and bond-women of them and their little ones; they have obliged our brethren to labor, kept them in utter ignorance, nourished them in vice, and raised them in degradation; and now that we have enriched their soil, and filled their coffers, they say that we are not capable of becoming like white men, and that we never can rise to respectability in this country. They would drive us to a strange land. But before I go, the bayonet shall pierce me through. African rights and liberty is a subject that ought to fire the breast of every free man of color in these United States, and excite in his bosom a lively, deep, decided and heart-felt interest.

Part Two

Classical Black Nationalism, 1850–62

From The Condition, Elevation, Emigration, and Destiny of the Colored People of the United States (1852)

The Fugitive Slave Act of 1850 was a part of the so-called Compromise of 1850, in which the South allowed California to enter the Union as a free state in exchange for harsher treatment of suspected runaway slaves in the North. It was also the catalyst that led Martin R. Delany to produce his book on the condition of African Americans. In chapter 16, which is included here, he published the entire text of the law, along with his dismally accurate interpretation of it. The law allowed federal commissioners to try any black person, slave or free, without a jury, and provided for paying commissioners a double fee if the suspect were declared a fugitive slave. The law also prohibited testimony by the accused, and thus in effect reduced every Free African to a potential slave. Delany asserted that the only self-respecting response to the act was to leave the United States, but although he viewed African Americans as "a nation within a nation," and called for emigration, he was not yet fully committed to the formation of a black republic; Liberia, in any case, was out of the question. Chapter 17, which is also included in this selection, contained a notable diatribe against the republic and its president, Joseph Jenkins Roberts.

Delany supported the notion of emigration to Canada as a temporary measure, and from 1856 to 1858 he resided with his family in Chatham, Ontario, which had a black population of around 2,400 out of 12,000. Other black Canadian communities were founded on somewhat separatist principles, although their residents usually pledged their grateful allegiance to Queen Victoria. Delany considered seriously, but without result, the possibilities of migration to some portion of South America, a matter in which he claimed to see "the finger of God." As an afterthought, he also considered East Africa as a possible destination, and appended to his book a proposal for "A Project for an Expendition of Adventure to the Eastern Coast of Africa," also included in the present volume. In 1854 Delany organized the "National Emigration Convention" in Cleveland, where his address on "The Political Destiny of the Colored Race on the American Continent" included extracts from The Condition of the Colored People. *By that time, he was prepared to call less equivocally for the establishment of a black nation-*

From Martin R. Delany, *The Condition, Elevation, Emigration, and Destiny of the Colored People of the United States* (Philadelphia: Martin R. Delany, 1852).

state, and secret sessions of the convention were putatively dominated by discussion of African emigration.

Chapter XVI. *National Disfranchisement of Colored People*

We give below the Act of Congress, known as the "Fugitive Slave Law," for the benefit of the reader, as there are thousands of the American people of all classes, who have never read the provisions of this enactment; and consequently, have no conception of its enormity. We had originally intended, also, to have inserted here, the Act of Congress of 1793, but since this Bill includes all the provisions of that Act, in fact, although called a "supplement," is a substitute, *de facto,* it would be superfluous; therefore, we insert the Bill alone, with explanations following: —

An Act

To Amend and Supplementary to the Act, entitled, "An Act respecting Fugitives from justice,
and persons escaping from the service of their
masters," approved February 12, 1793.

Be it enacted by the Senate and House of Representatives of the United States of America in Congress assembled, That the persons who have been, or may hereafter be, appointed commissioners, in virtue of any act of Congress, by the circuit courts of the United States, and who, in consequence of such appointment, are authorized to exercise the powers that any justice of the peace or other magistrate of any of the United States may exercise in respect to offenders for any crime or offence against the United States, by arresting, imprisoning, or bailing the same under and by virtue of the thirty-third section of the act of the twenty-fourth of September, seventeen hundred and eighty-nine, entitled "An act to estab-lish the judicial courts of the United States," shall be, and are hereby authorized and required to exercise and discharge all the powers and duties conferred by this act.

Sec. 2. *And be it further enacted,* That the superior court of each organized territory of the United States shall have the same power to appoint commissioners to take acknowledgements of bail and affidavit, and to take depositions of witnesses in civil causes, which is now possessed by the circuit courts of the United States; and all commissioners who shall hereafter be appointed for such purposes by the superior court of any organized territory of the United States shall possess all the powers and exercise all the duties conferred by law upon the commissioners appointed by the circuit courts of the United States for similar purposes, and shall moreover exercise and discharge all the powers and duties conferred by this act.

SEC. 3. *And be it further enacted,* That the circuit courts of the United States, and the superior courts of each organized territory of the United States, shall from time to time enlarge the number of commissioners, with a view to afford reasonable facilities to reclaim fugitives from labor, and to the prompt discharge of the duties imposed by this act.

SEC. 4. *And be it further enacted,* That the commissioners above named shall have concurrent jurisdiction with the judges of the circuit and district courts of the United States, in their respective circuits and districts within the several States, and the judges of the superior courts of the Territories, severally and collectively, in term time and vacation; and shall grant certificates to such claimants, upon satisfactory proof being made, with authority to take and remove such fugitives from service or labor, under the restrictions herein contained, to the State or territory from which such persons may have escaped or fled.

SEC. 5. *And be it further enacted,* That it shall be the duty of all marshals and deputy marshals to obey and execute all warrants and precepts issued under the provisions of this act, when to them directed; and should any marshal or deputy marshal refuse to receive such warrant or other process, when tendered, or to use all proper means diligently to execute the same, he shall, on conviction thereof, be fined in the sum of one thousand dollars to the use of such claimant, on the motion of such claimant, by the circuit or district court for the district of such marshal; and after arrest of such fugitive by such marshal or his deputy, or whilst at any time in his custody, under the provisions of this act, should such fugitive escape, whether with or without the assent of such marshal or his deputy, such marshal shall be liable, on his official bond, to be prosecuted, for the benefit of such claimant for the full value of the service or labor of said fugitive in the State, Territory, or district whence he escaped; and the better to enable the said commissioners, when thus appointed, to execute their duties faithfully and efficiently, in conformity with the requirements of the constitution of the United States and of this act, they are hereby authorized and empowered, within their counties respectively, to appoint in writing under their hands, any one or more suitable persons, from time to time, to execute all such warrants and other process as may be issued by them in the lawful performance of their respective duties; with an authority to such commissioners, or the persons to be appointed by them, to execute process as aforesaid, to summon and call to their aid the bystanders, or *posse comitatus* of the proper county, when necessary to insure a faithful observance of the clause of the constitution referred to, in conformity with the provisions of this act: and all good citizens are hereby commanded to aid and assist in the prompt and efficient execution of this law, whenever their services may be required, as aforesaid, for that person; and said warrants shall run and be executed by said officers anywhere in the State within which they are issued.

Sec. 6. *And be it further enacted,* That when a person held to service or labor in any State or Territory of the United States has heretofore or shall hereafter escape into another State or Territory of the United States, the person or persons to whom such service or labor may be due, or his, her, or their agent or attorney, duly authorized, by power of attorney, in writing, acknowledged and certified under the seal of some legal office or court of the State or Territory in which the same may be executed, may pursue and reclaim such fugitive person, either by procuring a warrant from some one of the courts, judges, or commissioners aforesaid, of the proper circuit, district or county, for the apprehension of such fugitive from service or labor, or by seizing and arresting such fugitive, where the same can be done without process, and by taking and causing such person to be taken forthwith before such court, judge or commissioner, whose duty it shall be to hear and determine the case of such claimant in a summary manner; and upon satisfactory proof being made, by deposition or affidavit, in writing, to be taken and certified by such court, judge, or commissioner, or by other satisfactory testimony, duly taken and certified by some court, magistrate, justice of the peace, or other legal officer authorized to administer an oath, and take depositions under the laws of the State or Territory from which such person owing service or labor may have escaped, with a certificate of such magistracy or other authority, as aforesaid, with the seal of the proper court or officer thereto attached, which seal shall be sufficient to establish the competency of the proof, and with proof, also by affidavit, of the identity of the person whose service or labor is claimed to be due as aforesaid, that the person so arrested does in fact owe service or labor to the person or persons claiming him or her, in the State or Territory from which such fugitive may have escaped as aforesaid, and that said person escaped, to make out and deliver to such claimant, his or her agent or attorney, a certificate setting forth the substantial facts as to the service or labor due from such fugitive to the claimant, and of his or her escape from the State or Territory in which such service or labor was due to the State or Territory in which he or she was arrested, with authority to such claimant, or his or her agent or attorney to use such reasonable force and restraint as may be necessary under the circumstances of the case, to take and remove such fugitive person back to the State or Territory from whence he or she may have escaped as aforesaid. In no trial or hearing under this act shall the testimony of such alleged fugitive be admitted in evidence; and the certificates in this and the first section mentioned shall be conclusive of the right of the person or persons in whose favor granted to remove such fugitive to the State or Territory from which he escaped, and shall prevent all molestation of said person or persons by any process issued by any court, judge, magistrate, or other person whomsoever.

Sec. 7. *And be it further enacted,* That any person who shall knowingly and willingly obstruct, hinder, or prevent such claimant, his agent or attorney, or any person or persons lawfully assisting him, her, or them, from arresting such a fugitive from service or labor, either with or without process as aforesaid; or shall rescue, or attempt to rescue such fugitive from service or labor, from the custody of such claimant, his or her agent or attorney or other person or persons lawfully assisting as aforesaid, when so arrested, pursuant to the authority herein given and declared: or shall aid, abet, or assist such person, so owing service or labor as aforesaid, directly or indirectly, to escape from such claimant, his agent or attorney, or other person or persons, legally authorized as aforesaid; or shall harbor or conceal such fugitive, so as to prevent the discovery and arrest of such person, after notice or knowledge of the fact that such person was a fugitive from service or labor as aforesaid, shall, for either of said offences, be subject to a fine not exceeding one thousand dollars, and imprisonment not exceeding six months, by indictment and conviction before the district court of the United States for the district in which such offence may have been committed, or before the proper court of criminal jurisdiction, if committed within any one of the organized territories of the United

States; and shall moreover forfeit and pay, by way of civil damages to the party injured by such illegal conduct, the sum of one thousand dollars for each fugitive so lost as aforesaid, to be recovered by action of debt in any of the district or territorial courts aforesaid, within whose jurisdiction the said offence may have been committed.

SEC. 8. *And be it further enacted,* That the marshals, their deputies, and the clerks of the said district and territorial courts, shall be paid for their services the like fees as may be allowed to them for similar services in other cases; and where such services are rendered exclusively in the arrest, custody, and delivery of the fugitive to the claimant, his or her agent or attorney, or where such supposed fugitive may be discharged out of custody for the want of sufficient proof as aforesaid, then such fees are to be paid in the whole by such claimant, his agent or attorney; and in all cases where the proceedings are before a commissioner, he shall be entitled to a fee of ten dollars in full for his services in each case, upon delivery of the said certificate to the claimant, his or her agent or attorney; or a fee of five dollars in cases where the proof shall not, in the opinion of such commissioner, warrant such certificate and delivery, inclusive of all services incident to such arrest and examination, to be paid in either case, by the claimant, his or her agent or attorney. The person or persons authorized to execute the process to be issued by such commissioners for the arrest and detention of fugitives from service or labor as aforesaid, shall also be entitled to a fee of five dollars each for each person he or they may arrest and take before any such commissioner as aforesaid at the instance and request of such claimant, with such other fees as may be deemed reasonable by such commissioner for such other additional services as may be necessarily performed by him or them: such as attending to the examination, keeping the fugitive in custody, and providing him with food and lodging during his detention, and until the final determination of such commissioner; and in general for performing such other duties as may be required by such claimant, his or her attorney or agent, or commissioner in the premises; such fees to be made up in conformity with the fees usually charged by the officers of the courts of justice within the proper district or county, as near as may be practicable, and paid by such claimants, their agents or attorneys, whether such supposed fugitive from service or labor be ordered to be delivered to such claimants by the final determination of such commissioners or not.

SEC. 9. *And be it further enacted,* That upon affidavit made by the claimant of such fugitive, his agent or attorney, after such certificate has been issued, that he has reason to apprehend that such fugitive will be rescued by force from his or their possession before he can be taken beyond the limits of the State in which the arrest is made, it shall be the duty of the officer making the arrest to retain such fugitive in his custody, and to remove him to the State whence he fled, and there to deliver him to said claimant, his agent or attorney. And to this end the officer aforesaid is hereby authorized and required to employ so many persons as he may deem necessary, to overcome such force, and to retain them in his service so long as circumstances may require; the said officer and his assistants, while so employed, to receive the same compensation, and to be allowed the same expenses as are now allowed by law for the transportation of criminals, to be certified by the judge of the district within which the arrest is made, and paid out of the treasury of the United States.

SEC. 10. *And be it further enacted,* That when any person held to service or labor in any State or Territory, or in the District of Columbia, shall escape therefrom, the party to whom such service or labor shall be due, his, her, or their agent or attorney may apply to any court of record therein, or judge thereof, in vacation, and make satisfactory proof to such court, or judge, in vacation, of the escape aforesaid, and that the person escaping owed service or labor to such party. Whereupon the court shall cause a record to be made of the matters so proved, and also a general description of the person so escaping, with such convenient certainty as may be; and a transcript of such record authenticated by the attestation of the clerk, and of the seal of the said court, being produced in any other State, Territory, or District in which the person so escaping may be found, and being exhibited to any judge, commissioner, or other officer, authorized by the law of the United States to cause persons escaping from service or labor to be delivered up, shall be held and taken to be full and conclusive evidence of the fact of escape, and that the service or labor of the person escaping is due to the party in such record mentioned. And upon the production by the said party of other and further evidence, if necessary, either oral or by affidavit, in addition to what is contained in the said record of the identity of the person escaping, he or she shall be delivered up to the claimant. And the said court, commissioner, judge or other person authorized by this act to grant certificates to claimants of fugitives, shall, upon the production of the record and other evidences aforesaid, grant to such claimant a certificate of his right to take any such person identified and proved to be owing service or labor as aforesaid, which certificate shall authorize such claimant to seize or arrest and transport such person to the State or Territory from which he escaped: *Provided,* That nothing herein contained shall be construed as requiring the production of a transcript of such record as evidence as aforesaid; but in its absence, the claim shall be heard and determined upon other satisfactory proofs competent in law.

HOWELL COBB,
Speaker of the House of Representatives.
WILLIAM R. KING,
President of the Senate, pro temporé.
Approved September 18, 1850.

MILLARD FILLMORE.

The most prominent provisions of the Constitution of the United States, and those which form the fundamental basis of personal security, are they which provide, that every person shall be secure in their person and property: that no person may be deprived of liberty without due process of law, and that for crime or misdemeanor; that there may be no process of law that shall work corruption of blood. By corruption of blood is meant, that process, by which a person is *degraded* and deprived of rights common to the enfranchised citizen—of the rights of an elector, and of eligibility to the office of a representative of the people; in a word, that no person nor their posterity, may ever be debased beneath the level of the recognised basis of American citizenship. This debasement and degradation is "corruption of blood;" politically understood—a legal acknowledgement of inferiority of birth.

Heretofore, it ever has been denied, that the United States recognised or knew any difference between the people—that the Constitution makes no distinction, but includes in its provisions, all the people alike. This is not true, and certainly is blind absurdity in us at least, who have suffered the dread consequences of this delusion, not now to see it.

By the provisions of this bill, the colored people of the United States are positively degraded beneath the level of the whites—are made liable at any time, in any place, and under all circumstances, to be arrested—and upon the claim of any white person, without the privilege, even of making a defence, sent into endless bondage. Let no visionary nonsense about *habeas corpus,* or a *fair trial,* deceive us; there are no such rights granted in this bill, and except where the commissioner is too ignorant to understand when reading it, or too stupid to enforce it when he does understand, there is no earthly chance—no hope under heaven for the colored person who is brought before one of these officers of the law. Any leniency that may be expected, must proceed from the whims or caprice of the magistrate—in fact, it is optional with them; and *our* rights and liberty entirely at their disposal.

We are slaves in the midst of freedom, waiting patiently, and unconcernedly—indifferently, and stupidly, for masters to come and lay claim to us, trusting to their generosity, whether or not they will own us and carry us into endless bondage.

The slave is more secure than we; he knows who holds the heel upon his bosom—we know not the wretch who may grasp us by the throat. His master may be a man of some conscientious scruples; ours may be unmerciful. Good or bad, mild or harsh, easy or hard, lenient or severe, saint or satan—whenever that master demands any one of us—even our affectionate wives and darling little children, *we must go into slavery*—there is *no alternative.* The *will* of the man who sits in judgment on our liberty, is the law. To him is given *all power* to say, whether or not we have a right to enjoy freedom. This is the power over the slave in the South—this is now extended to the North. The will of the man who sits in judgment over us is the law; because it is explicitly provided that the *decision* of the commissioner shall be final, from which there can be no appeal.

The freed man of the South is even more secure than the freeborn of the North; because such persons usually have their records in the slave states, bringing their "papers" with them; and the slaveholders will be faithful to their own acts. The Northern freeman knows no records; he despises the "papers."

Depend upon no promised protection of citizens in any quarter. Their own property and liberty are jeopardised, and they will not sacrifice them for us. This we may not expect them to do.

Besides, there are no people who ever lived, love their country and obey their laws as the Americans.

Their country is their Heaven—their Laws their Scriptures— and the decrees of their Magistrates obeyed as the fiat of God. It is the most consummate delusion and misdirected confidence to depend upon them for protection; and for a moment suppose even our children safe while walking in the streets among them.

A people capable of originating and sustaining such a law as this, are not the people to whom we are willing to entrust our liberty at discretion.

What can we do?—What shall we do? This is the great and important question:—Shall we submit to be dragged like brutes before heartless men, and sent into degradation and bondage?— Shall we fly, or shall we resist? Ponder well and reflect.

A learned jurist in the United States, (Chief Justice John Gibson of Pennsylvania,) lays down this as a fundamental right in the United States: that "Every man's house is his castle, and he has the right to defend it unto the taking of life, against any attempt to enter it against his will, except for crime," by well authenticated process.

But we have no such right. It was not intended for us, any more than any other provision of the law, intended for the protection of Americans. The policy is against us—it is useless to contend against it.

This is the law of the land and must be obeyed; and we candidly advise that it is useless for us to contend against it. To suppose its repeal, is to anticipate an overthrow of the Confederative Union; and we must be allowed an expression of opinion, when we say, that candidly we believe, the existence of the Fugitive Slave Law *necessary* to the continuance of the National Compact. This Law is the foundation of the Compromise—remove it, and the consequences are easily determined. We say necessary to the continuance of the National Compact: certainly we will not be understood as meaning that the enactment of such a Law was *really* necessary, or as favoring in the least this political monstrosity of the THIRTY-FIRST CONGRESS of the UNITED STATES of AMERICA—surely not at all; but we speak logically and politically, leaving morality and right out of the question—taking our position on the acknowledged popular basis of American Policy; arguing from premise to conclusion. We must abandon all vague theory, and look at *facts* as they really are; viewing ourselves in our true political position in the body politic. To imagine ourselves to be included in the body politic, except by express legislation, is at war with common sense, and contrary to fact. Legislation, the administration of the laws of the country, and the exercise of rights by the people, all prove to the contrary. We are politically, not of them, but aliens to the laws and political privileges of the country. These are truths—fixed facts, that quaint theory and exhausted moralising, are impregnable to, and fall harmlessly before.

It is useless to talk about our rights in individual States: we can have no rights there as citizens, not recognised in our common country; as the citizens of one State, are entitled to all the rights and privileges of an American citizen in all the States—the nullity of the one necessarily implying the nullity of the other. These provisions then do not include the colored people of the United States; since there is no power left in them, whereby they may protect us as their own citizens. Our descent, by the laws of the country, stamps us with inferiority—upon us has this law worked *corruption of blood*. We are in the hands of the General Government, and no State can rescue us. The Army and Navy stand at the service of our enslavers, the whole force of which, may at any moment—even in the dead of night, as has been done—when sunk in the depth of slumber, called out for the purpose of forcing our mothers, sisters, wives, and children, or ourselves, into hopeless servitude, there to weary out a miserable life, a relief from which, death would be hailed with joy. Heaven and earth—God and Humanity!—are not these sufficient to arouse the most worthless among mankind, of whatever descent, to a sense of their true position? These laws apply to us—shall we not be aroused?

Chapter XVII. Emigration of the Colored People of the United States

That there have been people in all ages under certain circumstances, that may be benefited by emigration, will be admitted; and that there are circumstances under which emigration is absolutely necessary to their political elevation, cannot be disputed.

This we see in the Exodus of the Jews from Egypt to the land of Judea; in the expedition of Dido and her followers from Tyre to Mauritania; and not to dwell upon hundreds of modern European examples—also in the ever memorable emigration of the Puritans, in 1620, from Great Britain, the land of their birth, to the wilderness of the New World, at which may be fixed the beginning of emigration to this continent as a permanent residence.

This may be acknowledged; but to advocate the emigration of the colored people of the United States from their native homes, is a new feature in our history, and at first view, may be considered objectionable, as pernicious to our interests. This objection is at once removed, when reflecting on our condition as incontrovertibly shown in a foregoing part of this work. And we shall proceed at once to give the advantages to be derived from emigration, to us as a people, in preference to any other policy that we may adopt. This granted, the question will then be, Where shall we go? This we conceive to be all-important—of paramount consideration, and shall endeavor to show the most advantageous locality; and premise the recommendation, with the strictest advice against any countenance whatever, to the emigration scheme of the so called Republic of Liberia.

Chapter XVIII. "Republic of Liberia"

That we desire the civilization and enlightenment of Africa—the high and elevated position of Liberia among the nations of the earth, may not be doubted, as the writer was among the first, seven or eight years ago, to make the suggestion and call upon the Liberians to hold up their heads like men; take courage, having confidence in their own capacity to govern themselves, and come out from their disparaging position, by formally declaring their Independence. . . .

[Delany inserts at this point a lengthy extract from the "First Annual Report of the Trustees of Donations for Education in Liberia," which described the number and types of schools that had been established in Liberia as of 1850 and the number of pupils enrolled in these various institutions at that time. The report recommended the establishment of a "higher seminary," that is, a liberal arts college or university. Delany seems rather impatient in anticipating results, as his critique of Liberia was published less than two years after the report of the trustees was issued. Edward W. Blyden and Alexander Crummell toured the United States seeking donations for the University of Liberia in collaboration with the "Trustees of Donations" during the early 1860s. Some discussion of these efforts is presented in Wilson J. Moses, Alexander Crummell: A Study of Civilization and Discontent.*]*

However foreign to the designs of the writer of ever making that country or any other out of America, his home; had this been done, and honorably maintained, the Republic of Liberia would have met with words of encouragement, not only from himself, an humble individual, but we dare assert, from the leading spirits among, if not from the whole colored population of the United States. Because they would have been willing to overlook the circumstances under which they went there, so that in the end, they were willing to take their stand as men, and thereby throw off the degradation of slaves, still under the control of American slave-holders, and American slave-ships. But in this, we were disappointed—grievously disappointed, and proceed to show in short, our objections to Liberia.

Its geographical position, in the first place, is objectionable, being located in the *sixth degree* of latitude North of the equator, in a district signally unhealthy, rendering it objectionable as a place of destination for the colored people of the United States. We shall say nothing about other parts of the African coast, and the reasons for its location where it is: it is enough for us to know the facts as they are, to justify an unqualified objection to Liberia.

In the second place, it originated in a deep laid scheme of the slaveholders of the country, to *exterminate* the free colored of the American continent; the origin being sufficient to justify us in impugning the motives.

Thirdly and lastly—Liberia is not an Independent Republic: in fact, *it is not* an independent nation at all; but a poor *miserable mockery*— a *burlesque* on a government—a pitiful dependency on the American Colonizationists, the Colonization Board at Washington city, in the District of Columbia, being the Executive and Government, and the principal man, called President, in Liberia, being the echo—a mere parrot of Rev. Robert R. Gurley, Elliot Cresson, Esq., Governor Pinney, and other leaders of the Colonization scheme—to do as they bid, and say what they tell him. This we see in all of his doings.

Does he go to France and England, and enter into solemn treaties of an honorable recognition of the independence of his country; before his own nation has any knowledge of the result, this man called President, dispatches an official report to the Colonizationists of the United States, asking their gracious approval? Does king Grando, or a party of fishermen besiege a village and murder some of the inhabitants, this same "President," dispatches an official report to the American Colonization Board, asking for instructions—who call an Executive Session of the Board, and immediately decide that war must be waged against the enemy, placing ten thousand dollars at his disposal—and war *actually declared in Liberia,* by virtue of the *instructions* of the *American Colonization Society.* A mockery of a government—a disgrace to the office pretended to be held—a parody on the position assumed. Liberia in Africa, is a mere dependency of Southern slaveholders, and American Colonizationists, and unworthy of any respectful consideration from us.

What would be thought of the people of Hayti, and their heads of government, if their instructions emanated from the American Anti-Slavery Society, or the British Foreign Missionary Board? Should they be respected at all as a nation? Would they be worthy of it? Certainly not. We do not expect Liberia to be all that Hayti is; but we ask and expect of her, to have a decent respect for herself—to endeavor to be freemen instead of voluntary slaves. Liberia is no place for the colored freemen of the United States; and we dismiss the subject with a single remark of caution against any advice contained in a pamphlet, which we have not seen, written by Hon. James G. Birney, in favor of Liberian emigration. Mr. Birney is like the generality of white Americans, who suppose that we are too ignorant to understand what we want; whenever they wish to get rid of us, would drive us any where, so that we left them. Don't adhere to a word therein contained; we will think for ourselves. Let Mr. Birney go his way, and we will go ours. This is one of those confounded gratuities that is forced in our faces at every turn we make. We dismiss it without further comment—and with it Colonization *in toto*—and Mr. Birney *de facto*.

But to return to emigration: Where shall we go? We must not leave this continent; America is our destination and our home.

That the continent of America seems to have been designed by Providence as an asylum for all the various nations of the earth, is very apparent. From the earliest discovery, various nations sent a representation here, either as adventurers and speculators, or employed seamen and soldiers, hired to do the work of their employers. And among the earliest and most numerous class who found their way to the New World, were those of the African race. And it is now ascertained to our mind, beyond a peradventure, that when the continent was discovered, there were found in Central America, a tribe of the black race, of fine looking people, having characteristics of color and hair, identifying them originally of the African race—no doubt being a remnant of the Africans who, with the Carthaginian expedition, were adventitiously cast upon this continent, in their memorable excursion to the "Great Island," after sailing many miles distant to the West of the Pillars of Hercules.

We are not inclined to be superstitious, but say, that we can see the "finger of God" in all this; and if the European race may with propriety, boast and claim, that this continent is better adapted to their development, than their own father-land; surely, it does not necessarily detract from our father-land, to claim the superior advantages to the African race, to be derived from this continent. But be that as it may, the world belongs to mankind—his common Father created it for his common good—his temporal destiny is here; and our present warfare, is not upon European rights, nor for European countries; but for the common rights of man, based upon the great principles of common humanity—taking our chance in the world of rights, and claiming to have originally more right to this continent, than the European race. And had we no other claims than those set forth in a former part of this work, they are sufficient to cause every colored man on the continent, to stand upon the soil unshaken and unmoved. The aboriginee of the continent, is more closely allied to us by consanguinity, than to the European—being descended from the Asiatic, whose alliance in matrimony with the African is very common—therefore, we have even greater claims to this continent on that account, and should unite and make common cause in elevation, with our similarly oppressed brother, the Indian.

The advantages of this continent are superior, because it presents every variety of climate, soil, and production of the earth, with every variety of mineral production, with all kinds of water privileges, and ocean coast on all sides, presenting every commercial advantage. Upon the American continent we are determined to stay, in spite of every odds against us. What part of the great continent shall our destination be—shall we emigrate to the North or South? . . .

Chapter XX. The Canadas

This is one of the most beautiful portions of North America. Canada East, formerly known as Lower Canada, is not quite so favorable, the climate being cold and severe in winter, the springs being late, the summers rather short, and the soil not so productive. But Canada West, formerly called Upper Canada, is equal to any portion of the Northern States. The climate being milder than that of the Northern portions of New York, Ohio, Michigan, Indiana, Illinois, or any of the States bordering on the lakes, the soil is prolific in productions of every description. Grains, vegetables, fruits, and cattle, are of the very best kind; from a short tour by the writer, in that country in the fall, 1851, one year ago, he prefers Canada West to any part of North America, as a destination for the colored people. But there is a serious objection to the Canadas—a political objection. The Canadians are descended from the same common parentage as the Americans on this side of the Lakes—and there is a manifest tendency on the part of the Canadians generally, to Americanism. That the Americans are determined to, and will have the Canadas, to a close observer, there is not a shadow of doubt; and our brethren should know this in time. This there would be no fear of, were not the Canadian people in favor of the project, neither would the Americans attempt an attack upon the provinces, without the move being favored by the people of those places.

Every act of the Americans, ostensibly as courtesy and friendship, tend to that end. This is seen in the policy pursued during the last two or three years, in the continual invitations, frequently reciprocated, that pass from the Americans to their "Canadian brethren"—always couched in affectionate language—to join them in their various celebrations, in different parts of the States. They have got them as far as Boston, and we may expect to hear of them going to New York, Philadelphia, Baltimore—and instead of the merrymaking over the beginning or ending of internal improvements, we may expect to see them ere long, wending their way to the seat of the federal government—it may be with William McKenzie, the memorable *patriot* and present member of the Colonial parliament, bearing in his hand the stars and stripes as their ensign—there to blend their voices in the loud shout of jubilee, in honor of the "bloodless victory," of Canadian annexation. This we forewarn the colored people, in time, is the inevitable and not far distant destiny of the Canadas. And let them come into the American Republic when they may, the fate of the colored man, however free before, is doomed, doomed, forever doomed. Disfranchisement, degradation, and a delivery up to slave catchers and kidnappers, are their only fate, let Canadian annexation take place when it will. The odious infamous fugitive slave law, will then be in full force with all of its terrors; and we have no doubt that fully in anticipation of this event, was the despicable law created.

Let not colored people be deceived and gulled by any visionary argument about original rights, or those of the people remaining the same as they were previous to cecession of the territory. The people can claim no rights than such as are known to exist previous to their annexation. This is manifestly the case with a large class of the former inhabitants of Mexico, who though citizens before, in the full exercise of their rights as such, so soon as the cecession of the territory took place, lost them entirely, as they could claim only such as were enjoyed by the people of a similar class, in the country to which they made their union. The laudatories heaped upon the Americans, within the hearing of the writer, while traveling the provinces the last fall, by one of the Canadian officiaries, in comparing their superior intelligence to what he termed the "stupid aristocracy," then returning from the Boston celebration, where there was a fair opportunity of comparing the intellect of their chief magistrate, his excellency, Lord Elgin, governor-general of the Canadas, and Sir Allen Napier McNab, knight baronet with that of some of the "plain republicans" who were present on the occasion, were extravagant. The Canadians generally were perfectly carried away with delight at their reception. They reminded us of some of our poor brethren, who had just made their escape from Southern bondage, and for the first time in their life, had been taken by the hand by a white man, who acknowledged them as equals. They don't know when to stop talking about it, they really annoy one with extravagant praises of them. This was the way with those gentlemen; and we dare predict, that from what we heard on that occasion, that Mr. McKenzie nor Big Bill Johnson, hero of the Forty Islands, are no greater *patriots* than these Canadian visitors to the Boston husa! We are satisfied that the Canadas are no place of safety for the colored people of the United States; otherwise we should have no objection to them.

But to the fugitive—our enslaved brethren flying from Southern despotism—we say, until we have a more preferable place—go on to Canada. Freedom, always; liberty any place and ever—before slavery. Continue to fly to the Canadas, and swell the number of the twenty-five thousand already there. Surely the British cannot, they will not look with indifference upon such a powerful auxiliary as these brave, bold, daring men—the very flower of the South, who have hazarded every consequence, many of whom have come from Arkansas and Florida in search of freedom. Worthy surely to be free, when gained at such a venture. Go on to the North, till the South is ready to receive you—for surely, he who can make his way from Arkansas to Canada, can find his way from Kentucky to Mexico. The moment his foot touches this land South, he is free. Let the bondman but be assured that he can find the same freedom South that there is in the North; the same liberty in Mexico, as in Canada, and he will prefer going South to going North. His risk is no greater in getting there. Go either way, and he in the majority of instances must run the gauntlet of the slave states. . . .

[Chapters 20 and 21 take up the topic of migration to some other part of the Americas. Delany asserts, "That country is best in which our manhood can be best developed; and that is Central and South America, and the West Indies—all belonging to this glorious continent." He expresses discomfort with the intention of some of his acquaintances to migrate to California, reminding them that the sea voyage to Nicaragua and New Grenada is shorter. He continues to speak of African migration as a plan of "our oppressors," and asserts that "God has, as certain as he has ever designed any thing, . . . designed this great portion of the New World for us, the colored races; and as certain as we stubborn our hearts and

stiffen our necks against it, his protecting arm and fostering care will be with-
drawn from us." In view of this remarkable statement, the appendix proposing an
expedition to East Africa comes as something of a surprise.]

Appendix. Project for an Expedition of Adventure, to the Eastern Coast of Africa

Every people should be the originators of their own designs, the projector of their own schemes, and creators of the events that lead to their destiny—the consummation of their desires.

Situated as we are, in the United States, many, and almost insurmountable obstacles present themselves. We are four-and-a-half millions in numbers, free and bond; six hundred thousand free, and three-and-a-half millions bond.

We have native hearts and virtues, just as other nations; which in their pristine purity are noble, potent, and worthy of example. We are a nation within a nation;—as the Poles in Russia, the Hungarians in Austria, the Welsh, Irish, and Scotch in the British dominions.

But we have been, by our oppressors, despoiled of our purity, and corrupted in our native characteristics, so that we have inherited their vices, and but few of their virtues, leaving us in character, really a *broken people*.

Being distinguished by complexion, we are still singled out—although having merged in the habits and customs of our oppressors—as a distinct nation of people; as the Poles, Hungarians, Irish, and others, who still retain their native peculiarities, of language, habits, and various other traits. The claims of no people, according to established policy and usage, are respected by any nation, until they are presented in a national capacity.

To accomplish so great and desirable an end, there should be held, a great representative gathering of the colored people of the United States; not what is termed a National Convention, represented en masse, such as have been, for the last few years, held at various times and places; but a true representation of the intelligence and wisdom of the colored freemen; because it will be futile and an utter failure, to attempt such a project without the highest grade of intelligence.

No great project was ever devised without the consultation of the most mature intelligence, and discreet discernment and precaution.

To effect this, and prevent intrusion and improper representation, there should be a CONFIDENTIAL COUNCIL held; and circulars issued, only to such persons as shall be *known* to the projectors to be equal to the desired object.

The authority from whence the call should originate, to be in this wise:—The originator of the scheme, to impart the contemplated Confidential Council, to a limited number of known, worthy gentlemen, who agreeing with the project, endorse at once the scheme, when becoming joint proprietors in interest, issue a *Confidential Circular,* leaving blanks for *date, time,* and *place* of *holding* the Council; sending them to trusty, worthy, and suitable colored freemen, in all parts of the United States, and the Canadas, inviting them to attend; who when met in Council, have the right to project any scheme they may think proper for the general good of the whole people—provided, that the project is laid before them after its maturity.

By this Council to be appointed, a Board of Commissioners, to consist of three, five, or such reasonable number as may be decided upon, one of whom shall be chosen as Principal or Conductor of the Board, whose duty and business shall be, to go on an expedition to the EASTERN COAST OF AFRICA, to make researches for a suitable location on that section of the coast, for the settlement of colored adventurers from the United States, and elsewhere. Their mission should be to all such places as might meet the approbation of the people; as South America, Mexico, the West Indies, &c.

The Commissioners all to be men of decided qualifications; to embody among them, the qualifications of physician, botanist, chemist, geologist, geographer, and surveyor,—having a sufficient knowledge of these sciences, for practical purposes.

Their business shall be, to make a topographical, geographical, geological, and botanical examination, into such part or parts as they may select, with all other useful information that may be obtained; to be recorded in a journal kept for that purpose.

The Council shall appoint a permanent Board of Directors, to manage and supervise the doings of the Commissioners, and to whom they shall be amenable for their doings, who shall hold their office until successors shall be appointed.

A National Confidential Council, to be held once in three years; and sooner, if necessity or emergency should demand it; the Board of Directors giving at least three months' notice, by circulars and newspapers. And should they fail to perform their duty, twenty-five of the representatives from any six States, of the former Council, may issue a call, authentically bearing their names, as sufficient authority for such a call. But when the Council is held for the reception of the report of the Commissioners, a general mass convention should then take place, by popular representation.

Manner of Raising Funds

The National Council shall appoint one or two Special Commissioners, to England and France, to solicit, in the name of the Representatives of a Broken Nation, of four-and-a-half millions, the necessary outfit and support, for any period not exceeding three years, of such an expedition. Certainly, what England and France would do, for a little nation—mere nominal nation, of five thousand civilized Liberians, they would be willing and ready to do, for five millions; if they be but authentically represented, in a national capacity. What was due to Greece, enveloped by Turkey, should be due to US, enveloped by the United States; and we believe would be respected, if properly presented. To England and France, we should look for sustenance, and the people of those two nations— as they would have every thing to gain from such an adventure and eventual settlement on the EASTERN COAST OF AFRICA— the opening of an immense trade being the consequence. The whole Continent is rich in minerals, and the most precious metals, as but a superficial notice of the topographical and geological reports from that country, plainly show to any mind versed in the least, in the science of the earth.

The Eastern Coast of Africa has long been neglected, and never but little known, even to the ancients; but has ever been our choice part of the Continent. Bounded by the Red Sea, Arabian Sea, and Indian Ocean, it presents the greatest facilities for an immense trade, with China, Japan, Siam, Hindoostan, in short, all the East Indies—of any other country in the world. With a settlement of enlightened freemen, who with the immense facilities, must soon grow into a powerful nation. In the Province of Berbera, south of the Strait of Babelmandel, or the great pass, from the Arabian to the Red Sea, the whole commerce of the East must touch this point.

Also, a great rail road could be constructed from here, running with the Mountains of the Moon, clearing them entirely, except making one mountain pass, at the western extremity of the Mountains of the Moon, and the southeastern terminus of the Kong Mountains; entering the Province of Dahomey, and terminating on the Atlantic Ocean West; which would make the GREAT THOR-OUGHFARE for all the trade with the East Indies and Eastern Coast of Africa, and the Continent of America. All the world would pass through Africa upon this rail road, which would yield a revenue infinitely greater than any other investment in the world.

The means for prosecuting such a project—as stupendous as it may appear—will be fully realised in the prosecution of the work. Every mile of the road, will thrice pay for itself, in the development of the rich treasures that now lie hidden in the bowels of the earth. There is no doubt, that in some one section of twenty-five miles, the developments of gold would more than pay the expenses of any one thousand miles of the work. This calculation may, to those who have never given this subject a thought, appear extravagant, and visionary; but to one who has had his attention in this direction for years, it is clear enough. But a few years will witness a development of gold, precious metals, and minerals in Eastern Africa, the Moon and Kong Mountains, ten-fold greater than all the rich productions of California.

There is one great physiological fact in regard to the colored race—which, while it may not apply to all colored persons, is true of those having black skins—that they can bear *more different* climates than the white race. They bear *all* the temperates and extremes, while the other can only bear the temperates and *one* of the extremes. The black race is endowed with natural properties, that adapt and fit them for temperate, cold, and hot climates; while the white race is only endowed with properties that adapt them to temperate and cold climates; being unable to stand the warmer climates; in them, the white race cannot work, but become perfectly indolent, requiring somebody to work for them—and these, are always people of the black race.

The black race may be found, inhabiting in healthful improvement, every part of the globe where the white race reside; while there are parts of the globe where the black race reside, that the white race cannot live in health.

What part of mankind is the "denizen of every soil, and the lord of terrestrial creation," if it be not the black race? The Creator has indisputably adapted us for the "denizens of *every soil*," all that is left for us to do, is to *make* ourselves the "*lords* of terrestrial creation." The land is ours—there it lies with inexhaustible resources; let us go and possess it. In Eastern Africa must rise up a nation, to whom all the world must pay commercial tribute.

We must MAKE an ISSUE, CREATE an EVENT, and ESTABLISH a NATIONAL POSITION for OURSELVES; and never may expect to be respected as men and women, until we have undertaken, some fearless, bold, and adventurous deeds of daring—contending against every odds—regardless of every consequence.

9

From Obiter Dictum on the Dred Scott Case (1857)

The obiter dictum *by Roger B. Taney (Chief Justice of the Supreme Court) on the Dred Scott case illustrates much of the reasoning that went into the position of white colonizationists. In essence, the United States was founded by Europeans, who never intended that Africans should be citizens of the United States. Few if any black leaders of the period accepted Taney's argument that African Americans were not citizens, but they were certainly aware that many of the founding fathers had viewed them as a separate and unassimilable category of the American population. Justice Taney's opinion was painful to African Americans, but its logic is strong, if not incontestable.*

It is important to note that Taney describes African Americans as a "class," and holds that it was the intention of the founding fathers to deal with them as a class. There is no mention of African Americans as individuals, who might, as individuals, be capable of meriting the rights and duties of citizens. The African American individual, in this case Dred Scott, is not considered a citizen, because he belongs to a separate class whose members were not considered citizens or capable of becoming citizens by the founding fathers.

Ironically, Justice Taney quotes the celebrated lines from the Declaration of Independence that deal with "all men" being "created equal" and endowed "with certain inalienable rights" as evidence that African Americans were not considered citizens by the founding fathers. He argues that the authors of these words would have been guilty of inconsistency if they had conceived the possibility of Africans enjoying American citizenship. As we have seen in an earlier document, Thomas Jefferson, the principal author of the declaration, held it to be self-evident that Africans, even if they were freed, could not be assimilated into the majority population. While Taney's opinion, as an obiter dictum, *was only a commentary and did not have the force of law, it was never decisively invalidated until Congress passed the Fourteenth Amendment to the Constitution, which finally declared that the African American population would legally hold citizenship, as would all other persons born or naturalized in the United States.*

From Roger B. Taney, Obiter Dictum on *Dred Scott v. Sanford, in Reports of Cases Argued and Adjudged in the Supreme Court of the United States,* vol. 19, December term, 1856 (New York: Banks and Brothers, 1883).

The question is simply this: Can a Negro, whose ancestors were imported into this country, and sold as slaves, become a member of the political community formed and brought into existence by the Constitution of the United States, and as such become entitled to all the rights, and privileges, and immunities, guaranteed by that instrument to the citizen? One of which rights is the privilege of suing in a court of the United States in the cases specified in the Constitution.

It will be observed, that the plea applies to that class of persons only whose ancestors were Negroes of the African race, and imported into this country, and sold and held as slaves. The only matter in issue before the court, therefore, is whether the descendants of such slaves, when they shall be emancipated, or who are born of parents who had become free before their birth, are citizens of a State, in the sense in which the word citizen is used in the Constitution of the United States. . . .

The words "people of the United States" and "citizens" are synonymous terms, and mean the same thing. They both describe the political body who, according to our republican institutions, form the sovereignty, and who hold the power and conduct the government through their representatives. They are what we familiarly call the "sovereign people," and every citizen is one of this people, and a constituent member of this sovereignty. The question before us is, whether the class of persons described in the plea in abatement compose a portion of this people, and are constituent members of this sovereignty? We think they are not, and that they are not included, and were not intended to be included, under the word "citizens" in the Constitution, and can, therefore, claim none of the rights and privileges which that instrument provides for and secures to citizens of the United States. On the contrary, they were at that time considered as a subordinate and inferior class of beings, who had been subjugated by the dominant race, and whether emancipated or not, yet remained subject to their authority, and had no rights or privileges but such as those who held the power and the government might choose to grant them. . . .

It is very clear, therefore, that no State can, by any Act or law of its own, passed since the adoption of the Constitution, introduce a new member into the political community created by the Constitution of the United States. It cannot make him a member of this community by making him a member of its own. And for the same reason it cannot introduce any person, or description of persons, who were not intended to be embraced in this new political family, which the Constitution brought into existence, but were intended to be excluded from it. . . .

In the opinion of the court, the legislation and histories of the times, and the language used in the Declaration of Independence, show, that neither the class of persons who had been imported as slaves, nor their descendants, whether they had become free or not, were then acknowledged as a part of the people, nor intended to be included in the general words used in that memorable instrument.

It is difficult at this day to realize the state of public opinion in relation to that unfortunate race, which prevailed in the civilized and enlightened portions of the world at the time of the Declaration of Independence, and when the Constitution of the United States was framed and adopted. . . .

They had for more than a century before been regarded as beings of an inferior order and altogether unfit to associate with the white race, either in social or political relations; and so far inferior that they had no rights which the white man was bound to respect; and that the Negro might justly and lawfully be reduced to slavery for his benefit. He was bought and sold and treated as an ordinary article of merchandise and traffic whenever a profit could be made by it. This opinion was at that time fixed and universal in the civilized portion of the white race. It was regarded as an axiom in morals as well. . . .

. . . A Negro of the African race was regarded . . . as an article of property and held and bought and sold as such in every one of the thirteen Colonies which united in the Declaration of Independence and afterward formed the Constitution of the United States. The slaves were more or less numerous in the different Colonies, as slave labor was found more or less profitable. But no one seems to have doubted the correctness of the prevailing opinion of the time. . . .

The language of the Declaration of Independence is equally conclusive:

It begins by declaring that "When, in the course of human events, it becomes necessary for one people to dissolve the political bands which have connected them with another, and to assume, among the powers of the earth the separate and equal station to which the laws of nature and nature's God entitle them, a decent respect for the opinions of mankind requires that they should declare the causes which impel them to the separation."

It then proceeds to say: "We hold these truths to be self-evident: that all men are created equal; that they are endowed by their Creator with certain inalienable rights; that among these are life, liberty, and the pursuit of happiness; that to secure these rights, governments are instituted, deriving their just powers from the consent of the governed."

The general words above quoted would seem to embrace the whole human family, and if they were used in a similar instrument at this day would be so understood. But it is too clear for dispute that the enslaved African race were not intended to be included and formed no part of the people who framed and adopted this declaration; for if the language, as understood in that day, would embrace them, the conduct of the distinguished men who framed the Declaration of Independence would have been utterly and flagrantly inconsistent with the principles they asserted; and instead of the sympathy of mankind, to which they so confidently appealed, they would have deserved and received universal rebuke and reprobation.

Yet the men who framed this declaration were great men—high in literary acquirements—high in their sense of honor, and incapable of asserting principles inconsistent with those on which they were acting. They perfectly understood the meaning of the language they used and how it would be understood by others;

and they knew that it would not in any part of the civilized world be supposed to embrace the Negro race, which, by common consent, had been excluded from civilized governments and the family of nations and doomed to slavery. They spoke and acted according to the then established doctrine and principles and in the ordinary language of the day, and no one misunderstood them. The unhappy black race were separated from the white by indelible marks, and laws long before established, and were never thought of or spoken of except as property and when the claims of the owner or the profit of the trader were supposed to need protection.

This state of public opinion had undergone no change when the Constitution was adopted, as is equally evident from its provisions and language.

The brief preamble sets forth by whom it was formed, for what purposes, and for whose benefit and protection. It declares that it is formed by the *people* of the United States; that is to say, by those who were members of the different political communities in the several states; and its great object is declared to be to secure the blessing of liberty to themselves and their posterity. It speaks in general terms of the *people* of the United States, and of *citizens* of the several states, when it is providing for the exercise of the powers granted or the privileges secured to the citizen. It does not define what description of persons are intended to be included under these terms, or who shall be regarded as a citizen and one of the people. It uses them as terms so well understood that no further description or definition was necessary. . . .

But there are two clauses in the Constitution which point directly and specifically to the Negro race as a separate class of persons, and show clearly that they were not regarded as a portion of the people or citizens of the Government then formed.

One of these clauses reserves to each of the thirteen States the right to import slaves until the year 1808, if it thinks it proper. And the importation which it thus sanctions was unquestionably of persons of the race of which we are speaking, as the traffic in slaves in the United States had always been confined to them. And by the other provision the States pledge themselves to each other to maintain the right of property of the master, by delivering up to him any slave who may have escaped from his service, and be found within their respective territories. . . . And these two provisions show, conclusively, that neither the description of persons therein referred to, nor their descendants, were embraced in any of the other provisions of the Constitution; for certainly these two clauses were not intended to confer on them or their posterity the blessings of liberty, or any of the personal rights so carefully provided for the citizen. . . .

Indeed, when we look to the condition of this race in the several States at the time, it is impossible to believe that these rights and privileges were intended to be extended to them. . . .

The legislation of the States therefore shows, in a manner not to be mistaken, the inferior and subject condition of that race at the time the Constitution was adopted, and long afterwards, throughout the thirteen States by which that instrument was framed; and it is hardly consistent with the respect due to these States, to suppose that they regarded at that time, as fellow-citizens and members of the sovereignty, a class of beings whom they had thus stigmatized.

10

From A Vindication of the Capacity of the Negro Race for Self-Government and Civilized Progress (1857)

In this document James T. Holly presents us with an adaptation of the doctrine of "manifest destiny" and a mystical and theological argument for emigration to Haiti. The belief in manifest destiny was popular among white Americans; its adherents claimed that the United States was manifestly destined to expand westward until it reached the Pacific (a short treatment of manifest destiny can be found in the Columbia Encyclopedia, 5th ed.). *In his novel adaptation of the doctrine, Holly asserts that black nationalism can realize its mission as a progressive force only by moving in the progressive westerly direction.*

But our historical investigations are at an end, and we must hasten to bring our reflections to a conclusion. I have now fulfilled my design in vindicating the capacity of the negro race for self-government and civilized progress against the unjust aspersions of our unprincipled oppressors, by boldly examining the facts of Haytian history and deducing legitimate conclusions therefrom. I have summoned the sable heroes and statesmen of that independent isle of the Caribbean Sea, and tried them by the high standard of modern civilization, fearlessly comparing them with the most illustrious men of the most enlightened nations of the earth;—and in this examination and comparison the negro race has not fallen one whit behind their contemporaries. And in this investigation I have made no allowance for the negroes just emerging from a barbarous condition and out of the brutish ignorance of West Indian slavery.

From James T. Holly, *A Vindication of the Capacity of the Negro Race for Self-Government and Civilized Progress as Demonstrated by Historical Events of the Haytian Revolution; and the Subsequent Acts of that People since Their National Independance* (n.p., 1857).

I have been careful not to make such an allowance, for fear that instead of proving negro equality only, I should prove negro superiority. I shun the point of making this allowance to the negro, as it might reverse the case of the question entirely, that I have been combatting and instead of disproving his alleged inferiority only, would on the other hand, go farther, and establish his superiority. Therefore as it is my design to banish the words "superiority" and "inferiority" from the vocabulary of the world, when applied to the natural capacity of races of men, I claim no allowance for them on the score of their condition and circumstances.

Having now presented the preceding array of facts and arguments to establish, before the world, the negro's equality with the white man in carrying forward the great principles of self-government and civilized progress; I would now have these facts exert their legitimate influence over the minds of my race, in this country, in producing that most desirable object of arousing them to a full consciousness of their own inherent dignity; and thereby increasing among them that self-respect which shall urge them on to the performance of those great deeds which the age and the race now demand at their hands.

Our brethren of Hayti, who stand in the vanguard of the race, have already made a name, and a fame for us, that is as imperishable as the world's history. They exercise sovereign authority over an island, that in natural advantages, is the Eden of America, and the garden spot of the world. Her rich resources invite the capacity of 10,000,000 human beings to adequately use them. It becomes then an important question for the negro race in America to well consider the weighty responsibility that the present exigency devolves upon them, to contribute to the continued advancement of this negro nationality of the New World until its glory and renown shall overspread and cover the whole earth, and redeem and regenerate by its influence in the future, the benighted Fatherland of the race in Africa.

Here in this black nationality of the New World, erected under such glorious auspices, is the stand point that must be occupied, and the lever that must be exerted, to regenerate and disenthrall the oppression and ignorance of the race, throughout the world. We must not overlook this practical vantage ground which Providence has raised up for us out of the depths of the sea, for any man-made and utopian scheme that is prematurely forced upon us, to send us across the ocean, to rummage the graves of our ancestors, in fruitless, and ill-directed efforts at the wrong end of human progress. Civilization and Christianity is passing from the East to the West; and its pristine splendor will only be rekindled in the ancient nations of the Old World, after it has belted the globe in its westward course, and revisted the Orient again. The serpentine trail of civilization and Christianity, like the ancient philosophic symbol of eternity, must coil backward to its fountain head. God, therefore in permitting the accursed slave traffic to transplant so many millions of the race, to the New World, and educing therefrom such a negro nationality as Hayti, indicates thereby, that we have a work now to do here in the Western World, which in his own good time shall shed its orient beams upon the Fatherland of the race. Let us see to it, that we meet the exigency now imposed upon us, as nobly on our part at this time as the Haytians met theirs at the opening of the present century. And in seeking to perform this duty, it may well be a question with us, whether it is not our duty, to go and identify our destiny with our heroic brethren in that independent isle of the Caribbean Sea, carrying with us such of the arts, sciences and genius of modern civilization, as we may gain from this hardy and enterprising Anglo-American race, in order to add to Haytian advancement; rather than to indolently remain here, asking for political rights, which, if granted, a social proscription stronger than conventional legislation will ever render nugatory and of no avail for the manly elevation and general well-being of the race. If one powerful and civilized negro sovereignty can be developed to the summit of national grandeur in the West Indies, where the keys to the commerce of both hemispheres can be held; this fact will solve all questions respecting the negro, whether they be those of slavery, prejudice or proscription, and wheresoever on the face of the globe such questions shall present themselves for a satisfactory solution.

A concentration and combination of the negro race, of the Western Hemisphere in Hayti, can produce just such a national development. The duty to do so, is therefore incumbent on them. And the responsibility of leading off in this gigantic enterprise Providence seems to have made our peculiar task by the eligibility of our situation in this country, as a point for gaining an easy access to that island. Then let us boldly enlist in this high pathway of duty, while the watchwords that shall cheer and inspire us in our noble and glorious undertaking, shall be the soul-stirring anthem of GOD and HUMANITY.

African Civilization Society (1859)

Frederick Douglass, a militant abolitionist and brilliant orator, vehemently opposed the African Civilization Society, which was founded in 1858 with Henry Highland Garnet as president. The society's membership, which was open to whites, included liberal whites like Francis Wayland, a former president of Brown University, and Benjamin Coates, a Quaker merchant, at one time a member of the liberal wing of the American Colonization Society. Douglass could not overlook the fact that Delany's and Garnet's enterprises were similar to those of the American Colonization Society.

"But I entreated you to tell your readers what your objections are to the civilization and christianization of Africa. What objection have you to colored men in this country engaging in agriculture, lawful trade, and commerce in the land of my forefathers? What objection have you to an organization that shall endeavor to check and destroy the African slavetrade, and that desires to co-operate with anti-slavery men and women of every grade in our own land, and to toil with them for the overthrow of American slavery? — Tell us, I pray you, tell us in your clear and manly style. 'Gird up thy loins, and answer thou me, if thou canst.' " — Letter from Henry Highland Garnet.

Hitherto we have allowed ourselves but little space for discussing the claims of this new scheme for the civilization of Africa, doing little more than indicating our dissent from the new movement, yet leaving our columns as free to its friends as to its opponents. We shall not depart from this course, while the various writers bring good temper and ability to the discussion, and shall keep themselves within reasonable limits. We hope the same impartiality will be shown in the management of the *Provincial Freeman,*

Frederick Douglass, "African Civilization Society," *Douglass' Monthly,* February 1859.

the adopted organ of the African Civilization Society. We need discussion among ourselves, discussion to rouse our souls to intenser life and activity.—"Communipaw" did capital service when he gave the subtle brain of Wm. Whipper a little work to do, and our readers the pleasure of seeing it done. Anything to promote earnest thinking among our people may be held as a good thing in itself, whether we assent to or dissent from the proposition which calls it forth.

We say this much before entering upon a compliance with the request of our friend Garnet, lest any should infer that the discussion now going on is distasteful to us, or that we desire to avoid it. The letter in question from Mr. Garnet is well calculated to make that impression. He evidently enjoys a wholesome confidence, not only in the goodness of his own cause, but in his own ability to defend it.—Sallying out before us, as if in "complete steel," he entreats us to appear "in manly style," to *"gird up our loins,"* as if the contest were one requiring all our strength and activity. "Answer thou me if thou canst?"—As if an answer were impossible. Not content with this, he reminds us of his former similar entreaties, thus making it our duty to reply to him, if for no better reason than respect and courtesy towards himself.

The first question put to us by Mr. Garnet is a strange and almost preposterous one. He asks for our "objections to the civilization and christianization of Africa." The answer we have to make here is very easy and very ready, and can be given without even taking the trouble to observe the generous advice to "gird up our loins." We have not, dear brother, the least possible objection either to the civilization or to the christianization of Africa, and the question is just about as absurd and ridiculous as if you had asked us to "gird up our loins," and tell the world what objection Frederick Douglass has to the abolition of slavery, or the elevation of the free people of color in the United States! We not only have no objection to the civilization and christianization of Africa, but rejoice to know that through the instrumentality of commerce, and the labors of faithful missionaries, those very desirable blessings are already being realized in the land of my fathers Africa.

Brother Garnet is a prudent man, and we admire his tact and address in presenting the issue before us, while we cannot assent entirely to its fairness. *"I did not ask you for a statement of your preference of America to Africa."* That is very aptly said, but is it impartially said? Does brother Garnet think such a preference, in view of all the circumstances, a wise and proper one? Or is he wholly indifferent as to the one preference or the other? He seems to think that our preferences have nothing to do with the question between us and the African Civilization Society, while we think that this preference touches the very bone of contention. The African Civilization Society says to us, go to Africa, raise cotton, civilize the natives, become planters, merchants, compete with the slave States in the Liverpool cotton market, and thus break down American slavery. To which we simply and briefly reply, "we prefer to remain in America"; and we do insist upon it, in the very face of our respected friend, that that is both a direct and candid answer. There is no dodging, no equivocation, but so far as we are concerned, the whole matter is ended. *You* go there, *we* stay here, is just the difference between us and the African Civilization Society, and the true issue upon which co-operation with it or opposition to it must turn.

Brother Garnet will pardon us for thinking it somewhat cool in him to ask us to give our objections to this new scheme. Our objections to it have been stated in substance, repeatedly. It has been no fault of ours if he has not read them.

As long ago as last September, we gave our views at large on this subject, in answer to an eloquent letter from Benjamin Coates, Esq., the real, but not the ostensible head of the African Civilization movement.

Meanwhile we will state briefly, for the benefit of friend Garnet, seven considerations, which prevent our co-operation with the African Civilization Society.

1. No one idea has given rise to more oppression and persecution toward the colored people of this country, than that which makes Africa, not America, their home. It is that wolfish idea that elbows us off the side walk, and denies us the rights of citizenship. The life and soul of this

abominable idea would have been thrashed out of it long ago, but for the jesuitical and persistent teaching of the American Colonization Society. The natural and unfailing tendency of the African Civilization Society, by sending *"around the hat"* in all our towns and cities for money to send colored men to Africa, will be to keep life and power in this narrow, bitter and persecuting idea, that Africa, not America, is the Negro's true home.

2. The abolition of American slavery, and the moral, mental and social improvement of our people, are objects of immediate, pressing and transcendent importance, involving a direct and positive issue with the pride and selfishness of the American people. The prosecution of this grand issue against all the principalities and powers of church and state, furnishes ample occupation for all our time and talents; and we instinctively shrink from any movement which involves a substitution of a doubtful and indirect issue, for one which is direct and certain, for we believe that the demand for the abolition of slavery now made in the name of humanity, and according to the law of the Living God, though long delayed, will, if faithfully pressed, certainly triumph.—The African Civilization Society proposes to plant its guns too far from the battlements of slavery for us. Its doctrines and measures are those of doubt and retreat, and it must land just where the American Colonization movement landed, upon the lying assumption, that white and black people can never live in the same land on terms of equality. Detesting this heresy as we do, and believing it to be full of all "deceivableness' of unrighteousness, we shun the paths that lead to it, no matter what taking names they bear, or how excellent the men who bid us to walk in them.

3. Among all the obstacles to the progress of civilization and of christianity in Africa, there is not one so difficult to overcome as the African slave trade. No argument is needed to make this position evident. The African Civilization Society will doubtless assent to its truth. Now, so regarding the slave trade, and believing that the existence of slavery in this country is one of the strongest props of the African slave trade, we hold that the best way to put down the slave trade, and to build up civilization in Africa, is to stand our ground and labor for the abolition of slavery in the U.S. But for slavery here, the slave trade would have been long since swept from the ocean by the united navies of Great Britain, France and the United States. The work, therefore, to which we are naturally and logically conducted, as the one of primary importance, is to abolish slavery. We thus get the example of a great nation on the right side, and

break up, so far as America is concerned, a demand for the slave trade. More will have been done. The enlightened conscience of our nation, through its church and government, and its press, will be let loose against slavery and the slave trade wherever practiced.

4. One of the chief considerations upon which the African Civilization Society is recommended to our favorable regard, is its tendency to break up the slave trade. We have looked at this recommendation, and find no reason to believe that any one man in Africa can do more for the abolition of that trade, while living in Africa, than while living in America. If we cannot make Virginia, with all her enlightenment and christianity, believe that there are better uses for her energies than employing them in breeding slaves for the market, we see not how we can expect to make Guinea, with its ignorance and savage selfishness, adopt our notions of political economy. Depend upon it, the savage chiefs on the western coast of Africa, who for ages have been accustomed to selling their captives into bondage, and pocketing the ready cash for them, will not more readily see and accept our moral and economical ideas, than the slave-traders of Maryland and Virginia. We are, therefore, less inclined to go to Africa to work against the slave-trade, than to stay here to work against it. Especially as the means for accomplishing our object are quite as promising here as there, and more especially since we are here already, with constitutions and habits suited to the country and its climate, and to its better institutions.

5. There are slaves in the United States to the number of four millions. They are stigmatized as an inferior race, fit only for slavery, incapable of improvement, and unable to take care of themselves. Now, it seems plain that here is the place, and we are the people to meet and put down these conclusions concerning our race. Certainly there is no place on the globe where the colored man can speak to a larger audience, either by precept or by example, than in the United States.

6. If slavery depended for its existence upon the cultivation of cotton, and were shut up to that single production, it might even then be fairly questioned whether any amount of cotton culture in Africa would materially affect the price of that article in this country, since demand and supply would go on together. But the case is very different. Slave labor can be employed in raising anything which human labor and the earth can produce. If one does not pay, another will. Christy says "Cotton is King," and our friends of the African Civilization movement are singing the same

tune; but clearly enough it must appear to common sense, that "King Cotton" in America has nothing to fear from King Cotton in Africa.

7. We object to enrolling ourselves among the friends of that new Colonization scheme, because we believe that our people should be let alone, and given a fair chance to work out their own destiny where they are. We are perpetually kept, with wandering eyes and open mouths, looking out for some mighty revolution in our affairs here, which is to remove us from this country. The consequence is, that we do not take a firm hold upon the advantages and opportunities about us. Permanent location is a mighty element of civilization. In a savage state men roam about, having no continued abiding place. They are *"going, going, going."* Towns and cities, houses and homes, are only built up by men who halt long enough to build them. There is a powerful motive for the cultivation of an honorable character, in the fact that we have a country, a neighborhood, a home. The full effect of this motive has not hitherto been experienced by our people. When in slavery, we were liable to perpetual sales, transfers and removals; and now that we are free, we are doomed to be constantly harassed with schemes to get us out of the country. We are quite tired of all this, and wish no more of it.

To all this it will be said that Douglass is opposed to our following the example of white men. They are pushing East, West, North and South. They are going to Oregon, Central America, Australia, South Africa and all over the world. Why should we not have the same right to better our condition that other men have and exercise? Any man who says that we deny this right, or even object to its exercise, only deceives the ignorant by such representations.

If colored men are convinced that they can better their condition by going to Africa, or anywhere else, we shall respect them if they will go, just as we respect others who have gone to California, Fraser Island, Oregon and the West Indies. They are self-moved, self-sustained, and their success or failure is their own individual concern. But widely different is the case, when men combine, in societies, under taking titles, send out agents to collect money, and call upon us to help them travel from continent to continent to promote some selfish or benevolent end. In the one case, it is none of our business where our people go.—They are of age, and can act for themselves.—But when they ask the public to go, or for money, sympathy, aid, or co-operation, or attempt to make it appear anybody's duty to go, the case ceases to be a private individual affair, and becomes a public question, and he who believes that he can make a better use of his time, talents, and influence, than such a movement proposes for him, may very properly say so, without in any measure calling in question the equal right of our people to migrate.

Again it may be said that we are opposed to sending the Gospel to benighted Africa; but this is not the case. The *American Missionary Society*, in its rooms at 48 Beekman Street, has never had occasion to complain of any such opposition, nor will it have such cause. But we will not anticipate the objections which may be brought to the foregoing views. They seem to us sober, rational, and true; but if otherwise, we shall be glad to have them honestly criticised.

12

From Address at Cooper's Institute (1860)

Henry Highland Garnet's African Civilization Society was under constant attack, from Frederick Douglass, George T. Downing, William Whipper, and other black abolitionists, who disingenuously sought to confuse it with the American Colonization Society. The following speech represents one of Garnet's attempts to clarify his position and that of the African Civilization Society.

We have among us men of talent and learning, but such is the prejudice against our race that they are not employed. The African Civilization Society proposes by the assistance of God to aid in the removal of those un-Christian barriers which are placed in the way of our race, by discovering fields for the full and free exercise of their talents and energies either in our own native land, in Central America, in Haiti, in any of the free West Indies Islands, or in Africa the land of our forefathers. We believe that Africa is to be redeemed by Christian civilization and that the great work is to be chiefly achieved by the free and voluntary emigration of enterprising colored people. We hold it to be the duty of the Christians and philanthropists in America, either to send or carry the gospel and civilization into Africa, to thus make some atonement for the wrong and crimes which the people of this country perpetrated upon that injured country. In our efforts to accomplish this work we offer no excuse for the unjust prejudices which exist towards us as a people. We reject the idea, entertained by many, that the black man can never enjoy equal privileges in this country with other classes. To admit this would be to distrust the power of the Gospel,

From Henry Highland Garnet, Address at Cooper's Institute, New York, N.Y., 1860, in *Weekly Anglo-African,* November 17, 1860.

and to doubt its universal triumph. We regard the enslavement of our race to be the highest crime against God and man, and we hope by teaching the Kings and Chiefs of Africa better things to induce them to exterminate the slave-trade and engage in lawful commerce, and in this way aid in destroying slavery in this and all other lands. In carrying out our objects we ask for volunteers and only for volunteers. We appeal to all on the broad grounds of humanity and Christian love. Our plan of operation in Africa is this:

1. To confirm the friendly relations already established by members of the society now there, with some of the chiefs in the Yoruba country, by sending out a company of virtuous, intelligent and enterprising colored people, who are now ready to act as pioneers, and who will proceed as soon as the necessary funds are raised.

2. To purchase lands at suitable points for the use of settlers to be given to them in equal limited quantities and to furnish the necessary mechanical and agricultural implements.

3. To erect school houses and houses of religious worship, to instruct the natives in the arts and sciences, and develop intelligence and industry, the natural resources of the country.

4. To promote lawful commerce upon the coast of Africa, and the growth of cotton and other tropical products by free labor.

With the blessing of God we hope to secure, as the result of our efforts, the diffusion of the Gospel in Africa, and the consequent overthrow of idolatry and superstition, the destruction of the African slave-trade, and the establishment of civil government by free colored men based upon true Christian principles, where ample scope may be afforded to all for the exercise of every mental and moral faculty.

In behalf of this important enterprise, we appeal to the patriot, the philanthropist and the Christian—believing that the generous sympathy of our nature will lead very many to act the part of the good Samaritan towards Africa, by contributing liberally to this object, and thus enabling the society to enter at once upon the work of African evangelization and civilization.

From the accounts recently received from the missionaries and explorers now in the field, the society is encouraged to commence a Christian industrial settlement in Yoruba, where the chiefs are willing to receive missionaries and settlers, and have proffered their friendship to do them good.

The society desires to raise $6,000 to enable this company, with their associates, to enter upon their work in Africa, and earnestly appeal to the friends of the African race for the needed amount, so that the enterprise may be speedily commenced.

I am happy to state that we last week received from our commissioners in Yoruba information that they had succeeded in effecting a treaty with the chiefs of that country for a large and sufficient tract of land, and that they are permitted to form their own municipal laws, subject only to the common law of that country. It is stated that the chiefs and kings are not only willing but anxious to have any number of intelligent colored men of this country, meet with them and settle there. Our plan is not to subvert the government and overthrow the reigning powers of those countries where in the providence of God we may be cast. We believe it would be preferable to sit down by their side, and not only teach the people by precept those principles which we desire them to cherish, but also to teach them by the power of example those things that will elevate their manhood and exalt their nature; and to make them feel that we are a part of themselves—interested in everything which promises to promote their happiness and increase their prosperity. I would state again, that we have now a number of men, of the proper sort, who are willing to embark in this glorious enterprise and who believe as I do, and as the officers and friends of this society believe, that there is a glorious future before Africa. We feel encouraged when we remember that Africa is one of the few countries whose future destiny is a subject of Divine prophecy, of which the Scriptures say, "Ethiopia shall soon stretch out her hands to God, and princes shall come out of Egypt."

13

From Official Report of the Niger Valley Exploring Party (1861)

On May 24, 1859, Martin R. Delany sailed for West Africa on the Mendi, *which flew the Liberian flag and carried forty-five passengers bound for Liberia. In the course of his travels, Delany merged his expedition with that of Robert Campbell, who claimed to represent Henry Highland Garnet's African Civilization Society. Historians agree that Campbell received some backing from that organization. Garnet first claimed, then later denied, that the African Civilization Society had any connection with the expedition(s), but Delany's name appeared shortly thereafter on the society's board of vice presidents. Delany and Campbell published separate reports of their travels. The excerpts from Delany's report reprinted here represent Delany's perspective on the "history of the project." They include his "Call for a National Emigration Convention of Colored Men," which met in 1854, and sections 3 and 4 of the report in their entirety. After his return from West Africa, Delany went on a lecture tour, appearing on the platform in "a long dark robe, with curious scrolls upon the neck as a collar. He said it was the wedding dress of a Chief, and that the embroidery was insignia, and had a special meaning well understood in African high circles. He wore it because he thought it becoming, and fitting the occasion"* (Liberator, *May 1, 1863).*

Political Movements

On or about the latter part of July, 1853, the following document was sent on, and shortly appeared in the columns of "FREDERICK DOUGLASS' PAPER," Rochester, N.Y., and the "ALIENED AMERICAN," published and edited by William Howard Day, Esq., M.A., at Cleveland, Ohio, U.S., which continued in those papers every issue, until the meeting of the Convention:

From Martin R. Delany, *Official Report of the Niger Valley Exploring Party* (New York: Thomas Hamilton, 1861).

Call for a National Emigration Convention of Colored Men

To be held in Cleveland, Ohio, on the 24th, 25th, and 26th of August, 1854

MEN AND BRETHREN: The time has fully come when we, as an oppressed people, should do something effectively, and use those means adequate to the attainment of the great and long desired end—do something to meet the actual demands of the present and prospective necessities of the rising generation of our people in this country. To do this, we must occupy a position of entire *equality*, of *unrestricted* rights, composing in fact, an acknowledged *necessary* part of the *ruling element* of society in which we live. The policy *necessary* to the *preservation* of this *element* must be *in our favor*, if ever we expect the enjoyment, freedom, sovereignty, and equality of rights anywhere. For this purpose, and to this end, then, all colored men in favor of Emigration out of the United States, and *opposed* to the American Colonization scheme of leaving the Western Hemisphere, are requested to meet in CLEVELAND, OHIO, TUESDAY, the 24th day of AUGUST, 1854, in a great NATIONAL CONVENTION, then and there to consider and decide upon the great and important subject of Emigration from the United States.

No person will be admitted to a seat in the Convention, who would introduce the subject of Emigration to the Eastern Hemisphere—either to Asia, Africa, or Europe—as our object and determination are to consider our claims to the West Indies, Central and South America, and the Canadas. This restriction has no reference to *personal* preference, or *individual* enterprise; but to the great question of national claims to come before the Convention.

All persons coming to the Convention must bring credentials properly authenticated, or bring verbal assurance to the Committee on Credentials—appointed for the purpose—of their fidelity to the measures and objects set forth in this call, as the Convention is specifically by and for the friends of Emigration, and none others—and no opposition to them will be entertained.

The question is not whether our condition can be bettered by emigration, but whether it can be made worse. If not, then, there is no part of the wide spread universe, where our social and political condition are not better than here in our native country, and nowhere in the world as here, proscribed on account of color.

We are friends to, and ever will stand shoulder to shoulder by our brethren, and all our friends in all good measures adopted by them for the bettering of our condition in this country, and surrender no rights but with our last breath; but as the subject of Emigration is of vital importance, and has ever been shunned by all delegated assemblages of our people as heretofore met, we cannot longer delay, and will not be farther baffled; and deny the right of our most sanguine friend or dearest brother, to prevent an intelligent inquiry into, and the carrying out of these measures, when this can be done, to our entire advantage, as we propose to show in Convention—as the West Indies, Central and South America—the majority of which are peopled by our brethren, or those identified with us in race, and what is more, *destiny*, on this continent—all stand with open arms and yearning hearts, importuning us in the name of suffering humanity to come—to make common cause, and share one common fate on the continent.

The Convention will meet without fail at the time fixed for assembling, as none but those favorable to Emigration are admissible; therefore no other gathering may prevent it. The number of delegates will not be restricted—except in the town where the Convention may be held—and there the number will be decided by the Convention when assembled, that they may not too far exceed the other delegations.

The time and place fixed for holding the Convention are ample; affording sufficient time, and a leisure season generally—and as Cleveland is now the centre of all directions—a good and favorable opportunity to all who desire to attend. Therefore, it may reasonably be the greatest gathering of the colored people ever before assembled in a Convention in the United States.

Colonizationists are advised, that no favors will be shown to them or their expatriating scheme, as we have no sympathy with the enemies of our race.

All colored men, East, West, North, and South, favorable to the measures set forth in this Call will send in their names (post-paid) to M. R. DELANY, or REV. WM. WEBB, Pittsburgh, Pa., that there may be arranged and attached to the Call, *five* names from each State.

We must make an issue, create an event, and establish a position *for ourselves*. It is glorious to think of, but far more glorious to carry out.

REV. WM. WEBB, M. R. DELANY, H. G. WEBB, THOS. A. BROWN, JOHN JONES, R. L. HAWKINS, SAMUEL VENERABLE, JOHN WILLIAMS, A. F. HAWKINS, S. W. SANDERS, JEFFERSON MILLER, *Pittsburgh, Pa.*:

REV. A. R. GREEN, P. L. JACKSON, J. H. MAHONEY, G. HARPER, JONATHAN GREEN, H. A. JACKSON, E. R. PARKER, SAMUEL BRUCE, *Alleghany City;* J. J. GOULD BIAS, M.D., REV. M. M. CLARK, A. M. SUMNER, JOHNSON WOODLIN, *Philadelphia;* JAMES M. WHITFIELD, JOHN N. STILL, STANLEY MATTHEWS, *New York.*

This Call was readily responded to by the addition of names from other States, which appeared in subsequent issues. . . .

History of the Project

In the winter of 1831–2, being then but a youth, I formed the design of going to Africa, the land of my ancestry; when in the succeeding winter of 1832–3, having then fully commenced to study, I entered into a solemn promise with the Rev. Molliston Madison Clark, then a student in Jefferson College, at Cannonsburg, Washington County, Pennsylvania, being but seventeen miles from Pittsburgh, where I resided (his vacations being spent in the latter place), to complete an education, and go on an independent and voluntary mission—to travel in Africa—I as a physician and he as a clergyman, for which he was then preparing.

During these vacations of about seven weeks each, Mr. Clark was of great advantage to me in my studies, he being then a man of probably thirty years of age, or more, and in his senior year (I think) at college.

This design I never abandoned, although in common with my race in America, I espoused the cause, and contended for our political and moral elevation on equality with the whites, believing then, as I do now, that merit alone should be the test of individual claims in the body politic. This cause I never have nor will abandon; believing that no man should hesitate or put off any duty for another time or place, but "act, act in the *living present,* act," *now* or *then*. This has been the rule of my life, and I hope ever shall be.

In 1850, I had fully matured a plan for an adventure, and to a number of select intelligent gentlemen (of African descent, of course) fully committed myself in favor of it. They all agreed that the scheme was good; and although neither of them entered personally into it, all fully sanctioned it, bidding me God-speed in my new adventure, as a powerful handmaid to their efforts in contending for our rights in America.

In 1854, at the great Emigration Convention in Cleveland, my paper, read and adopted as a "Report on the Political Destiny of the Colored Race on the American Continent," set forth fully my views on the advantages of Emigration.

Although the Call itself strictly prohibits the introduction of the question of emigration from the American Continent or Western Hemisphere, the qualification which directly follows—"This restriction has no reference to *personal* preference, or *individual* enterprise"—may readily be understood. It was a mere policy on the part of the authors of those documents, to confine their scheme to America (including the West Indies), whilst they were the leading advocates of the regeneration of Africa, lest they compromised themselves and their people to the avowed enemies of the race.

The Convention (at Cleveland, 1854), in its Secret Sessions made, Africa, with its rich, inexhaustible productions, and great facilities for checking the abominable Slave Trade, its most important point of dependence, though each individual was left to take the direction which in his judgment best suited him. Though our great gun was leveled, and the first shell thrown at the American Continent, driving a slaveholding faction into despair, and a political confusion from which they have been utterly unable to extricate themselves, but become more and more complicated every year, *Africa was held in reserve, until by the help of an All-wise Providence we could effect what has just been accomplished with signal success*—a work which the most sanguine friend of the cause believed would require at least the half of a century.

It is a curious, and not less singular historical fact, that a leading political journal, and the first newspaper which nominated Mr. James Buchanan, many years ago, for the Presidency of the United States; and at a time whilst he was yet at the Court of St. James (1854), as Envoy Extraordinary, this paper was strongly urging his claims as such, thus expresses itself, which gives a fair idea of the political pro-slavery press generally, especially in Pennsylvania, Mr. Buchanan's native State. I intended to give the article entire, as alarm will be seen even at the commencement; but pressure for space will prevent my quoting but a few sentences. It is from the Pittsburgh *Daily Morning Post,* Wednesday, October 18th, 1854:

A Grand Scheme for the Colored Race

In August last, a National Convention of colored people was held at Cleveland, Ohio. It was composed of delegates from most of the States. It was called the "National Emigration Convention," and its objects were to consider the political destinies of the black race; and recommend a plan of Emigration to countries where they can enjoy political liberty, and form nations "free and independent."

The Committee then proceeds to mark out a grand scheme by which the Negro race may be regenerated, and formed into free, intelligent, and prosperous nations. The West India Islands, Central America, and all the Northern and middle portions of South America, including the whole of Brazil, are designated as the regions desired; and that can be obtained as the seat of negro civilization and empire. These regions and islands together are represented as containing twenty-four and a half millions of population; but one-seventh of which, some three and a half millions, are whites of pure European extraction; and the remainder, nearly twenty-one millions, are colored people of African and Indian origin. This immense preponderance of the colored races in those regions, it is supposed, will enable them, with the aid of Emigration from the United States, to take possession of all those countries and islands, and become the ruling race in the empires to be formed out of those wide and fruitful realms. The Committee expresses full confidence in the practicability of this great undertaking; and that nothing is wanting to its success at no distant day but unanimity of sentiment and action among the masses of the colored people. The climate of those regions is represented as entirely congenial to the colored race, while to the European races it is enervating and destructive; and this fact, added to the present immense superiority of numbers on the part of the negroes, is relied on as a sure guarantee of the success of the great enterprise; and that their race could forever maintain the possession and control of those regions.

Other great events, it is supposed, will follow in the train of this mighty movement. With the West India Islands, and Central and South America, composing free negro nations, slavery in the United States would, they suppose, soon be at an end. The facility of escape, the near neighborhood of friends and aid, it is urged, would rapidly drain off from the Southern States all the most intelligent, robust, and bold of their slaves.

Dr. M. R. Delany, of Pittsburgh, was the chairman of the committee that made this report to the convention. It was, of course, adopted.

If Dr. D. drafted this report, it certainly does him much credit for learning and ability; and cannot fail to establish for him a reputation for vigor and brilliancy of imagination never yet surpassed. It is a vast conception of impossible birth. The Committee seem to have entirely overlooked the strength of the "powers on earth" that would oppose the Africanization of more than half the Western Hemisphere.

We have no motive in noticing this gorgeous dream of "the Committee," except to show its fallacy—its impracticability, in fact, its absurdity. No sensible man, whatever his color, should be for a moment deceived by such impracticable theories.

On the African coast already exists a thriving and prosperous Republic. It is the native home of the African race; and there he can enjoy the dignity of manhood, the rights of citizenship, and all the advantages of civilization and freedom. Every colored man in this country will be welcomed there as a free citizen; and there he can not only prosper, and secure his own comfort and happiness, but become a teacher and benefactor of his kindred races; and become an agent in carrying civilization and Christianity to a benighted continent. That any one will be turned aside from so noble a mission by the delusive dream of conquest and empire in the Western Hemisphere is an absurdity too monstrous and mischievous to be believed. Yet "the Committee's Report" was accepted, and adopted, and endorsed by a "National Convention;" and is published and sent forth to the world.

In July, 1855, Rev. James Theodore Holly, an accomplished black gentleman, now rector of St. Luke's Church, New Haven, Connecticut, U.S., was commissioned to Faustin Soulouque, Emperor of Hayti, where he was received at court with much attention, interchanging many official notes during a month's residence there, with favorable inducements to laborers to settle.

During the interval from the first convention, 1854 to 1858, as

President of the Council, I was actively engaged corresponding in every direction, among which were several States of Central and South America, as well as Jamaica and Cuba; the Rev. J. T. Holly, who, during two years of the time, filled the office of Foreign Secretary, contributing no small share in its accomplishment.

Immediately after the convention of 1856, from which I was absent by sickness, I commenced a general correspondence with individuals, imparting to each the basis of my adventure to Africa to obtain intelligent colleagues. During this time (the Spring of 1857), "Bowen's Central Africa" was published, giving an interesting and intelligent account of that extensive portion of Africa known on the large missionary map of that continent as Yoruba. Still more encouraged to carry out my scheme at this juncture, Livingstone's great work on Africa made its appearance, which seemed to have stimulated the Africo-Americans in many directions, among others, those of Wisconsin, from whom Mr. Jonathan J. Myers, a very respectable grocer, was delegated as their Chairman to counsel me on the subject. In the several councils held between Mr. Myers and myself, it was agreed and understood that I was to embody their cause and interests in my mission to Africa, they accepting of the policy of my scheme.

At this time, I made vigorous efforts to accomplish my design, and for this purpose, among others, endeavored to obtain goods in Philadelphia to embark for Loando de St. Paul, the Portuguese colony in Loango, South Africa, where the prospect seemed fair for a good trade in beeswax and ivory, though Lagos, West Central Africa, was my choice and destination. Robert Douglass, Esq., artist, an accomplished literary gentleman (landscape, portrait painter, and photographer) of Philadelphia, with whom I was in correspondence, sent me the following note:

Philadelphia, June 17, 1858

Mr. M. R. Delany:

Dear Sir—I think very highly of the intended Expedition to the "Valley of the Niger." I would be pleased to accompany it professionally, if I were to receive a proper outfit and salary. Dr. Wilson declines; but Mr.

Robert Campbell, of the "Institute for Colored Youth," a very accomplished Chemist, &c., &c., &c., says he will gladly accompany the Expedition, if a proper support for his family in his absence were assured. Rev. William Douglass, in conversation with me, has expressed very favorable views. Hoping you may be very successful, I remain in expectation of receiving more detailed accounts of the plan, its prospects and progress,

Your friend and well-wisher,
Robert Douglass

661, N. Thirteenth St., Phil.

Up to this time, I had never before known or heard of Mr. Campbell, who is a West India gentleman, native bred in Jamaica, but the recommendation of Mr. Douglass, an old acquaintance and gentleman of unsullied integrity, accompanied as it was by the following note from Dr. Wilson, also an accomplished gentleman of equal integrity, a physician, surgeon, and chemist, who, being selected by me as Surgeon and Naturalist of the party, also recommended Mr. Campbell in a detached note which has been mislaid, was sufficient at the time:

Philadelphia, June 7th, 1858

Dr. Delany:

Dear Sir—I received your note of May 25th, through the kindness of R. Douglass, Jr., and can truly say, I am highly gratified to learn of so laudable an enterprise and expedition; and would be happy and proud to be numbered with the noble hearts and brilliant minds, identified with it. Yet, whilst I acknowledge (and feel myself flattered by) the honor conferred upon me in being selected for so important and honorable position, I regret to inform you, that it will be wholly out of my power to accept.

Very respectfully,
James H. Wilson

838, Lombard Street.

I have been the more induced to give the letters of Mr. Douglass and Dr. Wilson in favor of Mr. Campbell, because some of my friends were disposed to think that I "went out of the way to make choice of an entire stranger, unknown to us, instead of old and tried acquaintances," as they were pleased to express it. I had but one object in view—the Moral, Social, and Political Elevation of Ourselves, and the Regeneration of Africa, for which I desired, as a *preference,* and indeed the only *adequate* and *essential* means by which it is to be accomplished, men of African descent, properly qualified and of pure and fixed principles. These I endeavored to select by corresponding only with such of my acquaintances.

At the Council which appointed me Commissioner to Africa, having presented the names of Messrs. Douglass and Campbell, asking that they also might be chosen; at a subsequent meeting the following action took place:

Whereas, Dr. Martin R. Delany, Commissioner to Africa, having presented the names of Messrs. Robert Douglass and Robert Campbell of Philadelphia, Pa., U.S., requesting that they be appointed Commissioners, the Board having made him Chief Commissioner with full power to appoint his own Assistants, do hereby sanction the appointment of these gentlemen as Assistant Commissioners.

A paper was then laid before the Council, presenting the name and scheme of the party, which was received and adopted.

Dr. Amos Aray, surgeon, a highly intelligent gentleman, and Mr. James W. Purnell, also an intelligent young gentleman, bred to mercantile pursuits, having subsequently sent in their names and received appointments by the Chief Commissioner, the following document was made out:

African Commission

The President and Officers of the General Board of Commissioners, viz: William H. Day, A.M., President; Matison F. Bailey, Vice-President; George W. Brodie, Secretary; James Madison Bell, Treasurer; Alfred Whipper, Auditor; Dr. Martin R. Delany, Special Foreign Secretary; Abram D. Shadd, James Henry Harris, and Isaac D. Shadd, the Executive Council in behalf of the organization for the promotion of the political and other interests of the Colored Inhabitants of North America, particularly the United States and Canada.

To all, unto whom these letters may come, greeting: The said General Board of Commissioners, in Executive Council assembled, have this day chosen, and by these presents do hereby appoint and authorize Dr. Martin Robison Delany, of Chatham, County of Kent, Province of Canada, Chief Commissioner; and Robert Douglass, Esq., Artist, and Prof. Robert Campbell, Naturalist, both of Philadelphia, Pennsylvania, one of the United States of America, to be Assistant Commissioners; Amos Aray, Surgeon; and James W. Purnell, Secretary and Commercial Reporter, both of Kent County, Canada West, of a Scientific Corps, to be known by the name of

The Niger Valley Exploring Party

The object of this Expedition is to make a Topographical, Geological and Geographical Examination of the Valley of the River Niger, in Africa, and an inquiry into the state and condition of the people of that Valley, and other parts of Africa, together with such other scientific inquiries as may by them be deemed expedient, for the purposes of science and for general information; and without any reference to, and with the Board being entirely opposed to any Emigration there as such. Provided, however, that nothing in this Instrument be so construed as to interfere with the right of the Commissioners to negotiate in their own behalf, or that of any other parties, or organization for territory.

The Chief-Commissioner is hereby authorized to add one or more competent Commissioners to their number; it being agreed and understood that this organization is, and is to be exempted from the pecuniary responsibility of sending out this Expedition.

Dated at the Office of the Executive Council, Chatham, county of Kent, Province of Canada, this Thirtieth day of August, in the year of our Lord, One Thousand Eight Hundred and Fifty-eight.

By the President,
William Howard Day
Isaac D. Shadd, Vice-President [1]
George W. Brodie, Secretary

So soon as these names with their destined mission were officially published, there arose at once from mistaken persons *(white)* in Philadelphia, a torrent of opposition, who presuming to know more about us (the blacks) and our own business than we did ourselves, went even so far as to speak to one of our party, and tell him that we were *not ready* for any such *important* undertaking, nor could be in *three years yet to come!* Of course, as necessary to sustain this, it was followed up with a dissertation on the *disqualification* of the Chief of the Party, mentally and physically, *external* appearances and all. So effectually was this opposition prosecuted, that colored people in many directions in the United States and the Canadas, were not only affected by it, but a "Party" of three had already been chosen and appointed to supersede us! Even without any knowledge on my part, claims were made in England in behalf of the "Niger Valley Exploring Party," solely through the instrumentality of these Philadelphians.

Such were the effects of this, that our preparatory progress was not only seriously retarded (I having to spend eight months in New York city to counteract the influence, where six weeks only would have been required), but three years originally intended to be spent in exploring had to be reduced to one, and the number of Commissioners from five to two, thereby depriving Mr. Robert Douglass from going, an old friend and most excellent gentleman, whose life, as well as that of his father before him, had been spent in efforts, not only of self-elevation, but the elevation also of his people. Many years ago, the accomplished articles of "Robet Douglass, Jun," to the *United States Gazette,* and other public journals, forced those negro-hating periodicals to respect at least the writer, if not his race. Dr. Aray, also an excellent gentleman who had given up business to join the party, was doomed to disappointment. And of Mr. Jas. W. Purnell—who met me in New York two weeks after my arrival, and through the whole eight months of adversity and doubtful progress, stood by me, performing the duty of Secretary, writing in every direction, copying, and from dictation for hours at a time—I cannot say too much. For a young gentleman inexperienced in such matters, he has no superior; and for integrity, trueheartedness, and trustworthiness, in my estimation, he has few if any rivals. To his great and good uncle, under whom he was brought up, much of his character is to be credited.

As an expression of the feelings of the most intelligent emigrationists with whom I corresponded generally in America, I give below two extracts from letters of Professor Freeman. The Professor is now as he then was, the Principal of Avery College.

Alleghany City, April 14, 1858

My Dear Friend—Your letter of condolence was duly received, for which we tender you our warmest thanks.

I have read Bowen's work, and shall to-day purchase Livingstone's. I am more and more convinced that Africa is the country to which all colored men who wish to attain the full stature of manhood, and bring up their children to be men and not creeping things, should turn their steps; and I feel more and more every day, that I made.a great mistake in not going there, when I was untrammelled by family ties, and had the opportunity.

Respectfully yours,
M. H. Freeman

Again the Professor says:

I see that Emigration has broken out in the East, and that ———— can notice one now without scoffing at, which he could not in 1854. Well, people can grow wondrously wiser in four years. But it will take several more *Olympiads* to bring the leaders among us up to the old Cleveland Platform of 1854.

All the fault of that movement was this, that it was at least one generation ahead of the colored *heads* of our people. We may, if we please, refuse to emigrate, and crouch like spaniels, to lick the hand that beats us; but children's children at the farthest, will have outgrown such pitiful meanness, and will dare to do all that others have dared and done for the sake of freedom and independence. Then all this cowardly cant about the unhealthy climate, the voracious beasts, and venomous reptiles of Africa, will be at a discount, instead of passing current as now for wisdom and prudence.

Mr. Campbell, who finally agreed voluntarily to be one of the "Niger Valley Exploring Party," spent some time with us in New York and some time in Philadelphia, but finally, in consequence of the doubtful prospects of my success, left, it would seem, at the suggestion and with the advice and recommendation of parties in Philadelphia, disconnected with and unknown to me, from whom he received letters of introduction for England. In justice to myself and party as organized, as well as the great cause and people whom I represent, I here simply remark, that this was no arrangement of mine nor our party, as such at the time; and whatever of success the visit was attended with, and benefit thereby accrued mutually to us in Africa, I as frankly decline any authority in the matter and credit to myself, as I should had the result proved what it might have done otherwise. I am only willing to claim that which is legitimately mine, and be responsible for my own doings whether good or bad; but this act the integrity of the Party was forced to acknowledge, as the following circular published in England will show:

Expedition to Africa
To Promote the Cultivation of Cotton and Other Products of Slave-Labor, By Emigrants from America

A party, consisting of Martin R. Delany, M.D., Robert Campbell, J. W. Purnell, Robert Douglass, and Amos Aray, M.D., (the last two subsequently omitted) has been commissioned by a Convention of Colored Persons, held at Chatham, C.W., to proceed to Africa, and select a location for the establishment of an Industrial Colony.

While such an enterprise is of importance in the Evangelization and Civilization of Africa, and in affording an asylum in which the oppressed descendants of that country may find the means of developing their mental and moral faculties unimpeded by unjust restrictions, it is regarded as of still greater importance in facilitating the production of those staples, particularly Cotton, which now are supplied to the world chiefly by Slave Labor. The effect of this would be to lessen the profits of Slavery, to render in time the slave a burden to his owner, and thus furnish an irresistible motive to Emancipation. Africa possesses resources which, properly developed, must doubtless render her eventually a great, if not the greatest, producer of all the products of Slave Labor. And how would all good men rejoice to see the blow which shall effectually prostrate the giant Slavery, struck by the Black Man's arm! It is necessary, however, that civilized influences be diffused in her midst, or, at least, that facilities for rendering available her products, be supplied equal to the demand for them.

It is the purpose of the party to proceed to Lagos, thence through Abbeokuta to Rabba, on the Niger, about 350 miles from the coast; to study the Agricultural and Commercial facilities of the country, and the disposition of the Natives towards strangers as settlers; also to negotiate for the grant or purchase of land, and to ascertain the conditions on which we might be protected in the usages of civilized life.

These objects being accomplished, the party will return and report the result of their labors, when a considerable number of intelligent and enterprising persons from the United States and Canada, many of them intimately acquainted with the production of Cotton, and its preparation for market, will be prepared to emigrate.

Towards defraying the expenses of this undertaking, £500 has been subscribed in America. This amount has been expended in providing for the families of two of the party in their absence; in paying the passage of Martin R. Delany and J. W. Purnell to Africa, direct from America, and providing them a few articles of outfit; in defraying the current expenses of the party since the 1st December ult., while engaged in soliciting subscriptions, and otherwise forwarding the objects of the Expedition; and in providing the Subscriber with the means of coming hither.

It is desired to raise in this country, in time to enable the Subscriber to depart for Africa in June by the steamer from Liverpool, an additional sum of £250, with which to provide other articles of outfit, and goods for trading with the natives for the means of subsistence, as well as to provide for other necessary and contingent expenses.

The Subscriber will take the liberty of calling upon you personally, at an early day, to solicit your aid in this enterprise.

Robert Campbell

Manchester, May 13th, 1859

Grant, for charity's sake, that it was done with the best of motives, it was flagrantly and fatally at variance with every principle of intelligent—to say nothing of enlightened—organizations among civilized men, and in perfect harmony with that mischievous interference by which the enemies of our race have ever sought to sow discord among us, to prove a natural contempt for the Negro and repugnance to his leadership, then taunt us with incapacity for self-government. These flambeaus and rockets directed with unerring precision, taking effect in the very centre of our magazine, did not cause, in those for whom it was intended, a falter nor a wince in their course, but steadily and determinedly they pressed their way to the completion of their object under prosecution. In this design the enemy was thwarted.

I drop every reflection and feeling of unpleasantness towards my young brother Campbell, who, being a West Indian, probably did not understand those *white Americans,* and formed his opinion of American *blacks* and their capacity to "lead," from the estimate they set upon them. I owe it to posterity, the destiny of my race, the great adventure into which I am embarked and the position I sustain to it, to make this record with all Christian (or *African,* if you please) forgiveness, against this most glaring and determined act of theirs to blast the negro's prospects in this his first effort in the Christian Era, to work out his own moral and political salvation, by the regeneration of his Fatherland, through the medium of a self-projected scheme; and thereby take the credit to themselves. It was too great an undertaking for negroes to have the credit of, and therefore they *must* go *under* the auspices of some white American Christians. To be black, it would seem, was necessarily to be "ungodly"; and to be white was necessarily to be "godly," or Christian, in the estimation of some.

With a grateful heart, I here as freely record as an equal duty I owe to posterity, my unfeigned thanks to all those gentlemen who took an active part and in any way aided the mission on my behalf, either from the pulpit, by the contribution of books, stationery, charts, instruments, or otherwise, especially those who made each the *one hundred dollar contribution,* and the two in New York, through whose instrumentality and influence these were obtained.

Those disinterested and voluntary acts of kindness I never shall forget whilst reason occupies her throne, and would here willingly record their names, had I their consent to do so.

I sailed from New York May 24th, in the fine *barque Mendi*—Captain M'Intyre—vessel and cargo owned by Johnson, Turpin and Dunbar, three enterprising colored gentlemen of Monrovia, Liberia, all formerly of New York, U.S. In the name of the General Board of Commissioners for the promotion of the political and other interest of the colored people of the United States and the Canadas, by self-exertion, I thank them.

I cannot close this section without expressing my obligations to Captain M'Intyre for his personal kindness to me; and also to his first officer, Captain Vernon Locke, (himself a ship-master, who took the position of first officer for the voyage, and who had been, for the last three or four years, collecting scientific information by astronomical, meteorological, and other observations, for Lieutenant Maury, Director of the Observatory at Washington, D.C., U.S.,) I am greatly indebted for many acts of kindness in facilitating my microscopic and other examinations and inquiries, during the voyage. Concerning the *nautilus and whale,* I learned more through this accomplished seaman than I had ever learned before. The first by examination of the mollusca, which were frequently caught by Captain L. for my accommodation—and of the latter, by oral information received from him (who had been a great whaler) on frequently observing those huge monsters during the voyage.[2]

Arrival and Reception in Liberia

Saturday, July 10th.—I landed on the beach at Grand Cape Mount, Robertsport, in company with Messrs. the Hon. John D. Johnson, Joseph Turpin, Dr. Dunbar, and Ellis A. Potter, amid the joyous acclamations of the numerous natives who stood along the beautiful shore, and a number of Liberians, among whom was Reverend Samuel Williams, who gave us a hearty reception. Here we passed through the town (over the side of the hill), returning to the vessel after night.

Monday, July 12th.—The roadstead of Monrovia was made about noon, when I, in company with B. E. Castendyk, Esq., a young German gentleman traveling for pleasure, took lodgings at Widow Moore's, the residence of Rev. John Seys, the United States consular agent, and commissioner for recaptured Africans.

On the day after my arrival, the following correspondence took place:

> Residence of the United States Consular Agent
> Monrovia, Liberia, July 12th, 1859

To His Excellency, the President of the Republic of Liberia:

Sir—By a Convention of Colored People of the United States and the Canadas, Martin R. Delany, Robert Douglass, Robert Campbell, Amos Aray, and James W. Purnell, were appointed as Commissioners under the name of the 'Niger Valley Exploring Party,' to make an Exploration through different parts of Africa.

I have arrived, Sir, near your Government, and expect soon to meet other members of the party. Any aid, orally, documentary, or in the person of an Official Commissioner, which you may please to give to facilitate the mission in Liberia will be gratefully and highly appreciated. I ask the favor of an interview with your Excellency, either privately or in Cabinet Council, or with any other gentlemen that the occasion may suggest, at such time as may be designated.

I am happy, Sir, of the opportunity of giving your Excellency assurance of my most distinguished consideration.

> *M. R. Delany*

His Excellency, President Benson.

■ ■ ■

> Government House, Monrovia, July 13, 1859

Sir—I have the honor to acknowledge the receipt of your note of the 12th instant, conveying to me the information of your appointment (in connection with colleagues expected soon to arrive), by a Convention of the colored people of the United States and the Canadas, 'Commissioners,' under the name of 'The Niger Valley Exploring Party;' and of your arrival near this Government. You have also been pleased to signify, that you will duly appreciate any aid, oral, documentary, or in the form of an official Commissioner this Government may feel disposed to afford you, in facilitation of the enterprise.

In reply, I have to express my deep regret, that the receipt of your very interesting note is on the very eve of my leaving this city on an official visit to the leeward counties, which will, for the present, deprive me of the pleasure I had anticipated of an interview with you on the very interesting and highly important objects of your mission.

The Hon. John N. Lewis, Secretary of State, with whom I will converse on the subject matter of your note before leaving, will be pleased to grant you an audience; and will, with pleasure, meet your wishes, so far as he can consistently.

Please be re-assured of the deep interest I feel in your very laudable enterprise; and that, if it were not for very important despatches received last week from the county of Maryland, which make it absolutely necessary that I should delay no time in reaching there, I would defer my departure a couple of days for the express purpose of consultation with you in person.

I have the honor to be most respectfully,
Your very obedient servant,
Stephen A. Benson

To M. R. Delany, Esq., &c.

▪ ▪ ▪

Monrovia, July 13, 1859

Martin R. Delany, Esq.:

Dear Sir—The undersigned, citizens of the city of Monrovia, having long heard of you and your efforts in the United States to elevate our down-trodden race, though those efforts were not unfrequently directed against Liberia, are glad to welcome you, in behalf of the community, to these shores; recognizing, as they do in you, an ardent and devoted lover of the African race, and an industrious agent in promoting their interests. And they take this opportunity of expressing to you their most cordial sympathy with the enterprise which has brought you to these shores, sincerely praying that your endeavors may be crowned with complete success.

The undersigned, further, in the name and behalf of the members of this community, respectfully request that you would favor the citizens with a lecture to-morrow evening, or on any other evening you may choose to appoint, at half-past seven o'clock, on any subject you may be pleased to select.

On receiving your reply notices will be issued accordingly.

B. P. Yates	*H. W. Dennis*
D. B. Warner	*Urias A. McGill*
Saml. F. McGill	*H. A. Johnson*
B. V. R. James	*Edw. W. Blyden*
Saml. Matthews	

▪ ▪ ▪

Residence of the United States Consular Agent,
Monrovia, July 13th, 1859

Gentlemen—Your note of to-day has been received, for the honor of which I thank you, and beg to say that numerous engagements prevent me from complying with your request on to-morrow evening.

You are mistaken, gentlemen, in supposing that I have ever spoken directly "against Liberia," as wherever I have been I have always acknowledged a unity of interests in our race wherever located; and any seeming opposition to Liberia could only be constructively such, for which I am not responsible.

Should it be your pleasure, I will do myself the honor of serving you on Monday evening next, or any other evening during the week, by a discourse on the "Political Destiny of the African Race," and assure you of the pleasure with which I have the honor to be,

Your most obedient servant,
M. R. Delany

Col. B. P. Yates; Hon. D. B. Warner; S. F. McGill, M.D.; Hon. B. V. R. James; Rev. Saml. Matthews; Urias McGill, Esq.; Rev. Edw. W. Blyden; H. W. Dennis, Esq.; H. A. Johnson, Esq., District Attorney.

▪ ▪ ▪

Monrovia, July 14, 1859

M. R. Delany, Esq.:

Sir—We have the honor to acknowledge your note of to-day in reply to an invitation of yesterday from us requesting that you would favor us, with many others, with an address on tomorrow evening, or at any other time agreeable to yourself. Having signified to us that next Monday evening you would be pleased to comply with the request, we tender you our thanks and will be happy to listen to a discourse on the "Political destiny of the African Race."

We have the honor to be, very respectfully, &c., yours,

B. V. R. James
Saml. Matthews
And others

On Monday evening, the 19th of July, having addressed a crowded audience in the Methodist Episcopal Church, Ex-Governor McGill in the chair, T. M. Chester, Esq., Secretary; Ex-President Roberts rose and in a short speech, in the name of the Liberians, welcomed me to Africa. By a vote of thanks and request to continue the discourse on a subsequent evening, this request was complied with on the following Tuesday evening.

Monrovia, July 28, 1859

Dr. M. R. Delany:

Dear Sir—The undersigned citizens of Monrovia having been much edified by listening to two very interesting lectures delivered by you in the Methodist church, avail themselves of this method to express their appreciation of the same, and to respectfully request that you will favor the community with a popular lecture on 'Physiology' on Friday evening, the 29th inst.

Henry J. Roberts	Henry W. Dennis
Saml. F. McGill	Edwd. W. Blyden
B. P. Yates	

The reply to this polite invitation of Doctors Roberts and McGill, and others, having been mislaid, I simply remark here that the request was complied with on the evening of August 3d, in the Methodist Church, to a crowded house of the most intelligent citizens of Monrovia, of both sexes and all ages.

On the evening of August 5th, I left Monrovia in the bark Mendi, stopping at Junk, Little Bassa, Grand Bassa mouth of St. John's River, Sinou, arriving at Cape Palmas Sabbath noon, August 20th.

Half an hour after my arrival, I was called upon by the Rev. Mr. Hoffman, Principal of the Female Orphan Asylum, at the residence of John Marshall, Esq., whose hospitality I was then receiving, and in the name of the white Missionaries welcomed to that part of Liberia. Before Mr. Hoffman left I was honored by a visit also from Rev. Alexander Crummell, Principal of Mount Vaughan High School, where, after partaking of the hospitality of Mr. Marshall during that day and evening, I took up my residence during a month's stay in this part of Liberia.

Having taken the *acclimating fever* on the 5th of the month, the day I left Monrovia, and besides regularly a dessert spoonful of a solution of the sulphate of *quinia* three times a day, and the night of my arrival two eight grain doses of Dover's Powder, the reference to "the state of my health" in the following correspondence, will be understood:

To Dr. M. R. Delany:

Dear Sir—We, the undersigned citizens of the county of Maryland, Liberia, beg to tender you a heartfelt welcome to our neighborhood, and to assure you of our warmest interest in the important mission which has called you to the coast of Africa. Perhaps you will consent, should your health permit, to favor us with a public interview before you leave. We would be most happy to hear your views concerning the interest of our race in general, and of your mission in particular. Moreover, by so doing, you will afford us an opportunity of paying you that respect which your reputation, talents, and noble mission command, and which it is our sincere desire to pay you.

If Thursday or Friday will suit your convenience it will be agreeable to us; but we leave the character of the meeting to be designated by yourself.

Aug. 23, 1859

Alex. Crummell

D. R. Fletcher	*Thos. Fuller*
B. J. Drayton	*Richd. W. Knight*
J. T. Gibson	*John Marshall*
C. H. Harmon	*Giles Elem*
S. B. D'Lyon	*T. S. Dent*
L. R. Hamilton	*A. Wood*
Benjamin Cook	*J. W. Williams*
H. W. Moulton	*Wm. W. Pearce*
Ansburn Tubman	*R. A. Gray*
James M. Moulton	*Jas. Adams*
N. Jackson, Jun.	*J. W. Cooper*
Jno. E. Moulton	

▪ ▪ ▪

Mount Vaughan, near Harper, Cape Palmas
August 27th, 1859

Gentlemen—Your note of the 23rd inst., requesting me, should my health permit, to appear before the citizens of your county, is before me, and for the sentiments therein expressed I thank you most kindly.

As I have reason to believe that I am now convalescent from my second attack of native fever, should my health continue to improve I shall start on an exploration for the head of Kavalla river on Monday next ensuing, to return on Friday evening.

Should it be your pleasure, gentlemen, and my health will permit, I will meet you on Monday, the 5th of September, the place and hour to be hereafter named according to circumstances.

I assure you of the pleasure, Gentlemen, with which I have the honor to be,

Your most obedient servant,
M. R. Delany

Gen. Wood; Judge Drayton; Rev. Alex. Crummell; John Marshall, Esq.; Hon. J. T. Gibson; C. H. Harmon, Esq.; J. W. Cooper, Esq.; Dr. Fletcher; Giles Elem, Esq.; Jas. M. Moulton, Esq.; Benjamin Cook, Esq.; S. B. D'Lyon, M.D., and others, Committee, &c., &c.

On the evening of the 14th, this request was complied with in the Methodist Church at Latrobe, an out-village of Harper, by addressing a crowded assemblage of both sexes and all ages of the most respectable people of the Cape, on the part of whom I was most cordially welcomed by Rev. Alexander Crummell.

Notes

1. Mr. Shadd was elected Vice-President in the place of Mr. Bailey, who left the Province for New Caledonia.

2. On the 16th day of June, lat 35 deg. 35 min., long. 38 deg. 39 min., a very large school (the largest Captain Locke said that he had ever seen or read of), probably *five hundred,* of sperm whales made their appearance in the segment of a circle to windward and leeward of the vessel about noon, continuing in sight, blowing and spouting, filling the air with spray for a long time, to our amusement and delight. The captain said, though an old whaler, he had never known of sperm whales in that latitude before; and from the immense number, and as they were frequently seen as we approached Africa many times on different days afterwards, that he thought a new whaling point had been discovered. Other whales were also seen frequently in these latitudes—lazy, shy "old bulls," which floated with their huge backs and part of their heads out of water, so as to expose their eyes, when they would suddenly disappear and as quickly appear again; but the great quantity of *squid spawn,* the peculiar *mollusca* upon which the sperm whale feeds, made it ominous, according to the opinion of Captain Locke, that a great new sperm whale fishery had been discovered, the spawn being seen during several days' sail before and after observing the great school.

NOTE.—I should not close this part of my report without stating that, during the year 1858, Mr. Myers wrote to the Royal Geographical Society, London; Thomas Clegg, Esq., Manchester; Dr. Livingstone, and perhaps others, all over *my name* as secretary and himself chairman. The letters referred to were written (without my knowledge) by a son of Mr. Myers; and I only mention the fact here because I am unwilling to claim the honor of the authorship of correspondence carried on through a lad of sixteen years of age.

14

The Progress of Civilization along the West Coast of Africa (1861)

Alexander Crummell spent sixteen years in Liberia, between 1853 and 1872, working as a farmer, educator, small businessman, and Episcopal missionary. He was visited by Martin R. Delany while he was principal of the missionary high school at Cape Palmas, and the two made a short expedition into the interior. The address reprinted here reveals the religious foundations of Crummell's black nationalism. It was delivered several times in the United States during an 1861 visit. Crummell is the subject of a biography by the editor of the present volume. See Wilson J. Moses, Alexander Crummell: A Study of Civilization and Discontent *(New York: Oxford, 1989).*

"The ways of Providence are not confined within narrow limits; he hurries not himself to display to-day the consequences of the principle that he yesterday laid down; he will draw it out in the lapse of ages when the hour is come."
—Guizot's *General History of Civilization, Lecture I.*

"Is it not apparent that civilization is the main fact, the general and definite fact, in which all others terminate, and are included? . . . This is so true, that, with respect to facts, *which are from their nature detestable, disastrous, a painful weight upon nations, as despotism and anarchy, for example,* if they have contributed in some degree to civilization, if they have given it a considerable impetus, up to a certain point *we excuse and pardon their injuries and their evil nature;* insomuch, that wherever we discover civilization, and the

---

Alexander Crummell, "The Progress of Civilization along the West Coast of Africa," in *The Future of Africa: Being Addresses, Sermons, Etc., Delivered in the Republic of Liberia* (New York: Charles Scribner, 1862).

facts which have tended to enrich it, *we are tempted to forget the price it has cost.*"
—Guizot's *General History of Civilization, Lecture I.*

"In all things, Providence, to accomplish its designs, lavishes courage, virtues, *sacrifices man himself!*"
—Guizot's *General History of Civilization, Lecture VII.*

Three hundred years of misery have made West Africa the synonyme of every thing painful and horrible. So generally, nay, so universally, has this been the case, that it is difficult for us to connect ideas grateful and gracious with even *any* part of that continent. It seems to have an enstamped character which cannot admit of mitigating lights or relieving shades. Fact, and incident, and memory, and imagination, all serve but to breed suggestions that are distressful and agonizing.

The principle of association, moreover, is so tenacious and persistent a faculty that it is almost impossible, at times, to turn it from the channels in which it has been wont to flow, for generations or for ages. And the story of anguish, and rapine, and murder, which is the story of Africa for 300 years,—which has been so prolonged that it has seemed to be *destiny;* which has been so aggravated and intense that it has seemed to be *organic,*—it seems almost impossible to change this story into a cheering episode of blessedness and mercy.

It is not so, however. The great poet of our language tells us that

"The night is long that never sees the day."

Still more pertinent to my subject is the declaration of the Psalmist, "Though ye have lain among the pots, yet shall ye be as the wings of a dove covered with silver, and her feathers with yellow gold." A contrast as broad, and marked, and gracious as this, is now manifesting itself through the vast extents of that continent, and I desire to use my opportunity to set before you a few of its prominent characteristics.

Doubtless all intelligent persons have contemplated the fact of the long-continued and unbroken benightedness of the continent of Africa; but perhaps they have not had their attention called to the recent transitional state into which that continent is passing, on the way to enlightenment and salvation.

The facts pertaining to this subject are so distinct, so prominent, and so interesting, that I may be pardoned if I pause here, for a few moments, and endeavor to present them more minutely.

1. And here, *first* of all, we have to observe the sad and startling fact, that mental and moral benightedness has enshrouded the whole of the vast continent of Africa, through all the periods of time, far back to the earliest records of history. We know that since the Advent of our Lord Jesus Christ, although both civilization and Christianity have streamed out, with the Gospel, from the Holy Land, through all Europe, to various parts of Asia, across the Atlantic to America, and, at length, from both Europe and America, to the islands of the sea; yet Africa has remained, during the whole of the Christian era, almost entirely unvisited by the benignant rays, and the genial influences of our Holy Faith.

And then, standing at the very start of the Christian era, if we strive to penetrate the long lapse of ages, which anticipated the coming of the Lord, we meet vista upon vista of the deepest darkness, stretching out to the earliest dawn of the world's being. So far as *Western* Africa is concerned, there is no history. The long, long centuries of human existence, there, give us no intelligent disclosures. "Darkness covered the land, and gross darkness the people."

And, indeed, if you will examine the case, you will find no cause for wonder at this universal prevalence of benightedness through all Africa. I know, indeed, that the fact is often contrasted with the advance of both Europe and Asia in enlightenment; and the inference drawn, that is, of negro inferiority, as the cause of the seeming organic wretchedness of that vast continent. But you will remember that the civilization of all races has been conditioned on contact. It is the remark of a great German historian—perhaps the greatest historian of modern times: "There is not in history the record of a single indigenous civilization; there is nowhere, in any reliable document, the report of any people lifting themselves up out of barbarism. The historic civilizations are all exotic. The torches that blaze along the line of centuries were kindled, each by the one behind."[1]

Where peoples and nations have been so situated that they could be touched by influence and power, there men have gone upward and onward. And this accounts for the fact that newly-discovered islands in the seas have almost always been found low, degraded, and bestial; while, on the other hand, the peoples and races living on continents, generally exhibit the evidences of progress and improvement. But so far as contact with the elements of civilization is concerned, so far as the possibility of being touched by the mental and moral influences of superior and elevating forces is implied, Africa might as well have been an island as a continent. The Desert of Sahara has served as effectually to cut off Africa from the ancient civilizations, as the ocean, for long centuries, separated the Sandwich Islands from the world's enlightenment. Here is the solvement of Africa's benightedness. Physical causes have divorced her from the world's cultivation and improvement. A great ocean of sand has shut her off from that law of both national and individual growth, namely, that culture and enlightenment have got to be *brought* to all new peoples, and made indigenous among them.

Thrown thus back upon herself, unvisited by either the mission of letters, or of grace, poor Africa, all the ages through, has been generating, and then reproducing, the whole brood and progeny of superstitions, idolatries, and paganisms, through all her quarters. And hence the most pitiful, the most abject of all human conditions! And hence the most sorrowful of all histories! The most miserable, even now, of all spectacles!

2. But, as I have remarked, the Christian and civilized world,

within a more recent period, has become both assured and hopeful by the fact of an evident transitional state, in Africa, from her night and gloom, to blessedness and glory. The long night of her darkness and misery has been broken in upon, during a little more than a half century, by the opening light of a brighter day of blessedness. Among the several causes which have contributed to these hopes for Africa, have been the following:—

First among these, was the Abolition of the slave-trade, by this country, and then by the leading powers of Europe. Auxiliary to this was the noble effort to rescue the numerous victims of this murderous traffic, by the active fleets, sent by generous nations, on this errand of humanity. Merciful feeling, and humane effort for Africa, served to interest the Christian world in her interests and her well-being. Just in proportion as the nations were prompted to heal the wounds of this afflicted continent, just so have they been scattering darkness from her agonized brow, and hastening the day of her final relief and regeneration.

But *secondly,* in addition to these distinctive philanthropic efforts, I must needs mention here the earnest missionary endeavors which, within the last 70 years, have helped to change to hopefulness the condition of Africa. These streams of saving influence have flowed out from every powerful Protestant State in the world. The whole world's enlightened and reformed religion, has striven for the regeneration of Africa. Missionaries have gone thither from England and Germany, from America and France, from Switzerland and Holland. Their stations are scattered all along the coast of Africa, from the south border of the desert to the Cape of Good Hope.

3. I have described all this as transitional—but it is more than this. The transitional aspects were confined to a preceding period of some 40 or 50 years, dating from about 1790; but these have now passed away. The *remedial,* the *regenerative* state of the Negro race and the continent of Africa, has now assumed a positive form, and reached a normal, and in some spots, an organic state; with both Christian and civilizing features. And these forms of fixed, and abiding, civilization are growing stronger and stronger every

day, and taking deeper and deeper root. And there is an almost certain prospect, that a yet more thorough and radical growth will be theirs; as year by year, the work of grace, and the power of government and civilization go on, in the divers settlements of western Africa. All the auxiliaries fitted to these ends are now in use there, under the control of a most favoring providence. I beg to present here, in detail, these formative and creative agencies. (a) First of all *there is the beneficent operation of legitimate Commerce.* For nigh 3 centuries, commerce, on the coast of Africa, was divested of every feature, humane, generous, and gracious. Commerce then was a robber; commerce was a marauder; commerce was a devastator; a thief; a murderer! But commerce, now, under the beneficent influence of Christianity, has become the handmaid of religion; and all along the coast of Africa she aids in the development of the resources of that continent; and conveys to its rude inhabitants the aids and instruments to civilization, to active industry, to domestic comfort, and to a budding social refinement. Without attempting any elaborate verification of these general statements, relative to West African commerce; I will merely present a few items which will show the progressive expansion and the real importance of African trade. I shall merely speak of two prime articles of that trade, namely *Cotton* and *Palm Oil.*

(1) Cotton. It is not very generally known that West Africa, that is, that section of the continent of Africa which is called *Negroland;* is a vast cotton growing country. The cotton that is grown there is manufactured on simple native looms, into cotton cloths; and these cloths enter into an extensive *home* barter, as also into the *foreign* trade, for the supply of the Brazilian slaves. Upwards of 200,000 of these manufactured cloths, weighing on the average 2½ lbs. apiece, pass out of the port of Lagos. Their value is stated by Mr. Consul Campbell, late consul at Lagos, at £250,000.

About 30,000 find their way from the interior to Monrovia, and the other ports of Liberia. A like number are brought and sold at Therbro.

The fact of this great growth of cotton in interior Africa, has not escaped the anxious eye of commerce; and within a few years efforts have been made by English houses, through missionaries and traders, to secure the *raw* material. The signal success of this movement is seen in the Abbeokutan country; where, from an exportation, 8 *years ago,* of about 235 *lbs.* of raw cotton, it has been increased to 3,447 *bales,* for the year 1859.

(2) PALM OIL. In 1808 the quantity of Palm oil, imported into *England,* was only 200 tons. "The quantity that reached Great Britain during the year 1860 was 804,326 cwt." The estimate of the annual amount, from the whole of West Africa, is 60,000 tons.

This exposition of trade you will observe, has reference to but *two* articles. Its real importance would be greatly exaggerated, if I could give you the items which pertain to the trade in other oils beside the Palm: in Ivory, of which 3,000 cwt. are annually exported; in Teak, Ebony, and Camwood, and in Gum-Arabic.

(3) I venture, however, to call attention to one more commercial fact, which will serve to show the growing value of this West African trade. In a recent number of the "African Times," published in London, I see that "the value of the exports of British produce and manufactures to British possessions on the west coast of Africa, has advanced from £263,725 in 1858 to £340,311 in 1860,"—that is, they have increased in value nigh $400,000 in two years.

I add here that such is the increasing value of the trade that the English steam-line on the West coast, earned the latter part of 1861 a dividend of 7 per cent., in addition to $10,000, which was laid aside as a sinking fund.

(b) Next to this, I may mention *the active spirit of travel and inquiry which marks the age.* Adventurous spirits are starting off from every civilized land for Africa; anxious to dissipate the spell, which for centuries has divorced her crowded populations from the world's brotherhood and enlightenment; and eager to guarantee them the advantages of culture, which, during the ages, has raised *them* from rudeness and degradation, and carried them up to the heights of grace and refinement.

Fifty years ago Africa was but little better known than it was in the days of Herodotus. Even the adventures of Bruce were regarded as splendid fictions; and he himself was often refused the courtesies due of society, from the supposed mendacity of his narrative. But the travels of Park and Clapperton, of Ledyard and the Landers, of Richardson and Barth, of Kraft and Livingston; have rectified the geographical errors which existed concerning the Nile and its several branches; have unfolded to the greedy gaze of commerce a vast interior route for trade and barter, by the river Niger, more than rivalling your own Mississippi, in its tropical richness and untouched luxuriant resources; — have modified the degrading prejudices concerning the negro, by contrasting him as free, dignified, powerful, and ingenious, in his native superiority, with the miserable caricature of him, shorn of his manhood, ludicrous, and benighted, in chains and slavery; and have led to the discovery of superior peoples, mighty nations, vast kingdoms, and populous cities with from 50 to 100,000 inhabitants in the interior, subject to law and authority, given to enterprise, and engaged in manufactures, agriculture, and extensive commerce.

And thus, by these adventures, vast millions of that continent have been brought into contact with civilized men; with the fabrics of civilized nations; with the quickening ideas of superior men; and the whole continent itself, save a slight belt on either side of the Equator, has been opened to the scrutiny of travellers; and even this has been recently trenched upon by Burton and Speke in the East, directly upon the Equator.

(c.) Another effective agency now in use in West Africa for a permanent work of regeneration, *is the missions and missionary schools scattered along some 2,000 miles and more of that coast, and which are giving, mostly, English instruction to many thousands of native African children.* These mission stations are those of the Church of England and the Wesleyans, both north and south of Liberia; and which form a complete cordon of spiritual posts from about the fifteenth degree of north latitude to Liberia; and from the southern limits of Liberia to ten degrees of south latitude. The most *northern* mission station is that of Gambia.

Here the English Church and the Wesleyans have important stations, with several ministers and catechists; stations on the coast, and *interior* stations some 600 miles up the river Gambia.

About 400 miles lower down the coast, the English Church commenced, in 1856, a mission on the Pongas River, among both pagans and Mohammedans; which has had such real success that it may now be regarded as established.

At about the eighth degree of north latitude is the great missionary stronghold Sierra Leone. The English Church here has a Bishop, and the Church Missionary Society of England conduct, from that point, their extensive operations in Western Africa. Between 30 and 40 clergymen, the majority of whom are native-born Africans, and upwards of 60 lay agents, are employed in their different stations, whether at Sierra Leone, or Lagos, or Abbeokuta, or on the Niger.

In Freetown, the capital, is a cathedral, and all through the colony are numerous, capacious stone churches and chapels. Two high schools, in connection with the Church of England, are in existence, one in Freetown and the other at Lagos, where, besides the ordinary branches of education, instruction is also given in elementary mathematics, and in Latin and Greek.

Upwards of 20 common schools are connected with their stations. Over 5,000 are on the roll of their churches. Upwards of 20 native young men, natives of the land, are being prepared, some while in active duty, for Holy Orders.

At a recent ordination the Bishop of Sierra Leone ordained, at one ordination, 12 or 14 deacons.

The importance of the great missionary station may be gathered from the fact that Sierra Leone has already become the mother of missions; for from this place have gone out the teachers and catechists, the farmers and traders, the missionaries and civilizers,— men of the negro race,—who have already introduced both the Gospel and civilized institutions at Lagos, made Abbeokuta a stronghold of missions, and churches, yea, and have carried schools and the Gospel to Rabba, 400 miles up the Niger.

This representation of the missionary character of Sierra Leone is incomplete, without a reference to the labors of the Wesleyans and the Lady Huntington connection; which two bodies maintain many ministers and catechists, have built several chapels, and have succeeded in converting to the faith near as large a body of members as the Church of England.

The WESLEYANS have 19 missionaries and assistants in all their stations, including Sierra Leone, Lagos, Abbeokuta, &c.; about 300 lay agents, 54 chapels, 45 day schools, and near 9,000 church members.

At the distance of about 60 miles below Sierra Leone the American Missionary Association have important stations, in the Mendi country, which have already been fruitful in converts, have tended to the suppression of native wars, have prompted native industry, and have originated an active commercial spirit. Some idea of the extent of their operations may be gathered from the fact, that the expenditure for the Mendi mission for 1861 amounted to $16,000.

Lower down the coast, that is, from Sierra Leone to lat. 4°, is the territory of Liberia, where American Christians—Baptists, Methodists, Presbyterians and Episcopalians—have been maintaining their missions nigh 40 years, both among natives and colonists.

The result of these efforts is, that the METHODIST, the leading denomination of Christians, is now organized as a national church, with a bishop, a colored citizen, and 18 preachers, members of conference, and several local preachers; 19 week-day schools are maintained, for both natives and colonists; and *two* High Schools are in operation, where classical education is given to both boys and girls. This body of Christians has several missionary stations among the heathen; several native preachers, and has 32 *native* boys, who are placed in equal numbers in the families of its ministers "for instruction in letters and in home and industrial affairs."

The PRESBYTERIAN body is formed into a synod, with some 8 or 10 ministers. It maintains some 4 or 5 mission stations among the heathen; but is specially noted for the most important educational establishment in the Republic—THE ALEXANDER HIGH

SCHOOL, in Monrovia; where a number of youth have received a superior education; and now some of them are holding most responsible positions in the government, as well as in the churches, and in mercantile life.

The BAPTISTS have some 12 chapels and ministers; and a large membership throughout the Republic. In Monrovia they maintain an important High School, where both boys and girls receive a good and thorough English education, with mathematical training. They are united in a CONFERENCE, which meets annually in different parts of the Republic.

The EPISCOPALIANS are a missionary body, under the direction of the Board of Missions of the Protestant Episcopal Church of the United States.

The following will exhibit the agency and the work of this Mission:—

Missionaries, Foreign, (including the Bishop,) 3 〕 " Colonist, 6; Native, 1	Total 10
Assistant Missionaries: 1 Physician, (colored,) 3 White Ladies, 11 Colonist, 19 Native	34
Candidates for orders: Colonist, 3; Native, 3	6
Confirmations: Colonist, 53; Native, 21	74
Communicants (returns imperfect): Colonist, 175; Native, 143; Foreign, 14; total	332
Scholars: Colonist Boarding, 45; Day, 223 〕 " Native, " 130; " 208	606

1 High School.

In connection with the Mission are 6 organized Colonist congregations, six principal Native stations, and seven out-stations.

The gospel is preached with more or less regularity, to over 100,000 people.

(d) *Another most powerful auxiliary to the work of African regeneration, is the formation of important Christian colonies on that coast.* The history and the importance of these germs of civilization, on the African coast, are but little known in this country. Let me dwell upon this particular item for a few moments.

The traveller sailing down the coast of Africa, and visiting its various settlements, meets, first of all, with the French settlement of Goree, and then with a few Portuguese ports in the same neighborhood, that is, from the 14th to the 17th degree of north latitude; but after that, Anglo-Saxon authority, whether English or American, sways the coast for nigh 2,000 miles.

The English colony of Gambia is the next point of importance. This settlement comprises a well-built town on the coast, with schools, good churches and chapels, and several ambitious European houses; and another colony, several hundred miles up the Gambia river, in the interior, at McCarthy's island; which is reached by steamers and large sailing vessels, and which yields an important trade. A day's sail brings the traveller to Sierra Leone, the capital of West Africa, the settlement of recaptured Africans, with a population of over 60,000 inhabitants: its chief town, Freetown, with over 20,000 inhabitants—a capacious city, with numerous fine and even elegant houses; with a cathedral and many stone churches; large shipping, many merchants, and considerable wealth. Here is the Governor's residence, a substantial and capacious building; and here is to be seen, on an elevated site, the barracks for the several regiments of native African troops enrolled in the British army.

Just below Sierra Leone is the REPUBLIC of LIBERIA, founded by the American Colonization Society, with great sacrifice of precious life, and by the expenditure of large means and treasure. I cannot enter into minute statements concerning this young nation. But I beg to say that here is what I claim to be a most singular and striking phenomenon; of 15,000 simple and unlettered men, descendants of slaves, exiles from hereditary wrong and oppression, who, with, indeed, the aid of a large Christian philanthropy, have swept the slave-trade from 700 miles of the coast; have assimilated nigh 20,000 native Africans to them, to their own civilization and religion; have brought into the Christian faith, by baptism, several hundreds of their neighboring heathen; have built some 20 different towns and settlements, with brick, and stone, and frame dwellings; have cleared thousands of acres of lands, and are exporting, as the produce thereof, sugar and coffee to foreign lands; whose merchants are the owners of 40 vessels, engaged in commerce, manned and officered by their own citizens; and who have demonstrated their moral strength and the political capacity of the nation, by the reception in less than 18 months—and that without any disturbance, without any disorganization, but by the turning it into an element of strength and advantage—by the reception, into the bosom of the State, of 5,000 heathen captives rescued, in nakedness and barbarism, by the cruisers of your own nation, from cruel slavers! I do not think I can exaggerate the importance of the Republic of Liberia. There are two or three facts of special importance, which I feel I cannot do otherwise than present in bold relief. *One* of these is, the fact that this little nation, of only 15,000 civilized black Americans has, during some 20 or 30 years, held under control nigh a half a million of bold and warlike heathen, and completely interdicted their participation in the slave-trade. *Second,* that although Liberia is one of the smallest of West African colonies, and its settlements are scattered along some 600 miles of coast; yet we are the *only* manufacturers of sugar and of bricks; we are the only ones who have saw-mills, and cut large quantities of lumber. And we present the singular fact, that is, that although we are the *least* of all the colonies on the coast in numbers; yet from the borders of the desert, to the Cape of Good Hope, Liberia is the only settlement which can meet demands for sugar, bricks, and lumber; and we can humbly claim, that for nigh 4,000 miles on that coast, we are the foremost of all people in enterprise, and that we own more vessels than all the sons of Africa, in all their settlements, along the whole line of the coast.

And now, through the munificence of citizens of Massachusetts and other states, a COLLEGE has been given to the Republic of Liberia; the college building, nobly situated on the heights of Montserrada, can be seen far distant on the ocean. The establishment of this college forms an epoch, not only in the history of Liberia, but also of West Africa; for already numbers of African children, the sons of native chiefs, and kings, and merchants, are sent to England and Scotland for education. I have myself seen 12 native African children in one school in England; and I have no doubt that at the present time there are fully 50 or 60 of such children in British schools: but alas, many die from the severity of the climate. The favorable position of Liberia College will, I have no doubt, give us advantage in this respect; and ere long, numbers of these children, from beyond our territory, as well as within, will be sent to us for instruction: and thus from Liberia, as a fountain-head, shall flow culture, learning, science, and enlightenment to many of the tribes of Africa, all along the coast, and up its rivers, to its most distant inland quarters!

Below the Republic of Liberia are the several forts, settlements, and colonies of the English; lying some two or three hundred miles apart; namely, Cape Coast Castle, Accra, Badagy, and the important town of Lagos, which bids fair to be the New York of West Africa. At all these places the English have chaplains; missions are planted by the Church of England and the Wesleyans; schools are sustained, and the whole work of evangelization is vigorously prosecuted.

I close this part of my subject with this brief summary of the results of labor, on the West coast of Africa, during the last 40 or 50 years; the several items of which I have gathered from divers sources.

Over 150 churches have been erected; nearly 200 schools are in operation; 20,000 children have been instructed in English; nigh 20,000 baptized persons are members of different bodies of Christians; 25 dialects have been reduced to writing; between 60 and 70 settlements have been formed—the centres of civilization, English-speaking our tongue, with schools, and churches, agricultural operations, and commerce.

The facts I have stated serve to bring before us a few marked principles and conclusions:

1. The *whole of Negroland seems, without doubt, to be given up to the English language, and hence to the influence of Anglo-Saxon life*

and civilization. It is a most singular providence that that very people, who have most largely participated in the slave-trade, should have been brought, by the power of God's dealings, and in the workings of His plans, to bear the weighty burden of lifting up this large section of humanity to manhood, and of illuminating them with Christian light and knowledge. Does any one here doubt this providence? Do any of you question the obligation? Just look then at that large portion of Africa which is bounded on the north by the desert, on the west and south by the Atlantic, and on the east by the river Niger; that immense territory which probably contains a population of from 30 to 50,000,000 of people, and which has been the seat of the slave-trade nigh three centuries; and then notice the other fact, that almost the only forts, settlements, colonies, and missions, along the whole line of its coast, are EN-GLISH-SPEAKING, namely Gambia, Pongas, Sierra Leone, Mendi, Liberia, Accra, and Lagos. Can any one doubt that God has thrown the responsibility of evangelizing this people upon the Anglo-Saxon race? Does it not seem manifest that God has laid this people's spiritual burden upon the sensitive Christian heart of England and America? What if this grand cause should prove the agency for neutralizing their national prejudices; or for producing a union, for love and human well-being, such as the world has never before witnessed?

2. Again, I would add, that *the evangelization of Africa is manifestly to be effected contemporaneously with its civilization.* Unlike most of the missionary and evangelizing movements of modern times, God evidently purposes the redemption of *Africa,* in connection with the use of all the appliances of culture, learning, trade, industry, and commerce. All these *are* already being used, in West Africa, as handmaids of religion. Civilization is to be a most marked agent in the process of evangelization, among the million masses of that vast continent. We shall see, in West Africa, in these our own days, and on a large scale, that primitive mode of propagating Christianity over a whole continent, which characterized the rapid progress of the faith in Apostolic times; when the Spirit of God

seized upon an actual, though pagan civilization; and ran, with an almost electric speed, through Palestine, through Asia Minor, through Greece, through the Roman provinces, through the Roman Empire; until, in less than three centuries, the Christian faith became the master influence of the world; and the diadem of the Cæsars had to bow in submission to the cross of Christ!

So, most probably, will it be in West Africa. The day of Africa's agony is being closed up by the simultaneous entrance of Christian churches and civilized colonies, all along her coasts, and through all her interior quarters!

3. You see here also the important fact that *the main agency God is employing for the ends I have pointed out, is black men themselves.* It is, indeed, in West Africa, as everywhere else in all history, namely, that the primal training, the early preparation come from advanced and superior people. *They* always plant the germs of a new faith, or are the pioneers of a new civilization. *But the work itself is always effected by indigenous agencies.* So in Africa, the work of these settlements, colonies, and mission, is being done by Negroes. Some of these came from the British West Indies: numbers of them are recaptured Africans, trained in English schools: thousands of them are *American* black men, educated in the missions of Liberia, or amid the institutions and in the schools of this country: and all of whom, thus enlightened, are Presidents, Judges, Senators, Merchants, Civilians, Planters, and a host of Priests, and Deacons, and Catechists—sons of Africa! How mighty is the hand of God in the affairs of earth! How wonderful is His providence amid the disastrous and destructive doings of men! The slave-trade has been carried on for centuries by cruel, ruthless men, without a thought of mercy. The system of slavery, in the lands of the black man's thraldom, has been a system of greed, and overwork, and lust, and premature decay, and death, with but slight and incidental alleviations. And yet there *have been* alleviations. God never allows any evils on earth to be entirely aggregations of evil, without their incidents of good. So here, in this matter, God has raised up, even

in their lands of servitude, a class of black men who have already gone from America, from the British West Indies, and from Sierra Leone; the pioneers of civilization and Christianity, to the land of their fathers. Thus God overrules the wrath of man. Thus from blasting, deadly evil, is He ever educing good. Thus does He pluck the sting of malignant intent out of the disastrous histories of men; and transforms those histories into benignant providences.

I know full well how wickedly, how blasphemously, all this story has been used to justify the wrongs of the Negro, and to fasten it all upon the will of God. But when Joseph told his brethren—"it was not you that sent me hither, but God," he did not mean that they had not acted brutally toward him; but only that, in all the dark deeds of men, there is a higher, mightier, more masterful hand than theirs, although unseen;—distracting their evil counsels, and directing them to goodly issues. God, although not the author of sin, is, nevertheless, the omnipotent and gracious disposer of it. Let us bless God for that master hand of His, which checks, and rules, and guides the policies and histories of men! "Alleluia! for the Lord God, omnipotent reigneth."

And here we may see, in *two* special points, how God shows himself Sovereign and Governor in this world, amid the sore vicissitudes and the bitter trials of men. For *first,* we have disclosed herein the workings of that great law of God, that is, the *call to suffering and endurance, to the end of greatness and noble duty,* in any race or people whom He has elected to greatness, and might, and future empire. For without doubt, the black man, in the lands of his thraldom, has been in the school of suffering; yea, tried in the fiery furnace, that being tried, he might secure therefrom the strength, the character, and the ability which might fit him for a civilizer and a teacher. Not for death, as the Indian, not for destruction, as the Sandwich islander, has the Negro been placed in juxtaposition with the Caucasian; but rather that he might seize upon civilization; that he might obtain hardiment of soul; that he might develop those singular vital forces, both of the living spirit and the hardy frame, in which I claim the Negro is unrivalled; and thus, himself, be enabled to go forth, the creator of new civilizations in distant quarters, and the founder, for Christ, of new churches!

And *next*, we may see in all this *that law of compensation which God vouchsafes the wronged and suffering, for all their woes and suffering*. After being afflicted, by nigh three centuries of servitude, God calls chosen men of this race, from all the lands of their thraldom— men laden with gifts, and intelligence, and piety—to the grand and noble mission, which they only can fulfil, even to plant colonies, establish Churches, found Missions, and lay the foundations of Universities along the shores, and beside the banks of the great rivers of Africa. He lifts up this people from lowly degradation, to the great work of evangelizing the vast continent of Africa, so that the grandeur and dignity of their duties may neutralize all the long, sad, memories of their servitude and sorrows.

4th, and lastly: I remark that the facts I have referred to *are full of promise of that future glory in Christ which is promised, and which will surely be given to Africa*. She has passed, sadly, wearily, through long ages of agony and woe; but the end is approaching. "The night is far spent: the day is at hand." The day when civilization and true religion shall make triumphal march through all her quarters, is rapidly drawing nigh. Yea, the time has already come when rudeness and barbarism shall be replaced by culture and refinement. Schools shall be filled by ten thousands of joyous children; Trades shall be pursued by her crowded populations; Agriculture shall pour forth its gifts and offerings for distant marts; Commerce shall bear multitudinous treasures to foreign climes; and Art shall multiply its blandishments, to

"Soften the rude and calm the boisterous mind."

It was a remark of the great William Pitt: "We may live to behold the nations of Africa engaged in the calm occupations of industry, and in the pursuit of a just and legitimate commerce; we may behold the beams of science and philosophy breaking in upon their land, which at some happier period, in still later times, may blaze with full lustre, and joining their influence to that of PURE RELIGION, may illuminate and invigorate the most distant extremities of that immense continent."

And already have these noble words been somewhat realized. I myself, with my own eyes, have seen the fulfilment, in partial degrees, of this grand prediction. Large masses of native children are now being trained in Christian schools. A great company of native catechists have gone forth from their homes to train and evangelize their heathen kin. A host of native priests and deacons have been commissioned to go forth as missionaries, in divers tongues to preach the gospel: already have they penetrated the wilds of the interior; already have they reached the banks of the Niger; and soon the full picture painted by the great orator, shall assume the features of grand reality, "and science and philosophy, with pure religion, illuminate and invigorate extremities of that immense continent."

But nobler words and a more glorious prediction have been uttered concerning Africa, than even the glowing words of the great British orator: for the words I now utter are the words of inspiration, they come from God Himself: "Ethiopia"—from the Atlantic Ocean to the Indian—from the Mediterranean to the Cape, "shall soon stretch out her hands unto God!"

Note

1. Niebuhr.

15

The Call of Providence to the Descendants of Africa in America (1862)

This essay is important in that it reveals the Christian mysticism that was omnipresent in nineteenth-century black nationalism. Edward Wilmot Blyden's nationalism, like that of Crummell, was essentially religious. Both men believed that it was the manifest and God-given destiny of African Americans to contribute to the progress of Africa through emigration. Although he was a Presbyterian minister, Blyden was sympathetic to the spread of Islam in Africa during his later career, because he believed that Islam would pave the way for Christianity.

> "BEHOLD, the Lord thy God hath set the land be-forethee: go up and possess it, as the Lord God of thy fathers hath said unto thee; fear not, neither be discouraged." DEUTERONOMY 1:21.

Among the descendants of Africa in this country the persuasion seems to prevail, though not now to the same extent as formerly, that they owe no special duty to the land of their forefathers; that their ancestors having been brought to this country against their will, and themselves having been born in the land, they are in duty bound to remain here and give their attention exclusively to the acquiring for themselves, and perpetuating to their posterity, social and political rights, notwithstanding the urgency of the call which their fatherland, by its forlorn and degraded moral condition, makes upon them for their assistance.

Edward Wilmot Blyden, "The Call of Providence to the Descendants of Africa in America" in *Liberia's Offering* (New York: John A. Gray, 1862).

All other people feel a pride in their ancestral land, and do everything in their power to create for it, if it has not already, an honorable name. But many of the descendants of Africa, on the contrary, speak disparagingly of their country; are ashamed to acknowledge any connection with that land, and would turn indignantly upon any who would bid them go up and take possession of the land of their fathers.

It is a sad feature in the residence of Africans in this country, that it has begotten in them a forgetfulness of Africa—a want of sympathy with her in her moral and intellectual desolation, and a clinging to the land which for centuries has been the scene of their thralldom. A shrewd European observer [1] of American society, says of the Negro in this country, that he "makes a thousand fruitless efforts to insinuate himself among men who repulse him; he conforms to the taste of his oppressors, adopts their opinions, and hopes by imitating them to form a part of their community. Having been told from infancy that his race is naturally inferior to that of the whites, he assents to the proposition, and is ashamed of his own nature. In each of his features he discovers a trace of slavery, and, if it were in his power, he would willingly rid himself of everything that makes him what he is."

It can not be denied that some very important advantages have accrued to the black man from his deportation to this land, but it has been at the expense of his manhood. Our nature in this country is not the same as it appears among the lordly natives of the interior of Africa, who have never felt the trammels of a foreign yoke. We have been dragged into depths of degradation. We have been taught a cringing servility. We have been drilled into contentment with the most undignified circumstances. Our finer sensibilities have been blunted. There has been an almost utter extinction of all that delicacy of feeling and sentiment which adorns character. The temperament of our souls has become harder or coarser, so that we can walk forth here, in this land of indignities, in ease and in complacency, while our complexion furnishes ground for every species of social insult which an intolerant prejudice may choose to inflict.

But a change is coming over us. The tendency of events is directing the attention of the colored people to some other scene, and Africa is beginning to receive the attention, which has so long been turned away from her; and as she throws open her portals and shows the inexhaustible means of comfort and independence within, the black man begins to feel dissatisfied with the annoyances by which he is here surrounded, and looks with longing eyes to his fatherland. I venture to predict that, within a very brief period, that down-trodden land instead of being regarded with prejudice and distaste, will largely attract the attention and engage the warmest interest of every man of color. A few have always sympathized with Africa, but it has been an indolent and unmeaning sympathy—a sympathy which put forth no effort, made no sacrifices, endured no self-denial, braved no obloquy for the sake of advancing African interests. But the scale is turning, and Africa is becoming the all-absorbing topic.

It is my desire, on the present occasion, to endeavor to set before you the work which, it is becoming more and more apparent, devolves upon the black men of the United States; and to guide my thoughts, I have chosen the words of the text: "Behold, the Lord thy God hath set the land before thee: go up and possess it, as the Lord God of thy fathers hath said unto thee; fear not, neither be discouraged."

You will at once perceive that I do not believe that the work to be done by black men is in this country. I believe that their field of operation is in some other and distant scene. Their work is far nobler and loftier than that which they are now doing in this country. It is theirs to betake themselves to injured Africa, and bless those outraged shores, and quiet those distracted families with the blessings of Christianity and civilization. It is theirs to bear with them to that land the arts of industry and peace, and counteract the influence of those horrid abominations which an inhuman avarice has introduced—to roll back the appalling cloud of ignorance and superstition which overspreads the land, and to rear on those shores an asylum of liberty for the down-trodden sons of Africa wherever found. This is the work to which Providence is obviously calling the black men of this country.

I am aware that some, against all experience, are hoping for the day when they will enjoy equal social and political rights in this land. We do not blame them for so believing and trusting. But we would remind them that there is a faith against reason, against experience, which consists in believing or pretending to believe very important propositions upon very slender proofs, and in maintaining opinions without any proper grounds. It ought to be clear to every thinking and impartial mind, that there can never occur in this country an equality, social or political, between whites and blacks. The whites have for a long time had the advantage. All the affairs of the country are in their hands. They make and administer the laws; they teach the schools; here, in the North, they ply all the trades, they own all the stores, they have possession of all the banks, they own all the ships and navigate them; they are the printers, proprietors, and editors of the leading newspapers, and they shape public opinion. Having always had the lead, they have acquired an ascendency they will ever maintain. The blacks have very few or no agencies in operation to counteract the ascendant influence of the Europeans. And instead of employing what little they have by a unity of effort to alleviate their condition, they turn all their power against themselves by their endless jealousies, and rivalries, and competition; everyone who is able to "pass" being emulous of a place among Europeans or Indians. This is the effect of their circumstances. It is the influence of the dominant class upon them. It argues no essential inferiority in them—no more than the disadvantages of the Israelites in Egypt argued their essential inferiority to the Egyptians. They are the weaker class overshadowed and depressed by the stronger. They are the feeble oak dwarfed by the overspreadings of a large tree, having not the advantage of rain, and sunshine, and fertilizing dews.

Before the weaker people God has set the land of their forefathers, and bids them go up and possess it without fear or discouragement. Before the tender plant he sets an open field, where, in the unobstructed air and sunshine, it may grow and flourish in all its native luxuriance.

There are two ways in which God speaks to men: one is by his word and the other by his providence. He has not sent any Moses, with signs and wonders, to cause an exodus of the descendants of Africa to their fatherland, yet he has loudly spoken to them as to their duty in the matter. He has spoken by his providence. First; By suffering them to be brought here and placed in circumstances where they could receive a training fitting them for the work of civilizing and evangelizing the land whence they were torn, and by preserving them under the severest trials and afflictions. Secondly; By allowing them, notwithstanding all the services they have rendered to this country, to be treated as strangers and aliens, so as to cause them to have anguish of spirit, as was the case with the Jews in Egypt, and to make them long for some refuge from their social and civil deprivations. Thirdly; By bearing a portion of them across the tempestuous seas back to Africa, by preserving them through the process of acclimation, and by establishing them in the land, despite the attempts of misguided men to drive them away. Fourthly; By keeping their fatherland in reserve for them in their absence.

The manner in which Africa has been kept from invasion is truly astounding. Known for ages, it is yet unknown. For centuries its inhabitants have been the victims of the cupidity of foreigners. The country has been rifled of its population. It has been left in some portions almost wholly unoccupied, but it has remained unmolested by foreigners. It has been very near the crowded countries of the world, yet none has relieved itself to any great extent of its overflowing population by seizing upon its domains. Europe, from the North, looks wishfully and with longing eyes across the narrow straits of Gilbraltar. Asia, with its teeming millions, is connected with us by an isthmus wide enough to admit of her throwing thousands into the country. But, notwithstanding the known wealth of the resources of the land, of which the report has gone into all the earth, there is still a terrible veil between us and our neighbors, the all-conquering Europeans, which they are only now essaying to lift; while the teeming millions of Asia have not even attempted to leave their boundaries to penetrate our borders. Neither alluring visions of glorious conquests, nor brilliant hopes of rapid enrichment, could induce them to invade the country. It has been preserved alike from the boastful civilization of Europe, and the effete and barbarous institutions of Asia. We call it, then, a Providential interposition, that while the owners of the soil have been abroad, passing through the fearful ordeal of a most grinding oppression, the land, though entirely unprotected, has lain uninvaded. We regard it as a providential call to Africans every where, to "go up and possess the land"; so that in a sense that is not merely constructive and figurative, but truly literal, God says to the black men of this country, with reference to Africa: "Behold, I set the land before you, go up and possess it."

Of course it can not be expected that this subject of the duty of colored men to go up and take possession of their fatherland, will be at once clear to every mind. Men look at objects from different points of view, and form their opinions according to the points from which they look, and are guided in their actions according to the opinions they form. As I have already said, the majority of exiled Africans do not seem to appreciate the great privilege of going and taking possession of the land. They seem to have lost all interest in that land, and to prefer living in subordinate and inferior positions in a strange land among oppressors, to encountering the risks involved in emigrating to a distant country. As I walk the streets of these cities, visit the hotels, go on board the steamboats, I am grieved to notice how much intelligence, how much strength and energy is frittered away in those trifling employments, which, if thrown into Africa, might elevate the millions of that land from their degradation, tribes at a time, and create an African power which would command the respect of the world, and place in the possession of Africans, its rightful owners, the wealth which is now diverted to other quarters. Most of the wealth that could be drawn from that land, during the last six centuries, has passed into the hands of Europeans, while many of Africa's own sons, sufficiently intelligent to control those immense resources, are sitting down in poverty and dependence in the land of strangers—exiles when they have so rich a domain from which they have never been expatriated, but which is willing, nay, anxious to welcome them home again.

We need some African power, some great center of the race where our physical, pecuniary, and intellectual strength may be collected. We need some spot whence such an influence may go forth in behalf of the race as shall be felt by the nations. We are now so scattered and divided that we can do nothing. The imposition begun last year by a foreign power upon Hayti, and which is still persisted in, fills every black man who has heard of it with indignation, but we are not strong enough to speak out effectually for that land. When the same power attempted an outrage upon the Liberians, there was no African power strong enough to interpose. So long as we remain thus divided, we may expect impositions. So long as we live simply by the sufferance of the nations, we must expect to be subject to their caprices.

Among the free portion of the descendants of Africa, numbering about four or five millions, there is enough talent, wealth, and enterprise, to form a respectable nationality on the continent of Africa. For nigh three hundred years their skill and industry have been expended in building up the southern countries of the New World, the poor, frail constitution of the Caucasian not allowing him to endure the fatigue and toil involved in such labors. Africans and their descendants have been the laborers, and the mechanics, and the artisans in the greater portion of this hemisphere. By the results of their labor the European countries have been sustained and enriched. All the cotton, coffee, indigo, sugar, tobacco, etc., which have formed the most important articles of European commerce, have been raised and prepared for market by the labor of the black man. Dr. Palmer of New-Orleans, bears the same testimony.[2] And all this labor they have done, for the most part not only without compensation, but with abuse, and contempt, and insult, as their reward.

Now, while Europeans are looking to our fatherland with such eagerness of desire, and are hastening to explore and take away its riches, ought not Africans in the Western hemisphere to turn their regards thither also? We need to collect the scattered forces of the race, and there is no rallying-ground more favorable than Africa. There

"No pent-up Utica contracts our powers,
The whole boundless continent is ours."

Ours as a gift from the Almighty when he drove asunder the nations and assigned them their boundaries; and ours by peculiar physical adaptation.

An African nationality is our great need, and God tells us by his providence that he has set the land before us, and bids us go up and possess it. We shall never receive the respect of other races until we establish a powerful nationality. We should not content ourselves with living among other races, simply by their permission or their endurance, as Africans live in this country. We must build up Negro states; we must establish and maintain the various institutions; we must make and administer laws, erect and preserve churches, and support the worship of God; we must have governments; we must have legislation of our own; we must build ships and navigate them; we must ply the trades, instruct the schools, control the press, and thus aid in shaping the opinions and guiding the destinies of mankind. Nationality is an ordinance of Nature. The heart of every true Negro yearns after a distinct and separate nationality.

Impoverished, feeble, and alone, Liberia is striving to establish and build up such a nationality in the home of the race. Can any descendant of Africa turn contemptuously upon a scene where such efforts are making? Would not every right-thinking Negro rather lift up his voice and direct the attention of his brethren to that land? Liberia, with outstretched arms, earnestly invites all to come. We call them forth out of all nations; we bid them take up their all and leave the countries of their exile, as of old the Israelites went forth from Egypt, taking with them their trades and their treasures, their intelligence, their mastery of arts, their knowledge of the sciences, their practical wisdom, and every thing that will render them useful in building up a nationality. We summon them from these States, from the Canadas, from the East and West-Indies, from South-America, from every where, to come and take part with us in our great work.

But those whom we call are under the influence of various opinions, having different and conflicting views of their relations and duty to Africa, according to the different stand-points they occupy. So it was with another people who, like ourselves, were suffering from the effects of protracted thralldom, when on the borders of the land to which God was leading them. When Moses sent out spies to search the land of Canaan, every man, on his return, seemed to be influenced in his report by his peculiar temperament, previous habits of thought, by the degree of his physical courage, or by something peculiar in his point of observation. All agreed, indeed, that it was an exceedingly rich land, "flowing with milk and honey," for they carried with them on their return, a proof of its amazing fertility. But a part, and a larger part, too, saw only giants and walled towns, and barbarians and cannibals. "Surely," said they, "it floweth with milk and honey. Nevertheless the people be strong that dwell in the land, and the cities are walled, and very great; and moreover we saw the children of Anak there. The land through which we have gone to search it, is a land that eateth up the inhabitants thereof; and all the people that we saw in it are men of a great stature. And there we saw the giants, the sons of Anak, which come of the giants: and we were in our own sight as grasshoppers, and so we were in their sight." It was only a small minority of that company that saw things in a more favorable light. "Caleb stilled the people before Moses, and said,

Let us go up at once and possess it; for we be well able to overcome it." (Numbers 13.)

In like manner there is division among the colored people of this country with regard to Africa, that land which the providence of God is bidding them go up and possess. Spies sent from different sections of this country by the colored people—and many a spy not commissioned—have gone to that land, and have returned and reported. Like the Hebrew spies, they have put forth diverse views. Most believe Africa to be a fertile and rich country, and an African nationality a desirable thing. But some affirm that the land is not fit to dwell in, for "it is a land that eateth up the inhabitants thereof," notwithstanding the millions of strong and vigorous aborigines who throng all parts of the country, and the thousands of colonists who are settled along the coast; some see in the inhabitants incorrigible barbarism, degradation, and superstition, and insuperable hostility to civilization; others suggest that the dangers and risks to be encountered, and the self-denial to be endured, are too great for the slender advantages which, as it appears to them, will accrue from immigration. A few only report that the land is open to us on every hand—that "every prospect pleases," and that the natives are so tractable that it would be a comparatively easy matter for civilized and Christianized black men to secure all the land to Christian law, liberty, and civilization.

I come to-day to defend the report of the minority. The thousands of our own race, emigrants from this country, settled for more than forty years in that land, agree with the minority report. Dr. Barth, and other travelers to the east and south-east of Liberia, indorse the sentiment of the minority, and testify to the beauty, and healthfulness, and productiveness of the country, and to the mildness and hospitality of its inhabitants. In Liberia we hear from natives, who are constantly coming to our settlements from the far interior, of land exuberantly fertile, of large, numerous, and wealthy tribes, athletic and industrious; not the descendants of Europeans—according to Bowen's insane theory—but *black* men, pure Negroes, who live in large towns, cultivate the soil, and carry on extensive traffic, maintaining amicable relations with each other and with men from a distance.

The ideas that formerly prevailed of the interior of Africa, which suited the purposes of poetry and sensation writing, have been proved entirely erroneous. Poets may no longer sing with impunity of Africa:

> *"A region of drought, where no river glides,*
> *Nor rippling brook with osiered sides;*
> *Where sedgy pool, nor bubbling fount,*
> *Nor tree, nor cloud, nor misty mount,*
> *Appears to refresh the aching eye,*
> *But barren earth and the burning sky,*
> *And the blank horizon round and round."*

No; missionary and scientific enterprises have disproved such fallacies. The land possesses every possible inducement. That extensive and beauteous domain which God has given us appeals to us and to black men every where, by its many blissful and benignant aspects; by its flowery landscapes, its beautiful rivers, its serene and peaceful skies; by all that attractive and perennial verdure which overspreads the hills and valleys; by its every prospect lighted up by delightful sunshine; by all its natural charms, it calls upon us to rescue it from the grasp of remorseless superstition, and introduce the blessings of the Gospel.

But there are some among the intelligent colored people of this country who, while they profess to have great love for Africa, and tell us that their souls are kindled when they hear of their fatherland, yet object to going themselves, because, as they affirm, the black man has a work to accomplish in this land—he has a destiny to fulfill. He, the representative of Africa, like the representatives from various parts of Europe, must act his part in building up this great composite nation. It is not difficult to see what the work of the black man is in this land. The most inexperienced observer may at once read his destiny. Look at the various departments of society here in the *free* North; look at the different branches of industry, and see how the black man is aiding to build up this nation. Look at the hotels, the saloons, the steamboats, the barbershops, and see how successfully he is carrying out his destiny! And there is an extreme likelihood that such are forever to be the exploits which he is destined to achieve in this country until he merges his African peculiarities in the Caucasian.

Others object to the *climate* of Africa, first, that it is unhealthy, and secondly, that it is not favorable to intellectual progress. To the first, we reply that it is not more insalubrious than other new countries. Persons going to Africa, who have not been broken down as to their constitutions in this country, stand as fair a chance of successful acclimation as in any other country of large, unbroken forests and extensively uncleared lands. In all new countries there are sufferings and privations. All those countries which have grown up during the last two centuries, in this hemisphere, have had as a foundation the groans, and tears, and blood of the pioneers. But what are the sufferings of pioneers, compared with the greatness of the results they accomplish for succeeding generations? Scarcely any great step in human progress is made without multitudes of victims. Every revolution that has been effected, every nationality that has been established, every country that has been rescued from the abominations of savagism, every colony that has been planted, has involved perplexities and sufferings to the generation who undertook it. In the evangelization of Africa, in the erection of African nationalities, we can expect no exceptions. The man, then, who is not able to suffer and to die for his fellows when necessity requires it, is not fit to be a pioneer in this great work.

We believe, as we have said, that the establishment of an African nationality in Africa is the great need of the African race; and the men who have gone, or may hereafter go to assist in laying the foundations of empire, so far from being dupes, or cowards, or traitors, as some have ignorantly called them, are the truest heroes of the race. They are the soldiers rushing first into the breach—physicians who at the risk of their own lives are first to explore an infectious disease. How much more nobly do they act than those who have held for years that it is nobler to sit here and patiently suffer with our brethren! Such sentimental inactivity finds no respect in these days of rapid movement. The world sees no merit in mere innocence. The man who contents himself to sit down and exemplify the virtue of patience and endurance will find no sympathy from the busy, restless crowd that rush by him. Even the "sick man" must get out of the way when he hears the tramp of the approaching host, or be crushed by the heedless and massive car of progress. Blind Bartimeuses are silenced by the crowd. The world requires active service; it respects only productive workers. The days of hermits and monks have passed away. Action—work, work—is the order of the day. Heroes in the strife and struggle of humanity are the demand of the age.

"They who would be free, themselves *must* strike *the blow."*

With regard to the objection founded upon the unfavorableness of the climate to intellectual progress, I have only to say, that proper moral agencies, when set in operation, can not be overborne by physical causes. "We continually behold lower laws held in restraint by higher; mechanic by dynamic; chemical by vital; physical by moral."[3] It has not yet been proved that with the proper influences, the tropics will not produce men of "cerebral activity." Those races which have degenerated by a removal from the North to the tropics did not possess the proper moral power. They had in themselves the seed of degeneracy, and would have degenerated any where. It was not Anglo-Saxon blood, nor a temperate climate, that kept the first emigrants to this land from falling into the same indolence and inefficiency which have overtaken the European settlers in South-America, but the Anglo-Saxon Bible—the principles contained in that book, are the great conservative and elevating power. Man is the same, and the human mind is the same, whether existing beneath African suns or Arctic frosts. I can conceive of no difference. It is the moral influences brought to bear upon the man that make the difference in his progress.

"High degrees of moral sentiment," says a distinguished American writer,[4] "control the unfavorable influences of climate; and some of our grandest examples of men and of races come from the equatorial regions." Man is elevated by taking hold of that which is higher than himself. Unless this is done, climate, color, race, will avail nothing.

> "*—unless above himself he can*
> *Erect himself, how poor a thing is man!*"

For my own part, I believe that the brilliant world of the tropics, with its marvels of nature, must of necessity give to mankind a new career of letters, and new forms in the various arts, whenever the millions of men at present uncultivated shall enjoy the advantages of civilization.

Africa will furnish a development of civilization which the world has never yet witnessed. Its great peculiarity will be its moral element. The Gospel is to achieve some of its most beautiful triumphs in that land. "God shall enlarge Japheth, and he shall dwell in the tents of Shem," was the blessing upon the European and Asiatic races. Wonderfully have these predictions been fulfilled. The all-conquering descendants of Japheth have gone to every clime, and have planted themselves on almost every shore. By means fair and unfair, they have spread themselves, have grown wealthy and powerful. They have been truly "enlarged." God has "dwelt in the tents of Shem," for so some understand the passage. The Messiah—God manifest in the flesh—was of the tribe of Judah. He was born and dwelt in the tents of Shem. The promise to Ethiopia, or Ham, is like that to Shem, of a spiritual kind. It refers not to physical strength, not to large and extensive domains, not to foreign conquests, not to wide-spread domination, but to the possession of spiritual qualities, to the elevation of the soul heavenward, to spiritual aspirations and divine communications. "Ethiopia shall stretch forth her hands unto God." Blessed, glorious promise! Our trust is not to be in chariots or horses, not in our own skill or power, but our help is to be in the name of the Lord. And surely, in reviewing our history as a people, whether we consider our preservation in the lands of our exile, or the preservation of our fatherland from invasion, we are compelled to exclaim: "Hitherto hath the Lord helped us!" Let us, then, fear not the influences of climate. Let us go forth stretching out our hands to God, and if it be as hot as Nebuchadnezzar's furnace, there will be one in the midst like unto the Son of God, counteracting its deleterious influences.

Behold, then, the Lord our God has set the land before us, with its burning climate, with its privations, with its moral, intellectual, and political needs, and by his providence he bids us go up and possess it without fear or discouragement. Shall we go up at his bidding? If the black men of this country, through unbelief or indolence, or for any other cause, fail to lay hold of the blessings which God is proffering to them, and neglect to accomplish the work which devolves upon them, the work will be done, but others will be brought in to do it, and to take possession of the country.

For while the colored people here are tossed about by various and conflicting opinions as to their duty to that land, men are going thither from other quarters of the globe. They are entering the land from various quarters with various motives and designs, and may eventually so preöccupy the land as to cut us off from the fair inheritance which lies before us, unless we go forth without further delay and establish ourselves.

The enterprise and energy manifested by white men who, with uncongenial constitutions, go from a distance to endeavor to open up that land to the world, are far from creditable to the civilized and enlightened colored men of the United States, when contrasted with their indifference in the matter. A noble army of self-expatriated evangelists have gone to that land from Europe and America; and, while anxious to extend the blessings of true religion, they have in no slight degree promoted the cause of science and commerce. Many have fallen, either from the effects of the climate or by the hands of violence;[5] still the interest in the land is by no means diminished. The enamored worshiper of science, and the Christian philanthropist, are still laboring to solve the problem of

African geography, and to elevate its benighted tribes. They are not only disclosing to the world the mysteries of regions hitherto unexplored, but tribes whose very existence had not before been known to the civilized world have been brought, through their instrumentality, into contact with civilization and Christianity. They have discovered in the distant portions of that land countries as productive as any in Europe and America. They have informed the world of bold and lofty mountains, extensive lakes, noble rivers, falls rivaling Niagara, so that, as a result of their arduous, difficult, and philanthropic labors of exploration, the cause of Christianity, ethnology, geography, and commerce has been, in a very important degree, subserved.

Dr. Livingstone, the indefatigable African explorer, who, it is estimated, has passed over not less than eleven thousand miles of African ground, speaking of the motives which led him to those shores, and still keep him there in spite of privations and severe afflictions, says:

"I expect to find for myself no large fortune in that country; nor do I expect to explore any large portions of a new country; but I do hope to find a pathway, by means of the river Zambesi, which may lead to highlands, where Europeans may form a settlement, and where, by opening up communication and establishing commercial intercourse with the natives of Africa, they may slowly, but not the less surely, impart to the people of that country the knowledge and inestimable blessings of Christianity."

The recently formed Oxford, Cambridge, and Dublin Missionary Society state their object to be to spread Christianity among the untaught people of Central Africa, "so to operate among them as by mere teaching and influence to help *to build up native Christian states*." The idea of building up "native Christian states" is a very important one, and is exactly such an idea as would be carried out if there were a large influx of civilized blacks from abroad.

I am sorry to find that among some in this country, the opinion prevails that in Liberia a distinction is maintained between the colonists and the aborigines, so that the latter are shut out from the social and political privileges of the former. No candid person who has read the laws of Liberia, or who has visited that country, can affirm or believe such a thing. The idea no doubt arises from the fact that the aborigines of a country generally suffer from the settling of colonists among them. But the work of Liberia is somewhat different from that of other colonies which have been planted on foreign shores. The work achieved by other emigrants has usually been—the enhancement of their own immediate interests; the increase of their physical comforts and conveniences; the enlargement of their borders by the most speedy and available methods, without regard to the effect such a course might have upon the aborigines. Their interests sometimes coming into direct contact with those of the owners of the soil, they have not unfrequently, by their superior skill and power, reduced the poor native to servitude or complete annihilation. The Israelites could live in peace in the land of Canaan only by exterminating the indigenous inhabitants. The colony that went out from Phenicia, and that laid the foundations of empire on the northern shores of Africa, at first paid a yearly tax to the natives; with the increasing wealth and power of Carthage, however, the respective conditions of the Carthaginians and the natives were changed, and the Phenician adventurers assumed and maintained a dominion over the Lybians. The colonies from Europe which landed at Plymouth Rock, at Boston, and at Jamestown—which took possession of the West-India islands and of Mexico, treated the aborigines in the same manner. The natives of India, Australia, and New-Zealand are experiencing a similar treatment under the overpowering and domineering rule of the Anglo-Saxons. Eagerness for gain and the passion for territorial aggrandisement have appeared to the colonists necessary to their growth and progress.

The work of Liberia, as I have said, is different and far nobler. We, on the borders of our fatherland, can not, as the framers of our Constitution wisely intimated, allow ourselves to be influenced by "avaricious speculations," or by desires for "territorial aggrandisement." Our work there is moral and intellectual as well as physical. We have to work upon the *people*, as well as upon the *land*—upon *mind* as well as upon *matter*. Our prosperity depends as much upon the wholesome and elevating influence we exert upon the native population, as upon the progress we make in agriculture, commerce, and manufacture. Indeed the conviction prevails in Liberia among the thinking people that we can make no important progress in these things without the coöperation of the aborigines. We believe that no policy can be more suicidal in Liberia than that which would keep aloof from the natives around us. We believe that our life and strength will be to elevate and incorporate them among us as speedily as possible.

And, then, the aborigines are not a race alien from the colonists. We are a part of them. When alien and hostile races have come together, as we have just seen, one has had to succumb to the other; but when different peoples of the same family have been brought together, there has invariably been a fusion, and the result has been an improved and powerful class. When three branches of the great Teutonic family met on the soil of England, they united. It is true that at first there was a distinction of caste among them in consequence of the superiority in every respect of the great Norman people; but, as the others came up to their level, the distinctions were quietly effaced, and Norman, Saxon, and Dane easily amalgamated. Thus, "a people inferior to none existing in the world was formed by the mixture of three branches of the great Teutonic family with each other and the aboriginal Britons."[6]

In America we see how readily persons from all parts of Europe assimilate; but what great difficulty the Negro, the Chinese, and the Indian experience! We find here representatives from all the nations of Europe easily blending with each other. But we find elements that will not assimilate. The Negro, the Indian, and the Chinese, who do not belong to the same family, repel each other, and are repelled by the Europeans. "The antagonistic elements are in contact, but refuse to unite, and as yet no agent has been found sufficiently potent to reduce them to unity."

But the case with America-Liberians and the aborigines is quite different. We are all descendants of Africa. In Liberia there may be found persons of almost every tribe in West-Africa, from Senegal to Congo. And not only do we and the natives belong to the same race, but we are also of the same family. The two peoples can no more be kept from assimilating and blending than water can be kept from mingling with its kindred elements. The policy of Liberia is to diffuse among them as rapidly as possible the principles of Christianity and civilization, to prepare them to take an active part in the duties of the nationality which we are endeavoring to erect. Whence, then, comes the slander which represents Liberians as "maintaining a distance from the aborigines—a constant and uniform separation"?

To take part in the noble work in which they are engaged on that coast, the government and people of Liberia earnestly invite the descendants of Africa in this country.[7] In all our feebleness, we have already accomplished something; but very little in comparison of what has to be done. A beginning has been made, however—a great deal of preparatory work accomplished. And if the intelligent and enterprising colored people of this country would emigrate in large numbers, an important work would be done in a short time. And we know exactly the kind of work that would be done. We know that where now stand unbroken forests would spring up towns and villages, with their schools and churches—that the natives would be taught the arts of civilization—that their energies would be properly directed—that their prejudices would disappear—that there would be a rapid and important revulsion from the practices of heathenism, and a radical change in their social condition—that the glorious principles of a Christian civilization would diffuse themselves throughout those benighted communities. Oh! that our people would take this matter into serious consideration, and think of the great privilege of kindling in the depths of the moral and spiritual gloom of Africa a glorious light—of causing the wilderness and the solitary place to be glad—the desert to bloom and blossom as the rose—and the whole land to be converted into a garden of the Lord.

Liberia, then, appeals to the colored men of this country for assistance in the noble work which she has begun. She appeals to those who believe that the descendants of Africa live in the serious neglect of their duty if they fail to help to raise the land of their forefathers from her degradation. She appeals to those who believe that a well-established African nationality is the most direct and efficient means of securing respectability and independence for the African race. She appeals to those who believe that a rich and fertile country, like Africa, which has lain so long under the cheerless gloom of ignorance, should not be left any longer without the influence of Christian civilization—to those who deem it a far more glorious work to save extensive tracts of country from barbarism and continued degradation than to amass for themselves the means of individual comfort and aggrandizement—to those who believe that there was a providence in the deportation of our forefathers from the land of their birth, and that that same providence now points to a work in Africa to be done by us their descendants. Finally, Liberia appeals to all African patriots and Christians—to all lovers of order and refinement—to lovers of industry and enterprise—of peace, comfort, and happiness—to those who having felt the power of the Gospel in opening up to them life and immortality, are desirous that their benighted kindred should share in the same blessings. "Behold, the Lord thy God hath set the land before thee: go up and possess it, as the Lord God of thy fathers hath said unto thee; fear not, neither be discouraged."

Notes

1. 1. De Tocqueville, *Democracy in America* [Vol. I, p. 346].

2. In the famous sermon of this distinguished divine on *Slavery a Divine Trust,* he says: "The enriching commerce which has built the splendid cities and marble palaces of England as well as of America, has been largely established upon the

products of Southern soil; and the blooms upon Southern fields, gathered by black hands, have fed the spindles and looms of Manchester and Birmingham not less than of Lawrence and Lowell."

3. Dean Trench, quoted by Baden Powell in *Essays and Reviews,* 1861.

4. R. W. Emerson, in the *Atlantic Monthly,* April, 1862.

5. The names of John Ledyard, Frederick Horneman, Dr. Walter Oudney, Captain Clapperton, Major Denman, John Richardson, and Dr. Overweg occur in the list of those who have fallen victims either to the climate or the hardships of their pilgrimage. But a more melancholy enumeration may be made. Major Houghton perished, or was murdered, in the basin of the Gambia. The truly admirable Mungo Park was killed in an attack of the natives, at a difficult passage of the Niger. The same fate befell Richard Lander in the lower course of the river. Major Laing was foully slain in his tent at a halting-place in the Sahara. John Davidson was assassinated soon after passing the fringe of the desert. Dr. Cowan and Captain Donovan disappeared in the wilds of South-Africa. Dr. Vogel was assassinated in the country about Lake Chad.—*Leisure Hour.*

6. Macaulay's History of England, vol. i. chap. 1.

7. The Legislature of Liberia, at its last session, 1861–62, passed an Act authorizing the appointment of Commissioners to "itinerate among and lecture to the people of color in the United States of North-America, to present to them the claims of Liberia, and its superior advantages as a desirable home for persons of African descent." The President appointed for this work, Professors Crummell and Blyden and J. D. Johnson, Esq.

16

Address on Colonization to a Deputation of Colored Men (1862)

President Abraham Lincoln's attitudes toward slavery and the African American population are frequently misunderstood. In the debates with Stephen A. Douglas, Lincoln made clear that while he did not believe in social and political equality for black Americans, he considered slavery a moral evil, to which he was unequivocally opposed. Lincoln agreed with the liberal wing of the American Colonization Society, which advocated colonization as a means of encouraging gradual emancipation of enslaved Africans. The Civil War was brought on when Southern extremists panicked shortly after Lincoln's election, wrongly believing that he advocated immediate abolition and interracial equality. By the middle of the Civil War, Lincoln, perhaps because he recognized the practical difficulties entailed in deporting four million people, no longer supported Liberian colonization. Edward Wilmot Blyden and Alexander Crummell, acting as representatives of the Liberian government in the United States, found it impossible to secure Lincoln's support for Liberian resettlement. The former president of Liberia, J. J. Roberts, met with Lincoln, but experienced no greater success. Congress had appropriated $600,000 for purposes of colonization, and representatives of Liberia were in Washington eager to make use of it, but rather than cooperating with the Liberians, Lincoln strangely chose to meet with a delegation of relatively obscure African Americans to announce that "the place I am thinking about having for a colony is in Central America."

August 14, 1862

This afternoon the President of the United States gave audience to a Committee of colored men at the White House. They were introduced by the Rev. J. Mitchell, Commissioner of Emigration. E. M. Thomas, the Chairman, remarked that they were there by

Abraham Lincoln, Address on Colonization to a Deputation of Colored Men, in *Abraham Lincoln, Complete Works: Comprising His Speeches, Letters, State Papers, and Miscellaneous Writings,* ed. John G. Nicolay and John Hay (New York: Century Co., 1894), 2:222–25.

invitation to hear what the Executive had to say to them. Having all been seated, the President, after a few preliminary observations, informed them that a sum of money had been appropriated by Congress, and placed at his disposition for the purpose of aiding the colonization in some country of the people, or a portion of them, of African descent, thereby making it his duty, as it had for a long time been his inclination, to favor that cause; and why, he asked, should the people of your race be colonized, and where? Why should they leave this country? This is, perhaps, the first question for proper consideration. You and we are different races. We have between us a broader difference than exists between almost any other two races. Whether it is right or wrong I need not discuss, but this physical difference is a great disadvantage to us both, as I think your race suffer very greatly, many of them by living among us, while ours suffer from your presence. In a word we suffer on each side. If this is admitted, it affords a reason at least why we should be separated. You here are freemen I suppose.

A Voice: Yes, sir.

The President—Perhaps you have long been free, or all your lives. Your race are suffering, in my judgment, the greatest wrong inflicted on any people. But even when you cease to be slaves, you are yet far removed from being placed on an equality with the white race. You are cut off from many of the advantages which the other race enjoy. The aspiration of men is to enjoy equality with the best when free, but on this broad continent, not a single man of your race is made the equal of a single man of ours. Go where you are treated the best, and the ban is still upon you.

I do not propose to discuss this, but to present it as a fact with which we have to deal. I cannot alter it if I would. It is a fact, about which we all think and feel alike, I and you. We look to our condition, owing to the existence of the two races on this continent. I need not recount to you the effects upon white men, growing out of the institution of Slavery. I believe in its general evil effects on the white race. See our present condition—the country engaged in war!—our white men cutting one another's throats, none knowing how far it will extend; and then consider what we know to be the truth. But for your race among us there could not be war, although many men engaged on either side do not care for you one way or the other. Nevertheless, I repeat, without the institution of Slavery and the colored race as a basis, the war could not have an existence.

It is better for us both, therefore, to be separated. I know that there are free men among you, who even if they could better their condition are not as much inclined to go out of the country as those, who being slaves could obtain their freedom on this condition. I suppose one of the principal difficulties in the way of colonization is that the free colored man cannot see that his comfort would be advanced by it. You may believe you can live in Washington or elsewhere in the United States the remainder of your life [as easily], perhaps more so than you can in any foreign country, and hence you may come to the conclusion that you have nothing to do with the idea of going to a foreign country. This is (I speak in no unkind sense) an extremely selfish view of the case.

But you ought to do something to help those who are not so fortunate as yourselves. There is an unwillingness on the part of our people, harsh as it may be, for you free colored people to remain with us. Now, if you could give a start to white people, you would open a wide door for many to be made free. If we deal with those who are not free at the beginning, and whose intellects are clouded by Slavery, we have very poor materials to start with. If intelligent colored men, such as are before me, would move in this matter, much might be accomplished. It is exceedingly important that we have men at the beginning capable of thinking as white men, and not those who have been systematically oppressed.

There is much to encourage you. For the sake of your race you should sacrifice something of your present comfort for the purpose of being as grand in that respect as the white people. It is a cheering thought throughout life that something can be done to ameliorate the condition of those who have been subject to the hard usage of the world. It is difficult to make a man miserable while he feels he is worthy of himself, and claims kindred to the great God who made him. In the American Revolutionary war sacrifices were made by men engaged in it; but they were cheered by the future. Gen. Washington himself endured greater physical hardships than if he had remained a British subject. Yet he was a happy man, because he was engaged in benefiting his race—something for the children of his neighbors, having none of his own.

The colony of Liberia has been in existence a long time. In a certain sense it is a success. The old President of Liberia, Roberts, has just been with me—the first time I ever saw him. He says they have within the bounds of that colony between 300,000 and 400,000 people, or more than in some of our old States, such as Rhode Island or Delaware, or in some of our newer States, and less than in some of our larger ones. They are not all American colonists, or their descendants. Something less than 12,000 have been sent thither from this country. Many of the original settlers have died, yet, like people elsewhere, their offspring outnumber those deceased.

The question is if the colored people are persuaded to go anywhere, why not there? One reason for an unwillingness to do so is that some of you would rather remain within reach of the country of your nativity. I do not know how much attachment you may have toward our race. It does not strike me that you have the greatest reason to love them. But still you are attached to them at all events.

The place I am thinking about having for a colony is in Central America. It is nearer to us than Liberia—not much more than one-fourth as far as Liberia, and within seven days' run by steamers. Unlike Liberia it is on a great line of travel—it is a highway. The country is a very excellent one for any people, and with great natural resources and advantages, and especially because of the similarity of climate with your native land—thus being suited to your physical condition.

The particular place I have in view is to be a great highway from the Atlantic or Caribbean Sea to the Pacific Ocean, and this particular place has all the advantages for a colony. On both sides there are harbors among the finest in the world. Again, there is evidence of very rich coal mines. A certain amount of coal is valuable in any country, and there may be more than enough for the wants of the country. Why I attach so much importance to coal is, it will afford an opportunity to the inhabitants for immediate employment till they get ready to settle permanently in their homes.

If you take colonists where there is no good landing, there is a bad show; and so where there is nothing to cultivate, and of which to make a farm. But if something is started so that you can get your daily bread as soon as you reach there, it is a great advantage. Coal land is the best thing I know of with which to commence an enterprise.

To return, you have been talked to upon this subject, and told that a speculation is intended by gentlemen, who have an interest in the country, including the coal mines. We have been mistaken all our lives if we do not know whites as well as blacks look to their self-interest. Unless among those deficient of intellect everybody you trade with makes something. You meet with these things here as elsewhere.

If such persons have what will be an advantage to them, the question is whether it cannot be made of advantage to you. You are intelligent, and know that success does not as much depend on external help as on self-reliance. Much, therefore, depends upon yourselves. As to the coal mines, I think I see the means available for your self-reliance.

I shall, if I get a sufficient number of you engaged, have provisions made that you shall not be wronged. If you will engage in the enterprise I will spend some of the money intrusted to me. I am not sure you will succeed. The Government may lose the money, but we cannot succeed unless we try; but we think, with care, we can succeed.

The political affairs in Central America are not in quite as satisfactory condition as I wish. There are contending factions in that quarter; but it is true all the factions are agreed alike on the subject of colonization, and want it, and are more generous than we are here. To your colored race they have no objection. Besides, I would endeavor to have you made equals, and have the best assurance that you should be the equals of the best.

The practical thing I want to ascertain is whether I can get a number of able-bodied men, with their wives and children, who are willing to go, when I present evidence of encouragement and protection. Could I get a hundred tolerably intelligent men, with their wives and children, to "cut their own fodder," so to speak? Can I have fifty? If I could find twenty-five able-bodied men, with a mixture of women and children, good things in the family relation, I think I could make a successful commencement.

I want you to let me know whether this can be done or not. This is the practical part of my wish to see you. These are subjects of very great importance, worthy of a month's study, [instead] of a speech delivered in an hour. I ask you then to consider seriously not pertaining to yourselves merely, nor for your race, and ours, for the present time, but as one of the things, if successfully managed, for the good of mankind—not confined to the present generation, but as

> From age to age descends the lay,
> To millions yet to be,
> Till far its echoes roll away,
> Into eternity.

The above is merely given as the substance of the President's remarks.

The Chairman of the delegation briefly replied that "they would hold a consultation and in a short time give an answer." The President said: "Take your full time—no hurry at all."

The delegation then withdrew.

An Open Letter to the Colored People
(1862)

Daniel Alexander Payne was a bishop of the African Methodist Episcopal Church and the founder of Wilberforce University in Ohio. He was a vice president of Garnet's African Civilization Society, and a respected abolitionist. The present text appeared originally in the Weekly Anglo African.

To the Colored People of the United States.

MEN, BRETHREN, SISTERS: A crisis is upon us which no one can enable us to meet, conquer, and convert into blessings for all concerned, but that God who builds up one nation and breaks down another.

For more than one generation, associations of white men, entitled Colonization Societies, have been engaged in plans and efforts for our expatriation; these have been met sometimes by denunciations, sometimes by ridicule, often by argument; but now the American government has assumed the work and responsibility of colonizing us in some foreign land within the torrid zone, and is now maturing measures to consummate this scheme of expatriation.

But let us never forget that there is a vast difference between voluntary associations of men and the legally constituted authorities of a country; while the former may be held in utter contempt, the latter must always be respected. To do so is a moral and religious, as well as a political duty.

Daniel A. Payne, "An Open Letter to the Colored People," in William Wells Brown, *The Black Man, His Antecedents, His Genius, and His Achievements* (New York: Thomas Hamilton, 1863).

The opinions of the government are based upon the ideas, that *white men and colored men cannot live together as equals in the same country;* and that unless a voluntary and peaceable separation is effected *now,* the time *must come when there will be a war of extermination* between the two races.

Now, in view of these opinions and purposes of the government, what shall we do? My humble advice is, before all, and first of all,—even before we say *yea* or *nay,*—let us seek from the mouth of God. Let every heart be humbled, and every knee bent in prayer before him. Throughout all this land of our captivity, in all this house of our bondage, let our cries ascend perpetually to Heaven for aid and direction.

To your knees, I say, O ye oppressed and enslaved ones of this Christian republic, to your knees, *and be there.*

Before the throne of God, if nowhere else, the black man can meet his white brother as an equal, and be heard.

It has been said that he is the God of the white man, and not of the black. This is horrible blasphemy—a *lie* from the pit that is bottomless—believe it not—no—never. Murmur not against the Lord on account of the cruelty and injustice of man. His almighty arm is already stretched out against slavery—against every man, every constitution, and every union that upholds it. His avenging chariot is now moving over the bloody fields of the doomed south, crushing beneath its massive wheels the very foundations of the blasphemous system. Soon slavery shall sink like Pharaoh—even like that brazen-hearted tyrant, it shall sink to rise no more forever.

Haste ye, then, O, hasten to your God; pour the sorrows of your crushed and bleeding hearts into his sympathizing bosom. It is true that "on the side of the oppressor there is power"—the power of the purse and the power of the sword. That is terrible. But listen to what is still *more terrible:* on the side of the oppressed there is the *strong arm* of the Lord, the Almighty God of Abraham, and Isaac, and Jacob—before his redeeming power the two contending armies, hostile to each other, and hostile to you, are like chaff before the whirlwind.

Fear not, but believe. He who is for you is more than they who are against you. Trust in him—hang upon his arm—go, hide beneath the shadow of his wings.

O God! Jehovah-jireh! wilt thou not hear us? We are poor, helpless, unarmed, despised. Is it not time for thee to hear the cry of the needy—to judge the poor of the people—to break in pieces the oppressor.

Be, O, be unto us what thou wast unto Israel in the land of Egypt, our Counsellor and Guide—our Shield and Buckler—*Our Great Deliverer—our Pillar of cloud by day—our Pillar of fire by night!*

Stand between us and our enemies, O thou angel of the Lord! Be unto us a shining light—to our enemies, confusion and impenetrable darkness. Stand between us till this Red Sea be crossed, and thy redeemed, *now* sighing, bleeding, weeping, shall shout and sing, for joy, the bold anthem of the free."

Part Three

Black Nationalist Revival, 1895–1925

18

The American Negro and His Fatherland
(1895)

Henry McNeal Turner, a bishop of the African Methodist Episcopal Church, supported colonization during the Civil War, and represented the most vocal of black nationalists after the Civil War. He was elected a vice president of the American Colonization Society in 1876. An inspired writer and able editor, he founded the Southern Christian Recorder *(1889), the* Voice of Missions *(1892), and the* Voice of the People *(1901). Turner is remembered for a clever editorial arguing that "God is a Negro," a theme later adopted by Marcus Garvey.*

It would be a waste of time to expend much labor, the few moments I have to devote to this subject, upon the present status of the Negroid race in the United States. It is too well-known already. However, I believe that the Negro was brought to this country in the providence of God to a heaven-permitted if not a divine-sanctioned manual laboring school, that he might have direct contact with the mightiest race that ever trod the face of the globe.

The heathen Africans, to my certain knowledge, I care not what others may say, eagerly yearn for that civilization which they believe will elevate them and make them potential for good. The African was not sent and brought to this country by chance, or by the avarice of the white man, single and alone. The white slave-purchaser went to the shores of that continent and bought our ancestors from their African masters. The bulk who were brought to this country were the children of parents who had been in slavery a thousand years. Yet hereditary slavery is not universal among the

Henry McNeal Turner, "The American Negro and His Fatherland," in *Africa and the American Negro,* ed. John W. E. Bowen (Atlanta: Gammon Theological Seminary, 1896).

African slaveholders. So that the argument often advanced, that the white man went to Africa and stole us, is not true. They bought us out of a slavery that still exists over a large portion of that continent. For there are millions and millions of slaves in Africa today. Thus the superior African sent us, and the white man brought us, and we remained in slavery as long as it was necessary to learn that a God, who is a spirit, made the world and controls it, and that that Supreme Being could be sought and found by the exercise of faith in His only begotten Son. Slavery then went down, and the colored man was thrown upon his own responsibility, and here he is today, in the providence of God, cultivating self-reliance and imbibing a knowledge of civil law in contradistinction to the dictum of one man, which was the law of the black man until slavery was overthrown. I believe that the Negroid race has been free long enough now to begin to think for himself and plan for better conditions than he can lay claim to in this country or ever will. *There is no manhood future in the United States for the Negro.* He may eke out an existence for generations to come, but he can never be a *man*—full, symmetrical and undwarfed. Upon this point I know thousands who make pretensions to scholarship, white and colored, will differ and may charge me with folly, while I in turn pity their ignorance of history and political and civil sociology. We beg here to itemize and give a cursory glance at a few facts calculated to convince any man who is not biased or lamentably ignorant. Let us note a few of them.

1. There is a great chasm between the white and black, not only in this country, but in the West India Islands, South America, and as much as has been said to the contrary, I have seen inklings of it in Ireland, in England, in France, in Germany, and even away down in southern Spain in sight of Morocco in Africa. We will not, however, deal with foreign nations, but let us note a few facts connected with the United States.

I repeat that a great chasm exists between the two race varieties in this country. The white people, neither North or South, will have social contact as a mass between themselves and any portion of the Negroid race. Although they may be as white in appearance as themselves, yet a drop of African blood imparts a taint, and the talk about two races remaining in the same country with mutual interest and responsibility in its institutions and progress, with no social contact, is the jargon of folly, and no man who has read the history of nations and the development of countries, and the agencies which have culminated in the homogeneity of racial variations, will proclaim such a doctrine. Senator Morgan, of Alabama, tells the truth when he says that the Negro has nothing to expect without social equality with the whites, and that the whites will never grant it.

This question must be examined and opinions reached in the light of history and sociological philosophy, and not by a mere think-so on the part of men devoid of learning. When I use the term learning, I do not refer to men who have graduated from some college and have a smattering knowledge of Greek, Latin, mathematics and a few school books, and have done nothing since but read the trashy articles of newspapers. That is not scholarship. Scholarship consists in wading through dusty volumes for forty and fifty years. That class of men would not dare to predict symmetrical manhood for the Negroid race in this or any other country, without social equality. The colored man who will stand up and in one breath say that the Negroid race does not want social equality and in the next predict a great future in the face of all the proscription of which the colored man is the victim, is either an ignoramus, or is an advocate of the perpetual servility and degradation of his race variety. I know, as Senator Morgan says, and as every white man in the land will say, that the whites will not grant social equality to the Negroid race, nor am I certain that God wants them to do it. And as such, I believe that two or three millions of us should return to the land of our ancestors, and establish our own nation, civilization, laws, customs, style of manufacture, and not only give the world, like other race varieties, the benefit of our individuality, but build up social conditions peculiarly our own, and cease to be grumblers, chronic complainers and a menace to the white man's country, or the country he claims and is bound to dominate.

The civil status of the Negro is simply what the white man grants of his own free will and accord. The black man can demand nothing. He is deposed from the jury and tried, convicted and sentenced by men who do not claim to be his peers. On the railroads, where the colored race is found in the largest numbers, he is the victim of proscription, and he must ride in the Jim Crow car or walk. The Supreme Court of the United States decided, October 15th, 1883, that the colored man had no civil rights under the general government, and the several States, from then until now, have been enacting laws which limit, curtail and deprive him of his civil rights, immunities and privileges, until he is now being disfranchised, and where it will end no one can divine.

They told me in the Geographical Institute in Paris, France, that according to their calculation there are not less than 400,000,000 of Africans and their descendants on the globe, so that we are not lacking in numbers to form a nationality of our own.

2. The environments of the Negroid race variety in this country tend to the inferiority of them, even if the argument can be established that we are equals with the white man in the aggregate, notwithstanding the same opportunities may be enjoyed in the schools. Let us note a few facts.

The discriminating laws, all will concede, are degrading to those against whom they operate, and the degrader will be degraded also. "For all acts are reactionary, and will return in curses upon those who curse," said Stephen A. Douglas, the great competitor of President Lincoln. Neither does it require a philosopher to inform you that degradation begets degradation. Any people oppressed, proscribed, belied, slandered, burned, flayed and lynched will not only become cowardly and servile, but will transmit that same servility to their posterity, and continue to do so *ad infinitum,* and as such will never make a bold and courageous people. The condition of the Negro in the United States is so repugnant to the instincts of respected manhood that thousands, yea hundreds of thousands, of miscegenated will pass for white, and snub the people with whom they are identified at every opportunity, thus destroying themselves, or at least *unracing* themselves. They do not want to be black because of its ignoble condition, and they cannot be white, thus they become monstrosities. Thousands of young men who are even educated by white teachers never have any respect for people of their own color and spend their days as devotees of white gods. Hundreds, if not thousands, of the terms employed by the white race in the English language are also degrading to the black man. Everything that is satanic, corrupt, base and infamous is denominated *black,* and all that constitutes virtue, purity, innocence, religion, and that which is divine and heavenly, is represented as *white.* Our Sabbath-school children, by the time they reach proper consciousness, are taught to sing to the laudation of white and to the contempt of black. Can any one with an ounce of common sense expect that these children, when they reach maturity, will ever have any respect for their black or colored faces, or the faces of their associates? But, without multiplying words, the terms used in our religious experience, and the hymns we sing in many instances, are degrading, and will be as long as the black man is surrounded by the idea that *white* represents God and black represents the devil. The Negro should, therefore, build up a nation of his own, and create a language in keeping with his color, as the whites have done. Nor will he ever respect himself until he does it.

3. In this country the colored man, with a few honorable exceptions, folds his arms and waits for the white man to propose, project, erect, invent, discover, combine, plan and execute everything connected with civilization, including machinery, finance, and indeed everything. This, in the nature of things, dwarfs the colored man and allows his great faculties to slumber from the cradle to the grave. Yet he possesses mechanical and inventive genius, I believe, equal to any race on earth. Much has been said about the natural inability of the colored race to engage in the professions of skilled labor. Yet before the war, right here in this

Southland he erected and completed all of the fine edifices in which the lords of the land luxuriated. It is idle talk to speak of a colored man not being a success in skilled labor or the fine arts. What the black man needs is a country and surroundings in harmony with his color and with respect for his manhood. Upon this point I would delight to dwell longer if I had time. Thousands of white people in this country are ever and anon advising the colored people to keep out of politics, but they do not advise themselves. If the Negro is a man in keeping with other men, why should he be less concerned about politics than any one else? Strange, too, that a number of would-be colored leaders are ignorant and debased enough to proclaim the same foolish jargon. For the Negro to stay out of politics is to level himself with a horse or a cow, which is no politician, and the Negro who does it proclaims his inability to take part in political affairs. If the Negro is to be a man, full and complete, he must take part in everything that belongs to manhood. If he omits a single duty, responsibility or privilege, to that extent he is limited and incomplete.

Time, however, forbids my continuing the discussion of this subject, roughly and hastily as these thoughts have been thrown together. Not being able to present a dozen or two more phases, which I would cheerfully and gladly do if opportunity permitted, I conclude by saying the argument that it would be impossible to transport the colored people of the United States back to Africa is an advertisement of folly. Two hundred millions of dollars would rid this country of the last member of the Negroid race, if such a thing was desirable, and two hundred and fifty millions would give every man, woman and child excellent fare, and the general government could furnish that amount and never miss it, and that would only be the pitiful sum of a million dollars a year for the time we labored for nothing, and for which somebody or some power is responsible. The emigrant agents at New York, Boston, Philadelphia, St. John, N.B., and Halifax, N.S., with whom I have talked, establish beyond contradiction, that over a million, and from that to twelve hundred thousand persons, come to this country every year, and yet there is no public stir about it. But in the case of African emigration, two or three millions only of self-reliant men and women would be necessary to establish the conditions we are advocating in Africa.

19

The Conservation of Races (1897)

W. E. B. Du Bois was a prolific scholar, educated at Fisk University, the University of Berlin, and Harvard University, where he earned a Ph.D. in 1896. In 1897, at the age of twenty-eight, he delivered his address "The Conservation of Races" at the initial meeting of the American Negro Academy before an audience of senior black men, including Alexander Crummell. The attitude of W. E. B. Du Bois toward black nationalism has been described as ambivalent. Throughout his career he consistently advocated separate institutions for black Americans, but as a founder of the NAACP he fought aggressively for integration and social equality between black and white. He revealed his ambivalence toward separatism in an editorial for Crisis *(January 1919). It was an essay remarkable for its employment of such terms as "paradox" and "dilemma," arising out of "contradictory facts." He maintained that it was "impossible to build up a logical scheme of a self-sufficing separate Negro America inside America or a Negro world with no close relations to the white world." At the same time he maintained that "if the Negro is to develop his own power and gifts . . . , then he must unite and work with Negroes and build a new and great Negro ethos." Du Bois eventually found it impossible to work with the NAACP, which opposed his endorsement of African American institutional separatism. He left the organization in 1934, and in 1940 published* Dusk of Dawn, *in which he further developed his ideas on the need for separate black institutions. Du Bois organized or participated in six international Pan-African conferences, and wrote several historical treatises in an Afrocentric vein, most notably* Black Folk Then and Now *(1939) and* The World and Africa *(1946). In 1961 he was invited to the Republic of Ghana by its president, Kwame Nkrumah, to direct the compilation of an* Encyclopedia Africana. *He spent the final twenty-two months of his life working on that project in Ghana, where he died in August 1963. "The Conservation of Races" reveals how concepts of black independence and racial destiny were present in his thinking from the beginning of his career.*

The American Negro has always felt an intense personal interest in discussions as to the origins and destinies of races: primarily be-

W. E. B. Du Bois, *The Conservation of Races*, American Negro Academy Occasional Papers, no. 2 (Washington, D.C., 1897).

cause back of most discussions of race with which he is familiar, have lurked certain assumptions as to his natural abilities, as to his political, intellectual and moral status, which he felt were wrong. He has, consequently, been led to deprecate and minimize race distinctions, to believe intensely that out of one blood God created all nations, and to speak of human brotherhood as though it were the possibility of an already dawning to-morrow.

Nevertheless, in our calmer moments we must acknowledge that human beings are divided into races; that in this country the two most extreme types of the world's races have met, and the resulting problem as to the future relations of these types is not only of intense and living interest to us, but forms an epoch in the history of mankind.

It is necessary, therefore, in planning our movements, in guiding our future development, that at times we rise above the pressing, but smaller questions of separate schools and cars, wage-discrimination and lynch law, to survey the whole question of race in human philosophy and to lay, on a basis of broad knowledge and careful insight, those large lines of policy and higher ideals which may form our guiding lines and boundaries in the practical difficulties of every day. For it is certain that all human striving must recognize the hard limits of natural law, and that any striving, no matter how intense and earnest, which is against the constitution of the world, is vain. The question, then, which we must seriously consider is this: What is the real meaning of Race; what has, in the past, been the law of race development, and what lessons has the past history of race development to teach the rising Negro people?

When we thus come to inquire into the essential difference of races we find it hard to come at once to any definite conclusion. Many criteria of race differences have in the past been proposed, as color, hair, cranial measurements and language. And manifestly, in each of these respects, human beings differ widely. They vary in color, for instance, from the marble-like pallor of the Scandinavian to the rich, dark brown of the Zulu, passing by the creamy Slav, the yellow Chinese, the light brown Sicilian and the brown Egyptian. Men vary, too, in the texture of hair from the obstinately straight hair of the Chinese to the obstinately tufted and frizzled hair of the Bushman. In measurement of heads, again, men vary; from the broad-headed Tartar to the medium-headed European and the narrow-headed Hottentot; or, again in language, from the highly-inflected Roman tongue to the monosyllabic Chinese. All these physical characteristics are patent enough, and if they agreed with each other it would be very easy to classify mankind. Unfortunately for scientists, however, these criteria of race are most exasperatingly intermingled. Color does not agree with texture of hair, for many of the dark races have straight hair; nor does color agree with the breadth of the head, for the yellow Tartar has a broader head than the German; nor, again, has the science of language as yet succeeded in clearing up the relative authority of these various and contradictory criteria. The final word of science, so far, is that we have at least two, perhaps three, great families of human beings—the whites and Negroes, possibly the yellow race. That other races have arisen from the intermingling of the blood of these two. This broad division of the world's races which men like Huxley and Raetzel have introduced as more nearly true than the old five-race scheme of Blumenbach, is nothing more than an acknowledgment that, so far as purely physical characteristics are concerned, the differences between men do not explain all the differences of their history. It declares, as Darwin himself said, that great as is the physical unlikeness of the various races of men their likenesses are greater, and upon this rests the whole scientific doctrine of Human Brotherhood.

Although the wonderful developments of human history teach that the grosser physical differences of color, hair and bone go but a short way toward explaining the different roles which groups of men have played in Human Progress, yet there are differences—subtle, delicate and elusive, though they may be—which have silently but definitely separated men into groups. While these subtle forces have generally followed the natural cleavage of common blood, descent and physical peculiarities, they have at other times swept across and ignored these. At all times, however, they have divided human beings into races, which, while they perhaps transcend scientific definition, nevertheless, are clearly defined to the eye of the Historian and Sociologist.

If this be true, then the history of the world is the history, not of individuals, but of groups, not of nations, but of races, and he who ignores or seeks to override the race idea in human history ignores and overrides the central thought of all history. What, then, is a race? It is a vast family of human beings, generally of common blood and language, always of common history, traditions and impulses, who are both voluntarily and involuntarily striving together for the accomplishment of certain more or less vividly conceived ideals of life.

Turning to real history, there can be no doubt, first, as to the widespread, nay, universal, prevalence of the race idea, the race spirit, the race ideal, and as to its efficiency as the vastest and most ingenious invention for human progress. We, who have been reared and trained under the individualistic philosophy of the Declaration of Independence and the laisser-faire philosophy of Adam Smith, are loath to see and loath to acknowledge this patent fact of human history. We see the Pharaohs, Caesars, Toussaints and Napoleons of history and forget the vast races of which they were but epitomized expressions. We are apt to think in our American impatience, that while it may have been true in the past that closed race groups made history, that here in conglomerate America *nous avons changer tout cela*—we have changed all that, and have no need of this ancient instrument of progress. This assumption of which the Negro people are especially fond, can not be established by a careful consideration of history.

We find upon the world's stage today eight distinctly differentiated races, in the sense in which History tells us the word must be used. They are, the Slavs of eastern Europe, the Teutons of middle Europe, the English of Great Britain and America, the Romance nations of Southern and Western Europe, the Negroes of Africa and America, the Semitic people of Western Asia and Northern

Africa, the Hindoos of Central Asia and the Mongolians of Eastern Asia. There are, of course, other minor race groups, as the American Indians, the Esquimaux and the South Sea Islanders; these larger races, too, are far from homogeneous; the Slav includes the Czech, the Magyar, the Pole and the Russian; the Teuton includes the German, the Scandinavian and the Dutch; the English include the Scotch, the Irish and the conglomerate American. Under Romance nations the widely-differing Frenchman, Italian, Sicilian and Spaniard are comprehended. The term Negro is, perhaps, the most indefinite of all, combining the Mulattoes and Zamboes of America and the Egyptians, Bantus and Bushmen of Africa. Among the Hindoos are traces of widely differing nations, while the great Chinese, Tartar, Corean and Japanese families fall under the one designation—Mongolian.

The question now is: What is the real distinction between these nations? Is it the physical differences of blood, color and cranial measurements? Certainly we must all acknowledge that physical differences play a great part, and that, with wide exceptions and qualifications, these eight great races of to-day follow the cleavage of physical race distinctions; the English and Teuton represent the white variety of mankind; the Mongolian, the yellow; the Negroes, the black. Between these are many crosses and mixtures, where Mongolian and Teuton have blended into the Slav, and other mixtures have produced the Romance nations and the Semites. But while race differences have followed mainly physical race lines, yet no mere physical distinctions would really define or explain the deeper differences—the cohesiveness and continuity of these groups. The deeper differences are spiritual, psychical, differences—undoubtedly based on the physical, but infinitely transcending them. The forces that bind together the Teuton nations are, then, first, their race identity and common blood; secondly, and more important, a common history, common laws and religion, similar habits of thought and a conscious striving together for certain ideals of life. The whole process which has brought about these race differentiations has been a growth, and the great characteristic of this growth has been the differentiation of spiritual and mental differences between great races of mankind and the integration of physical differences.

The age of nomadic tribes of closely related individuals represents the maximum of physical differences. They were practically vast families, and there were as many groups as families. As the families came together to form cities the physical differences lessened, purity of blood was replaced by the requirement of domicile, and all who lived within the city bounds became gradually to be regarded as members of the group; *i.e.*, there was a slight and slow breaking down of physical barriers. This, however, was accompanied by an increase of the spiritual and social differences between cities. This city became husbandmen, this, merchants, another warriors, and so on. The *ideals of life* for which the different cities struggled were different. When at last cities began to coalesce into nations there was another breaking down of barriers which separated groups of men. The larger and broader differences of color, hair and physical proportions were not by any means ignored, but myriads of minor differences disappeared, and the sociological and historical races of men began to approximate the present division of races as indicated by physical researches. At the same time the spiritual and physical differences of race groups which constituted the nations became deep and decisive. The English nation stood for constitutional liberty and commercial freedom; the German nation for science and philosophy; the Romance nations stood for literature and art, and the other race groups are striving, each in its own way, to develope for civilization its particular message, its particular ideal, which shall help to guide the world nearer and nearer that perfection of human life for which we all long, that

"one far off Divine event."

This has been the function of race differences up to the present time. What shall be its function in the future? Manifestly some of the great races of today—particularly the Negro race—have not as yet given to civilization the full spiritual message which they are capable of giving. I will not say that the Negro race has as yet given no message to the world, for it is still a mooted question among scientists as to just how far Egyptian civilization was Negro in its origin; if it was not wholly Negro, it was certainly very closely allied. Be that as it may, however the fact still remains that the full, complete Negro message of the whole Negro race has not as yet been given to the world: that the messages and ideal of the yellow race have not been completed, and that the striving of the mighty Slavs has but begun. The question is, then: How shall this message be delivered; how shall these various ideals be realized? The answer is plain: By the development of these race groups, not as individuals, but as races. For the development of Japanese genius, Japanese literature and art, Japanese spirit, only Japanese, bound and welded together, Japanese inspired by one vast ideal, can work out in its fullness the wonderful message which Japan has for the nations of the earth. For the development of Negro genius, of Negro literature and art, of Negro spirit, only Negroes bound and welded together, Negroes inspired by one vast ideal, can work out in its fullness the great message we have for humanity. We cannot reverse history; we are subject to the same natural laws as other races, and if the Negro is ever to be a factor in the world's history—if among the gaily-colored banners that deck the broad ramparts of civilization is to hang one uncompromising black, then it must be placed there by black hands, fashioned by black heads and hallowed by the travail of 200,000,000 black hearts beating in one glad song of jubilee.

For this reason, the advance guard of the Negro people—the 8,000,000 people of Negro blood in the United States of America—must soon come to realize that if they are to take their just place in the van of Pan-Negroism, then their destiny is *not* absorption by the white Americans. That if in America it is to be proven for the first time in the modern world that not only Negroes are capable of evolving individual men like Toussaint, the Saviour, but are a nation stored with wonderful possibilities of culture, then their destiny is not a servile imitation of Anglo-Saxon culture, but a stalwart originality which shall unswervingly follow Negro ideals.

It may, however, be objected here that the situation of our race in America renders this attitude impossible; that our sole hope of salvation lies in our being able to lose our race identity in the commingled blood of the nation; and that any other course would merely increase the friction of races which we call race prejudice, and against which we have so long and so earnestly fought.

Here, then, is the dilemma, and it is a puzzling one, I admit. No Negro who has given earnest thought to the situation of his people in America has failed, at some time in life, to find himself at these cross-roads; has failed to ask himself at some time: What, after all, am I? Am I an American or am I a Negro? Can I be both? Or is it my duty to cease to be a Negro as soon as possible and be an American? If I strive as a Negro, am I not perpetuating the very cleft that threatens and separates Black and White America? Is not my only possible practical aim the subduction of all that is Negro in me to the American? Does my black blood place upon me any more obligation to assert my nationality than German, or Irish or Italian blood would?

It is such incessant self-questioning and the hesitation that arises from it, that is making the present period a time of vacillation and contradiction for the American Negro; combined race action is stifled, race responsibility is shirked, race enterprises languish, and the best blood, the best talent, the best energy of the Negro people cannot be marshalled to do the bidding of the race. They stand back to make room for every rascal and demagogue who chooses to cloak his selfish deviltry under the veil of race pride.

Is this right? Is it rational? Is it good policy? Have we in America a distinct mission as a race—a distinct sphere of action and an opportunity for race development, or is self-obliteration the highest end to which Negro blood dare aspire?

If we carefully consider what race prejudice really is, we find it, historically, to be nothing but the friction between different groups of people; it is the difference in aim, in feeling, in ideals of two different races; if, now, this difference exists touching territory, laws, language, or even religion, it is manifest that these people cannot live in the same territory without fatal collision; but if, on the other hand, there is substantial agreement in laws, language and religion; if there is a satisfactory adjustment of economic life, then there is no reason why, in the same country and on the same street, two or three great national ideals might not thrive and develop, that men of different races might not strive together for their race ideals as well, perhaps even better, than in isolation. Here, it seems to me, is the reading of the riddle that puzzles so many of us. We are Americans, not only by birth and by citizenship, but by our political ideals, our language, our religion. Farther than that, our Americanism does not go. At that point, we are Negroes, members of a vast historic race that from the very dawn of creation has slept, but half awakening in the dark forests of its African fatherland. We are the first fruits of this new nation, the harbinger of that black to-morrow which is yet destined to soften the whiteness of the Teutonic to-day. We are that people whose subtle sense of song has given America its only American music, its only American fairy tales, its only touch of pathos and humor amid its mad money-getting plutocracy. As such, it is our duty to conserve our physical powers, our intellectual endowments, our spiritual ideals; as a race we must strive by race organization, by race solidarity, by race unity to the realization of that broader humanity which freely recognizes differences in men, but sternly deprecates inequality in their opportunities of development.

For the accomplishment of these ends we need race organizations: Negro colleges, Negro newspapers, Negro business organizations, a Negro school of literature and art, and an intellectual clearing house, for all these products of the Negro mind, which we may call a Negro Academy. Not only is all this necessary for positive advance, it is absolutely imperative for negative defense. Let us not deceive ourselves at our situation in this country. Weighted with a heritage of moral iniquity from our past history, hard pressed in the economic world by foreign immigrants and native prejudice, hated here, despised there and pitied everywhere; our one haven of refuge is ourselves, and but one means of advance, our own belief in our great destiny, our own implicit trust in our ability and worth. There is no power under God's high heaven that can stop the advance of eight thousand thousand honest, earnest, inspired and united people. But—and here is the rub—they *must* be honest, fearlessly criticising their own faults, zealously correcting them; they must be *earnest*. No people that laughs at itself, and ridicules itself, and wishes to God it was anything but itself ever wrote its name in history; it *must* be inspired with the Divine faith of our black mothers, that out of the blood and dust of battle will march a victorious host, a mighty nation, a peculiar people, to speak to the nations of earth a Divine truth that shall make them free. And such a people must be united; not merely united for the organized theft of political spoils, not united to disgrace religion with whoremongers and ward-heelers; not united merely to protest and pass resolutions, but united to stop the ravages of consumption among the Negro people, united to keep black boys from loafing, gambling and crime; united to guard the purity of black women and to reduce that vast army of black prostitutes that is today marching to hell; and united in serious organizations, to determine by careful conference and thoughtful interchange of opinion the broad lines of policy and action for the American Negro.

This, is the reason for being which the American Negro Academy has. It aims at once to be the epitome and expression of the intellect of the black-blooded people of America, the exponent of the race ideals of one of the world's great races. As such, the Academy must, if successful, be

(a). Representative in character.
(b). Impartial in conduct.
(c). Firm in leadership.

It must be representative in character; not in that it represents all interests or all factions, but in that it seeks to comprise something of the *best* thought, the most unselfish striving and the highest ideals. There are scattered in forgotten nooks and corners throughout the land, Negroes of some considerable training, of high minds, and high motives, who are unknown to their fellows, who exert far too little influence. These the Negro Academy should strive to bring into touch with each other and to give them a common mouthpiece.

The Academy should be impartial in conduct; while it aims to exalt the people it should aim to do so by truth—not by lies, by honesty—not by flattery. It should continually impress the fact upon the Negro people that they must not expect to have things done for them—they MUST DO FOR THEMSELVES; that they have on their hands a vast work of self-reformation to do, and that a little less complaint and whining, and a little more dogged work and manly striving would do us more credit and benefit than a thousand Force or Civil Rights bills.

Finally, the American Negro Academy must point out a practical path of advance to the Negro people; there lie before every Negro today hundreds of questions of policy and right which must be settled and which each one settles now, not in accordance with any rule, but by impulse or individual preference; for instance: What should be the attitude of Negroes toward the educational qualification for voters? What should be our attitude toward separate schools? How should we meet discriminations on railways and in hotels? Such questions need not so much specific answers for each part as a general expression of policy, and nobody should be better fitted to announce such a policy than a representative honest Negro Academy.

All this, however, must come in time after careful organization and long conference. The immediate work before us should be practical and have direct bearing upon the situation of the Negro. The historical work of collecting the laws of the United States and of the various States of the Union with regard to the Negro is a work of such magnitude and importance that no body but one like this could think of undertaking it. If we could accomplish that one task we would justify our existence.

In the field of Sociology an appalling work lies before us. First, we must unflinchingly and bravely face the truth, not with apologies, but with solemn earnestness. The Negro Academy ought to sound a note of warning that would echo in every black cabin in the land: *Unless we conquer our present vices they will conquer us;* we are diseased, we are developing criminal tendencies, and an alarmingly large percentage of our men and women are sexually impure. The Negro Academy should stand and proclaim this over the housetops, crying with Garrison: *I will not equivocate, I will not retreat a single inch, and I will be heard.* The Academy should seek to gather about it the talented, unselfish men, the pure and noble-minded women, to fight an army of devils that disgraces our manhood and our womanhood. There does not stand today upon God's earth a race more capable in muscle, in intellect, in morals, than the American Negro, if he will bend his energies in the right direction; if he will

> Burst his birth's invidious bar
> And grasp the skirts of happy chance,
> And breast the blows of circumstance,
> And grapple with his evil star.

In science and morals, I have indicated two fields of work for the Academy. Finally, in practical policy, I wish to suggest the following *Academy Creed:*

1. We believe that the Negro people, as a race, have a contribution to make to civilization and humanity, which no other race can make.

2. We believe it the duty of the Americans of Negro descent, as a body, to maintain their race identity until this mission of the Negro people is accomplished, and the ideal of human brotherhood has become a practical possibility.

3. We believe that, unless modern civilization is a failure, it is entirely feasible and practicable for two races in such essential political, economic and religious harmony as the white and colored people of America, to develop side by side in peace and mutual happiness, the peculiar contribution which each has to make to the culture of their common country.

4. As a means to this end we advocate, not such social equality be-

tween these races as would disregard human likes and dislikes, but such a social equilibrium as would, throughout all the complicated relations of life, give due and just consideration to culture, ability, and moral worth, whether they be found under white or black skins.

5. We believe that the first and greatest step toward the settlement of the present friction between the races—commonly called the Negro Problem—lies in the correction of the immorality, crime and laziness among the Negroes themselves, which still remains as a heritage from slavery. We believe that only earnest and long continued efforts on our own part can cure these social ills.

6. We believe that the second great step toward a better adjustment of the relations between the races, should be a more impartial selection of ability in the economic and intellectual world, and a greater respect for personal liberty and worth, regardless of race. We believe that only earnest efforts on the part of the white people of this country will bring much needed reform in these matters.

7. On the basis of the foregoing declaration, and firmly believing in our high destiny, we, as American Negroes, are resolved to strive in every honorable way for the realization of the best and highest aims, for the development of strong manhood and pure womanhood, and for the rearing of a race ideal in America and Africa, to the glory of God and the uplifting of the Negro people.

Address at Newport News (1919)

During and immediately following World War I, Marcus Moziah Garvey led the most successful black nationalist mass movement in the history of the United States. He founded the Universal Negro Improvement Association (UNIA), which encouraged black economic self-sufficiency and supported a number of business enterprises. His newspaper, Negro World, *was a successful publication of high quality, drawing on the talents of several excellent journalists, including William H. Ferris, John E. Bruce, J. A. Rogers, and T. Thomas Fortune. On the other hand, the Black Star Line, the UNIA's steamship corporation, made a series of disastrous investments in vessels that were dilapidated or downright unseaworthy. The* Yarmouth, *rechristened* Frederick Douglass, *purchased in 1919, was sold at public auction in 1921. The* Shadyside, *purchased in April 1920, sank while docked in the winter of 1920–21. The* Kanawha, *rechristened* Antonio Maceo, *purchased in April 1920, was abandoned in Cuba in the fall of 1921. The* Goethals, *rechristened* Booker T. *Washington, purchased in 1925, was sold at public auction in 1926. Garvey and the UNIA advocated selective repatriation of African Americans, and negotiated with the Liberian government toward that end. Garvey did much to nurture Pan-African sentiments among the black masses, but in 1925 he was imprisoned on trumped-up charges of using the mails to defraud. W. E. B. Du Bois, although shocked by many aspects of the Garvey movement, believed Garvey to have been well-intentioned, and found no evidence of personal dishonesty on Garvey's part.*

Mr. President, Officers and Members of the Newport News Division of the Universal Negro Improvement Association—Indeed, it is a pleasure to be with you. From the first time I visited your city I became impressed with your earnestness. Ever since I came here and went away an impression, an indelible impression, was made on me relative to your earnestness in the great onward and upward

Marcus Garvey, Address at Newport News, October 25, 1919, *Negro World*, November 1, 1919. Reprinted courtesy of Robert A. Hill, ed., *The Marcus Garvey and Universal Negro Improvement Association Papers* (Berkeley: University of California Press, 1983), 1:112–20.

movement engineered under the leadership of the Universal Negro Improvement Association.

Since I visited you last the Universal Negro Improvement Association has grown financially and otherwise, numerically, to the extent that tonight, this very hour the Universal Negro Improvement Association is regarded as the strongest Negro movement in the world. (Cheers.) We have been able to force entry into every civilized country where Negroes live, and tonight the colors that you and I are wearing in Newport News are being worn by Negroes all over the world.

U.N.I.A. Serious Movement

As I have told you in many addresses before, the Universal Negro Improvement Association is a very serious movement. We are out for serious business. We are out for the capturing of liberty and democracy. (Cheers.) Liberty is not yet captured, therefore we are still fighting. We are in a very great war, a great conflict, and we will never get liberty, we will never capture democracy, until we, like all the other peoples who have won liberty and democracy, shed our sacred blood. This liberty, this democracy, for which we Negroes of the world are hoping, is a thing that has caused blood as a sacrifice by every people who possess it today.

The Defeat of Germany

The white man of America who possesses his liberty and his democracy won it through the sacrifice of those thousands of soldiers who fought and fell under the leadership of George Washington. The French people, who are enjoying their liberty and their democracy today, are enjoying it because thousands of Frenchmen fought, bled and died to make France safe. That America, England and France have had peace with the world and with themselves is simply through the fact that they have defeated Germany and won for themselves liberty and democracy.

Liberty and Democracy Expensive

Therefore, you will realize that liberty and democracy are very expensive things, and you have to give life for it. And if we Negroes think we can get all these things without the shedding of blood for them we are making a dreadful mistake. You are not going to get anything unless you organize to fight for it. There are some things you can fight for constitutionally, such as your political rights, your civic rights, but to get liberty you have to shed some blood for it. And that is what the Universal Negro Improvement Association is preparing your minds for—to shed some blood so as to make your race a free and independent race. That blood we are not going to shed in Newport News, that blood we are not going to shed in America, because America will not be big enough to hold the Negro when the Negro gets ready. But that blood we are preparing to shed one day on the African battlefield, because it is the determination of the New Negro to re-possess himself of that country that God gave his forefathers. Africa is the richest continent in the world; it is the country that has given civilization to mankind and has made the white man what he is.

What the White Man Owes the Negro

After the white man is through abusing the Negro, when he gets back his sober senses, he will realize that he owes all he possesses today to the Negro. The Negro gave him science and art and literature and everything that is dear to him today, and the white man has kept them for thousands of years, and he has taken advantage of the world. He has even gone out of his way to reduce the African that gave him his civilization and kept him as a slave for two hundred and fifty years. But we feel that the time has come when we must take hold of that civilization that we once held. The hour has struck for the Negro to be once more a power in the world, and not all the white men in the world will be able to hold the Negro from becoming a power in the next century. Not even the powers of hell will be able to stop the Negro in his onward and upward movement. With Jesus as our standard bearer the Negro will march to victory.

The Negro Rules

There will be no democracy in the world until the Negro rules. We have given the white man a chance for thousands of years to show his feeling towards his fellowmen. And what has he done up to this twentieth century? He has murdered man; he has massacred man; he has deprived man of his rights even as God gave to man. The white man has shown himself an unfit subject to rule. Therefore he has to step off the stage of action.

I believe it is Shakespeare who said:

> "The Quality of mercy is not strained,
> It droppeth like the gentle rain from heaven
> Upon the place beneath;
> It is twice blessed;
> It blesseth him that gives and him that takes."

Has the white man any mercy? Not before the black man returns to power will there be any mercy in the world. The Negro has been the savior of all that has been good for mankind.

But the future portends great things. It portends a leadership of Negroes that will draw man nearer to his God, because in the Negroes' rule there will be mercy, love and charity to all.

Man Created for a Purpose

I want you colored men and women in Newport News to realize that you form a great part in this creation, for God has created you for a purpose; that purpose you have to keep in view; that purpose you must live. God said through the Psalmist that Ethiopia shall stretch forth her hands unto him and that princes shall come out of Ethiopia. I believe fervently that the hour has come for Ethiopia to stretch forth her hands unto God, and as we are stretching forth our hands unto God in New York, in Pennsylvania, in the West Indies, in Central America and in Africa and throughout the world I trust that you in Newport News are stretching forth your hands unto God.

Endless Chain of Negroes

There is an endless chain of Negroes all over the world, and wherever Negroes are to be found this day they are suffering from the brutality of the white man, and because Negroes are suffering all over the world we feel that the time has come for the four hundred millions of us scattered all over the world to link up our sentiment for one common purpose—to obtain liberty and democracy.

Africa Must Be Restored

I want you to understand that you have an association that is one of the greatest movements in the world. The New Negro, backed by the Universal Negro Improvement Association, is determined to restore Africa to the world, and you scattered children of Africa in Newport News, you children of Ethiopia, I want you to understand that the call is now made to you. What are you going to do? Are you going to remain to yourselves in Newport News and die? Or are you going to link up your strength, morally and financially, with the other Negroes of the world and let us all fight one battle unto victory? If you are prepared to do the latter, the battle is nearly won, because we of the Universal Negro Improvement Association intend within the next twelve months to roll up a sentiment in the United States of America that will be backed up by fifteen million black folks, so that when in the future you touch one Negro in Newport News you shall have touched fifteen million Negroes of the country. And within the next twenty-four months we intend to roll up an organization of nearly four hundred million people, so that when you touch any Negro in Newport News you touch four hundred million of Negroes all over the world at the same time.

Liberty or Death

It falls to the province of every black man and every black woman to be a member of the Universal Negro Improvement Association, because there is but one purpose before us, which is the purpose of liberty—that liberty that Patrick Henry spoke about in the legislature of Virginia over one hundred and forty years ago. We new Negroes of America declare that we desire liberty or we will take death. (Cheers.) They called us out but a few months ago to fight three thousand miles away in Europe to save civilization, to give liberty and democracy to the other peoples of the world. And we fought so splendidly, and after we died, after we gave up our blood, and some of us survived and returned to our respective countries, in America, in the West Indies, in Central America and in Africa, they told us, as they told us in the past, that this country is the white man's country. What is it but menial opportunities for you where you live in contact with white men? Because they have told us that in America, because they have told us that in France, because they have told us under the government of Great Britain that our opportunities are limited when we come in contact with white men, we say the war is not over yet. The war must go on; only that the war is not going on in France and Flanders, but the war will go on in the African plains, there to decide once and for all in the very near future whether black men are to be serfs and slaves or black men are to be free men.

Black Men Are Going to Be Free

We have decreed that black men are going to be free as white men are free or as yellow men are free. We have declared that if there is to be a British Empire, if there is to be a German Empire, if there is to be a Japanese Empire, if there is to be a French Republic and if there is to be an American Republic, then there must be a black republic of Africa. (Cheers.)

The White Man Hid the Book from the Negro

The New Negro has given up the idea of white leadership. The white man cannot lead the Negro any longer any more. He was able through our ignorance to lead us for over three hundred years since he took us from Africa, but the New Negro has learned enough now. When the white man took the black man from Africa he took him under a camouflage. He said to the Queen of England that he was taking the black man from Africa for the purpose of civilizing and Christianizing him. But that was not his purpose. The white man's purpose for taking the Negro from his native land was to make a slave of him, to have free labor. Some of us were brought to the Southern States of this country, some of our brothers and sisters were taken to Central America and others were taken to the West Indian Islands, and we labored under the bonds of slavery for 250 years. The white man never schooled us for the 250 years. He hid the book from us, even the very Bible, and never taught the Negro anything.

The Negro Made a Rush for the Book

But God moves in a mysterious way, and he brought about Lincoln and Victoria, and he said, "You must let those people free," and they did let us free. As soon as we were freed we made a rush to get the book, and we did get the book. We got the Bible first, and we began to sing songs and give praise to God, and that is why the Negro shouts so much in church. But after he was through with the first he got hold of the school book and went from his A B C to Z, and what has happened in fifty years? There is not a white man so educated that you cannot find a Negro to equal him. None in France, none in England, none in America to beat the Negro educationally, and because we stand equal with him we say no longer shall the white man lead us, but we shall lead ourselves.

The Negro and the Gun and Powder

If we had not a complete training in knowledge before 1914 in that we only knew the book and were only able to read and write, they of themselves gave us training and placed two million of us in the army and gave us gun and powder and taught us how to use them. That completed the education of the Negro. Therefore, tonight the Negro stands complete in education. He knows how to read his book, he knows how to figure out, and he knows how to use the sword and the gun. And because he can do these things so splendidly, he is determined that he shall carve the way for himself to true liberty and democracy which the white man denied him after he was called out to shed his blood on the battlefields of France and Flanders.

The Black Star Line Steamship Corporation

I did not come down to Newport News to talk to you merely from a sentimental standpoint. I have come to talk to you from a sentimental and business standpoint. We cannot live on sentiment. We have to live on the material production of the world. I am here representing the Black Star Line Steamship Corporation of the world. The purpose of the Black Star Line Steamship Corporation is to float a line of steamships to run between America, Canada, the West Indies, South and Central America and Africa, carrying freight and passengers, thus linking up the sentiment and wealth of the four hundred million Negroes of the world. Every day I spend away from New York means a financial loss of $5,000 a day; but I have sacrificed all that to come and speak to you in Newport News, because you in Newport News have a history in connection with the Black Star Line.

First Stock Sold

I want to say to you that on the 31st of this month the S.S. Frederick Douglass will sail out of New York harbor, the property of the Black Star Line—the property of the Negro peoples of the world. I also want you to understand that the first stock that was sold in the Black Star Line was sold in the Dixie Theatre in Newport News. (Cheers.) The first five hundred dollars that we sold was sold in Newport News. Therefore, you gave the real start to the Black Star Line, and as you started the Black Star Line we want you to finish the Black Star Line.

So that is why I took the chance of leaving New York to speak to you in Newport News. I telegraphed your President a few days ago and asked him up to a conference to let him see what New York is doing to come back and tell you. The Negroes are alive in New York and they are alive in Philadelphia also. New York is supplying its quota to the Black Star Line and so is Philadelphia. I have taken the chance to come to Newport News to find out if you are going to supply your quota towards the Black Star Line. I want you to understand that opportunity is now knocking at your door. You know that opportunity knocks but once at every man's door. The Black Star Line is the biggest industrial and commercial undertaking of the Negro of the Twentieth Century. The Black Star Line opens up the industrial and commercial avenues that were heretofore closed to Negroes.

The Negro Must Protect Himself

Every ship, every house, every store the white man builds, he has his gun and powder to protect them. The white man has surrounded himself with all the protection necessary to protect his property. The Japanese Government protects the yellow man, and the English, German, French and American Governments protect the white man, and the Negro has absolutely no protection. And that is why they lynch and burn us with impunity all over the world, and they will continue to do so until the Negro starts out to protect himself. The Negro cannot protect himself by living alone—he must organize. When you offend one white man in America, you offend ninety millions of white men. When you offend one Negro, the other Negroes are unconcerned because we are not organized. Not until you can offer protection to your race as the white man offers protection to his race, will you be a free and independent people in the world.

Index